CULTURE AND INTERNATIONAL
CONFLICT RESOLUTION

I0423086

New Approaches to Conflict Analysis

Series editor: Peter Lawler, Senior Lecturer in International Relations, Department of Government, University of Manchester

Until recently, the study of conflict and conflict resolution remained comparatively immune to broad developments in social and political theory. When the changing nature and locus of large-scale conflict in the post-Cold War era is also taken into account, the case for a reconsideration of the fundamentals of conflict analysis and conflict resolution becomes all the more stark.

New Approaches to Conflict Analysis promotes the development of new theoretical insights and their application to concrete cases of large-scale conflict, broadly defined. The series intends not to ignore established approaches to conflict analysis and conflict resolution, but to contribute to the reconstruction of the field through a dialogue between orthodoxy and its contemporary critics. Equally, the series reflects the contemporary porosity of intellectual borderlines rather than simply perpetuating rigid boundaries around the study of conflict and peace. *New Approaches to Conflict Analysis* seeks to uphold the normative commitment of the field's founders yet also recognises that the moral impulse to research is properly part of its subject matter. To these ends, the series is comprised of the highest quality work of scholars drawn from throughout the international academic community, and from a wide range of disciplines within the social sciences.

Culture and international conflict resolution

A critical analysis of the work of John Burton

TARJA VÄYRYNEN

Manchester University Press

MANCHESTER AND NEW YORK

distributed exclusively in the USA by Palgrave

The right of Tarja Väyrynen to be identified as the author of this work has been asserted by her in accordance with the Copyright, Designs and Patents Act 1988.

Published by Manchester University Press
Oxford Road, Manchester M13 9NR, UK
and Room 400, 175 Fifth Avenue, New York, NY 10010, USA
www.manchesteruniversitypress.co.uk

Distributed exclusively in the USA by
Palgrave, 175 Fifth Avenue, New York NY 10010, USA

Distributed exclusively in Canada by
UBC Press, University of British Columbia, 2029 West Mall,
Vancouver, BC, Canada V6T 1Z2

British Library Cataloguing-in-Publication Data
A catalogue record for this book is available from the British Library

Library of Congress Cataloging-in-Publication Data
A catalog record for this book is available from the Library of Congress

ISBN 13: 978 0 7190 8140 8

First published in hardback 2001 by Manchester University Press
This edition first published 2009

Printed by Lightning Source

CONTENTS

Acknowledgements — vii

Contents

ACKNOWLEDGEMENTS

I am grateful to Professor Chris Brown and Dr Keith Webb, who acted as the supervisors of my thesis, from which this work derives. I would like to express thanks also to Professor A. J. R. Groom and Professor Stephen Chan, from whom I received valuable advice and criticism, and Professor Andrew Linklater, who examined my thesis. Andrew Williams, Jarrod Wiener and Daniel Hiester read parts of the work and made useful suggestions. My special thanks to Professor John W. Burton, who read the first half of the study and encouraged me to continue my analysis. Thanks are also due to my colleagues both at the University of Kent at Canterbury and at Tampere University. I am indebted to my friends, and especially to Mr Y. Kanaya and Marko. They encouraged me, devoted long hours to discussions, let me test my ideas and refused to be easily impressed. Without the support of Irene and Anne, I would never have completed the last stage of this work.

T.V.

1

Introduction:
the problematique of culture
in international conflict analysis

One winter not long ago I participated in a workshop for resolving the Israeli–Palestinian conflict held at a distinguished American university. Our workshop was squeezed between similar workshops dealing with the 'Northern Ireland conflict' and the 'Cyprus conflict'. My frustration grew slowly until at a formal dinner I had one glass too many. I stood up and said to the organiser, a 'resolver' *par excellence*, 'I wonder if you know who we are at all. For all you care, we can be Zimbabweans, Basques, Arabs, Jews, Catholics, Protestants, Greeks, Turks. To you we are just guinea pigs to be tested, or at least best to be engineered.'[1]

What is required in a problem-solving forum is a 'filter' to screen out false assumptions and implications from existing knowledge, cultural and ideological orientations and personal prejudices. Probably the main task of the third party is to provide this filter. If the participants can use this filter, then they will be able to perceive realities accurately, to assess available theoretical and empirical knowledge, and arrive at reliable conclusions.[2]

THE PROBLEM-SOLVING workshop type of international conflict resolution has proved to be a promising approach in solving violent conflicts. The 'Oslo channel', where Norwegian social scientists facilitated a peace agreement between Israelis and Palestinians, is the most publicised example of the success of informal third-party conflict resolution. The Norwegian workshop was based on a branch of thinking – and acting – in peace and conflict studies which was developed in the 1960s. A number of studies were produced at that time which were devoted to improving inter-nation relations by improving communication and cultural understanding. They were mainly based on a broad social-psychological perspective which encouraged researchers to examine how to move from conflictual zero-sum games to more positive-sum games. Some of these studies involved practical applications in the form of conflict resolution workshops which brought together representatives of parties in a violent political conflict.

John Burton's work exemplifies this sort of approach to international relations and conflict resolution. He is one of the pioneering scholars and practitioners of problem-solving workshop conflict resolution, and his ideas have widely influenced academic works in the field of conflict and conflict resolution in general. His theory of the relationship between basic human needs and the development of protracted conflict has brought in a set of new issues and evoked a lively theoretical debate among conflict analysts. Burton's contribution is not limited to his version of human needs theory. For example, a variant of world society approaches owes much to the thought and influence of Burton. He argued very early that the emphasis in the study of international relations should be on transactions instead of states. Similarly, he has paid attention to functional cooperation as a tool of adaptation to changing international circumstances.

This book examines Burton's conflict and conflict resolution theory and its relation to his human needs theory. It is demonstrated that taking sociobiologically based human needs as a starting-point for conflict theory leads to the denial of culture and the socially constructed nature of human existence. The study seeks to critique the idea of problem-solving workshop conflict resolution by way of a critical analysis of Burton and the articulation of an alternative approach.

Totalist and 'non-totalist' views of conflict resolution

The problematique of culture is at the centre of both theorising and practising problem-solving workshop conflict resolution. The quotations which opened this chapter reveal two opposite views of the role of culture. The first criticises conflict resolution attempts which isolate conflict management from larger social and cultural contexts, whereas the other sees a degree of detachment as a necessary condition for successful resolution. The complaint levels the critique against the universalistic tendencies of conflict resolution which dismiss the role of culture in conflict management and underestimate the uniqueness of conflicts. For Burton, in the second quote, culture should not intrude into conflict resolution processes. The role of the conflict resolution facilitator, in Burton's view, is to act as a filter which purifies conflict management from cultural influences.

The quotations reveal also one of the most recent debates in the field of international conflict analysis, namely that between non-totalist conflict theories which emphasise the social as well as local construction of conflict and conflict resolution and 'human needs' theories which found the origin of conflict in biological human needs.[3] In the non-totalist conflict theories, culture is vital for becoming and being a moral person. Human needs theories, on the other hand, suggest that there are ontological human needs which are universal and, therewith, not relative to culture. Denying culture its constitutive role paves the way for the assumption that there are culture-free techniques of conflict resolution.

Conflict and conflict resolution theories based on human needs do note the existence of cultural values, as Burton's theory does, but cultural factors are seen to motivate behaviour in a limited sense. For example, the preservation of cultural values may lead individuals to defend their identities, but it is ultimately the pursuit of needs that is the reason for the formation of such valuable entities as identity groups. The emphasis on shared needs in human needs theories results in looking for similarities between the parties in conflict rather than encouraging the parties to accept and live with differences, the border between 'us' and 'them'.

The non-totalist approaches identify forces which make conflicts culturally constructed. Conflicts occur in cultural contexts, and human 'being' is culturally conditioned. The world is experienced in terms of typifications which categorise and classify the world to us in certain ways. These typifications are sedimented in our stocks of knowledge, which are socially and culturally derived and approved. As members of social groups we accept the ready-made standardised schemes of the cultural patterns of social groups as unquestioned guides for interpreting and acting in the social world. Groups and institutions participate in creating and defining realities for individuals: through intersubjective typifications and shared world-views realities, 'what is known as reality', are defined. Culture is given, thus, a fundamental role in understanding conflict and conflict resolution.

Culture in conflict resolution theories

There is a group of non-totalist studies in the field of international conflict analysis which desire to demonstrate the importance of culture in conflict and conflict resolution, and with which this book bears similarities. Unlike Burton's theory, they do not reduce culture to the status of a secondary variable which influences conflictual and cooperative behaviour. Rather, they see culture as constructing reality in one way or another. The approaches can be categorised under four sub-groups: social constructionist theories, feminist studies, frame analysis and discourse analysis.

First, a typical feature of the social constructionist view is the argument that culture is constitutive of human reality. Culture offers a grammar for acting in and interpreting the world, and it refers to widely shared practices and to commonly held assumptions and presuppositions that individuals and groups hold about the world. It involves the social structuring of both the world outside the self and the internal world. According to this view, since culture produces understandings of conflict and conflict resolution, the study of these is an important element of any meaningful analysis of conflict. In other words, international conflict analysis should be a form of cultural analysis.[4]

A branch of social constructionist studies holds that 'culture shapes what people consider valuable and worth fighting over'.[5] Conflict can be understood as cultural behaviour. Culture frames people's understanding of the world and shapes action in the social world. In order to study conflicts, a conflict analyst needs to examine 'social structural interests' and 'psychocultural interpretations'. Interests arise from social structures and determine the selection of the targets of conflictual behaviour. Psychocultural interpretations include dominant images and metaphors concerning what is at stake or the relationship between the parties in conflict. By using comparative methods it is possible to examine also how the culture of conflict – a society's relevant norms, practices and institutions – allows a society to manage conflict in characteristic ways.[6]

Since culture is a constitutive of social reality, conflict resolution is relative to culture. Conflicts are cultural events, evolving within frameworks of cultural norms and values which condition what is worth fighting for, what is the normal way to fight, what warrants conflictual action and what kinds of solution are acceptable. Perceptions of disputes and ways of dealing with them derive from habits and customs embedded in social groups and cultures. It follows – as Laura Nader notes on conflict resolution techniques – that 'if we are going to systematise or professionalise the job of third party, it has to be the situation that defines the distinctive features to be used'.[7]

Second, the gendered nature of reality as well as of conflict and conflict resolution practices is focused on by an increasing number of feminist writers. Their studies aim to demonstrate an interrogation of links between gender, identity and violence. The associations between men, militarism and masculinity, on the one hand, and women, peace and femininity on the other are problematised. This problematisation directs the research not solely towards women's own experiences but also towards the gendered production of war and peace. Feminist interventions reveal gender relations as central features of international relations, of identity conflicts, and of war. Although these studies do not employ the notion of culture as their key concept, they challenge totalist theorising in peace and conflict studies by emphasising the political, social and cultural construction of identities.[8]

Third, frame analysis argues that enemies in conflict have mutually exclusive frames of reference which preclude cooperation between them. These frames of reference are psychological frames which are dependent on persistent patterns of behaviour, i.e. they reflect social structures. Conflict resolution is, therefore, defined to mean the dissolution of conflictual frames and substitution of them by a joint (cooperative) frame.[9] Since conflict resolution is about creating a joint cooperative frame between the parties, conflict analysts need to examine the creation of shared meanings and the fusion of interpretative horizons of the parties in the conflict resolution process. The development of shared meaning is important in managing conflict, because through it 'we increase the prospect for mutual engagement in effective and productive resolution of differences'.[10] Relational empathy can provide a means of understanding how to manage differences effectively in conflict situations. Through the development of rela-

tional empathy in a conflict resolution process a series of successive approximations to the other's point of view can be achieved. These approximations can then
serve as a basis for the development of shared meaning.[11]

Interaction is seen in the frame analysis to be also an arena where actors
come together with potentially differing perspectives on the situation, its
meaning and the opportunities for achieving their goals. The meanings of the
behaviour and events are always open to different interpretations. This applies to
the mediators in relation to the parties, too: the basis upon which mediators
claim authority is always open to challenge. In order to impress the parties with
the practitioner's perspicacity, ability and skill, mediators convey symbolic mes-
sages about themselves. In other words, mediators create impressions about
themselves, their role and their abilities, and how these are sustained and supported. Since mediators often lack formal authority, 'much of their influence
stems from their expressive management of their expertise, their rapport with
the parties, and the parties' perceptions of their contributions to progress and
settlement in the current case and in others external to it'.[12]

Fourth, it is argued that language has a constitutive function in conflict resolution practices. It is thought to constitute 'reality' for the parties. Given the fundamentality of language, discourses are the main focus of discourse analysis.
Discourse is seen as the way in which social processes emerge, reconstitute themselves and change. In conflict analysis the approach based on discourse analysis
offers, for example, a 'perspective on the mediation process, one that addresses
the relationship between discourse and social processes and challenges the
objectivism at the core of our understandings about mediation and neutrality'.[13]
At the centre of the study is how mediators produce and support, in and through
the rhetoric of neutrality, dominant ideologies and positions of privilege. In other
words, what is examined is how a discursive practice actually functions to
obscure the workings of power in mediation and makes the political nature of the
mediation process invisible.[14]

In sum, the studies which emphasise the role of language, culture and identity in international conflict resolution demonstrate that conflicts do not arise
only from differences of interest. Rather, conflicts are over meaning, over the
social construction and management of meaning. Conflict resolution engages
the parties in an attempt to find shared meanings and frames for acting in the
social world. The third party has a highly political role in conflict resolution processes: mediators and facilitators provide interpretative frameworks for knowing
and constructing realities for the parties.

Burton and problem-solving conflict resolution

Burton's views on international conflict resolution represent universalising tendencies in theorising, and differ from approaches which assume culture to have

a major role in the formation of conflicts as well as in their resolution. Burton's conflict and conflict resolution theory assumes the origin of conflict to be in such human needs as identity, participation and security. It is claimed that people will pursue those needs regardless of the consequences to themselves or to a system. International conflicts arise from the failure of domestic systems to provide for the needs of people. Given that the origin of conflict is in basic human needs, the preconditions for conflict resolution, on the other hand, can be found in the analytical differentiation of needs from interests, in the improvement of communication between the parties in conflict and in the alteration of structures and institutions which hinder the processes of needs satisfaction. Burton considers problem-solving workshop conflict resolution to be the best means for the creation of such preconditions.

Burton's conflict resolution theory is founded on a version of human needs thinking. Burton gives needs priority over other characteristics – such as culture or language – of human 'being'. He assumes that basic needs form a fundamental stratum of the person which acts as the motive of behaviour. In his view, needs are equal to drives whose demands seek satisfaction at any cost, subject only to minor constraints. Burton's theory implies universal and biologically founded human nature and, thereby, it offers ways to defuse culturalism and contextualism.

As noted earlier, at the centre of Burton's theory is the notion of 'problem-solving conflict resolution'.[15] The term has recently come to denote any form of cooperative conflict resolution. When the concepts of 'problem-solving workshop' and 'controlled communication' were introduced to International Relations (IR) in the late 1960s and early 1970s by such scholars as John Burton, Herbert Kelman and Leonard Doob, they referred to international conflict resolution attempts which brought together representatives of nations or ethnic groups in an active conflict. The talks which took place in problem-solving workshops were designed to contribute directly to the resolution of an international conflict.

Several schools of problem-solving workshop conflict resolution have developed, but they share some basic ideas. For example, workshops are meant to bring together representatives of parties in conflict for direct communication in an unofficial setting. A panel of scholars which facilitates and promotes communication between the parties is an essential part of this type of conflict resolution. However, the role of the third party differs from that of the traditional mediator. Unlike many mediators, facilitators do not propose or impose solutions. The function of the third party in the problem-solving workshop is to create an atmosphere where innovative solutions can emerge out of the interaction between the parties themselves. The objective of the workshop is both to create analytical communication and to generate inputs into political processes. Although problem-solving workshop conflict resolution is not negotiation as such, it is often in practice a complementary and parallel process.

An element of training of the participants in conflict resolution skills is included in problem-solving workshop conflict resolution. Participants in a conflict are assumed to need skills and orientations to develop constructive solutions to their conflicts. They need the skills involved in establishing cooperative relationships, in communicating and in exploring creative solutions. The main task of the workshop is, however, to carry out a concrete task, to contribute to the resolution of a particular conflict.

There is a strong belief in rationality in traditional problem-solving conflict resolution. Since it is claimed that subjective (perceptions) and objective (human needs) elements play an important part in every conflict and form an obstacle to conflict resolution, it is thought that these elements have to be tackled in a rational way. It is assumed that human beings are capable of rational thinking and acting when an appropriate framework is offered. Problem-solving workshops are supposed to offer a framework for conflicting parties for scrutinising the nature of their relationship, for analysing the ultimate roots of their differences and, finally, for finding commonalities. The analysis is expected to take place by exercising both instrumental reasoning about means to ends and discursive reasoning[16] about definitions and values.

A non-totalist theory of international conflict resolution

A concern of this study is to identify unexplored and under-studied areas of international conflict resolution in general, and problem-solving conflict resolution in particular. In other words, it aims at providing an alternative language for the study of conflict resolution. Alfred Schutz's phenomenology and social constructionist theories of human 'being' are employed in order both to criticise Burton's views of human nature and to establish a conceptual framework which does not arise from human needs thinking. By applying phenomenological concepts, an understanding of conflict and conflict resolution can be gained which differs in many respects from Burton's theories. The most important point of departure is the account of culture, which Schutz's theories – unlike Burton's biologically based views – provide for conflict and conflict resolution theory.

Non-totalist theorising can be described in the following manner:

> One might seek, not to impose one reading on the field of discourse, but to elaborate a general reading that can contend with others by broadening the established terms of debates; not to create a transformation of international life grounded in a universal project, but to contribute to a general perspective that might support reconstitution of aspects of international life; not to root a theory in a transcendental ground, but to problematise the grounding any theory presupposes while it works out the implications of a particular set of themes; not merely in invert hierarchies in other theories (a useful task), but to construct alternative hierarchies that support modifications in relations between identity and difference.[17]

The phenomenological approach employed fulfils the criteria for non-totalist theories suggested by William Connolly in the quotation above. It broadens the established terms of problem-solving conflict resolution theorising, which derive mainly from sociobiological, sociopsychological and psychological discourses. By doing this, it contributes to a general perspective on conflict resolution which is an aspect of international life. The approach questions the ground of Burton's version of human needs theory and its relation to conflict resolution theory by suggesting an alternative image of human existence. Similarly, it constructs alternative hierarchies (e.g. culture/needs, society/nature, dialogue/strategic action) and new domains of study (e.g. socially constructed identity, discursive rationality).

In this study a non-totalist understanding of conflict and conflict resolution is built upon a social constructionist image of human 'being' which takes into account the organic relationships between the individual, social group and culture. It is demonstrated that there is no need to appeal to the existence of universal human needs in order to understand and practise problem-solving workshop conflict resolution. Phenomenological sociology suggests a theoretical language for the conceptualisation of problem-solving workshop conflict resolution: it offers a language which arises neither from sociobiology nor from psychology.

The approach employed shows how the participants bring to the conflict resolution situation their definitions of reality, conflict and conflict resolution, which are influenced, if not determined, by culturally and socially constructed typifications. Given the fundamentality of the social world and cultural patterns, the problem-solving workshop is not a filter where culture is filtered out, or put aside, as Burton argues. On the contrary, the dimensions of the social world continue to exist in the workshop. The workshop is a place where a cultural encounter takes place, and where the socially and culturally produced border between 'we' and 'they' can be reflected, not abolished.

Conflicts are characterised by a breakdown of shared reality. Cooperating with others, on the other hand, presupposes shared typifications through which a shared reality is defined. If typifications break down or are denied, the society faces *anomie* which may take the form of conflict. Applied to problem-solving conflict resolution, it is necessary that in the problem-solving workshop the participants can engage in 'negotiations' in which typifications are harmonised. The problem-solving workshop is, thus, an attempt to find a shared reality between the parties in conflict. It deals mainly with the interpretative schemes of the participants by offering them a framework for 'negotiations over meanings and realities'. The finding of a common language game both presupposes and facilitates the finding of a shared reality.

Interpretative method

Humans are self-interpreting and self-defining beings, who live in the world of cultural meaning. As a consequence, the object of the study of social science

8

must include the interpretations and definitions of the human subjects whose interaction makes up the social world. Interpretative approaches in social science start with the understanding that the social world is partly constituted by human self-interpretation, and that the methods and purposes of social science are different from the methods and aims of natural science.[18] Interpretative approaches clearly differ from the positivist tradition, whose main idea is the methodological unity of science. It is assumed in the positivist tradition that there is no fundamental difference between the social world and the natural world; both contain regularities independent of time and place. The ways of conducting scientific analysis in the natural world are thought to be appropriate to the social world too.

In addition to man being self-interpreting and self-defining, human 'being' is a self-interpreting activity itself. The activity involves an understanding of what 'being' means, and it is this understanding which opens a clearing in which human beings can encounter objects, institutions and other human beings. In other words, 'understanding is the original character of the being of human life itself'.[19] In the encounter the interpreter begins the analysis from within the practices he or she seeks to interpret. The choice of phenomena to be interpreted is guided by a traditional understanding of 'being' which has already made the interpreter what he or she is. Interpretation begins with preconceptions that are replaced by more suitable ones during the event of understanding. Understanding is ultimately an interplay between the movement of tradition and the movement of the interpreter.[20]

Encountering the social world often takes the form of encountering a text. A text – as a cultural product – is a work of discourse, which cannot be reduced to the sentences whereof it is composed. There is also a complex relationship between the author of the text and its interpreter. The text transcends its own sociopsychological conditions of production and, thereby, opens itself to an unlimited series of readings. The text 'decontextualises' itself in such a way that it can be 'recontextualised' in a new situation by the act of reading. In the case of the written text, the intention of the author does not coincide with the meaning of what is written. The 'objective' meaning of the text is something other than the 'subjective' intentions of its author and, therefore, the problem of the right understanding cannot be solved by a simple return to the alleged intention of the author. In short, the textual meaning cannot be derived from the psychological meaning.[21]

The act of interpretation culminates in an act of 'appropriation'. The act of 'appropriation' does not seek to rejoin the original intentions of the author, but rather to expand the conscious horizon of the reader by actualising the meaning of the text. The 'distanciation' of the text from the author is not abolished by 'appropriation'. On the contrary, 'appropriation' is understanding at and through distance, which is inevitably between the author and the interpreter. In 'appropriation' we do not impose our meaning on the text. Nor do we leave ourselves aside. Rather, we use our preconceptions so that the meaning of the text can be 'made to speak for us': we conjoin a new discourse to the discourse of the text. Interpretation can be described as a conversation with the text in which the horizon of the interpreter and the horizon of the text amalgamate.[22]

The text creates a version of a world or, rather, it 'makes a world': it does not reflect or represent a world. A world is created by dividing, combining, emphasising, ordering, deleting, filling in and filling out. Worlds are made not only by what is said literally but also by what is said metaphorically as well as by what is exemplified and expressed. The 'truth' of a version of a world produced by a text cannot be defined or tested against 'the world', for not only do truths differ for different worlds but the nature of the relationship between a version and a world apart from it is nebulous. The 'truth' of, for example, a theory is but one special feature and its importance is often overridden by the theory's cogency, compactness, comprehensiveness, informativeness and organising power. However, a version may be taken to be 'true'. For example, within a scientific frame of reference the version a theory offers appears to be true.[23]

The researcher participates in a 'world-making' acticity. Nelson Goodman describes scientific activities:

> The scientist who supposes that he is singlemindedly dedicated to the search for truth deceives himself. He is unconcerned with the trivial truths he could grind out endlessly; and he looks to the multifaceted and irregular results of observations for little more than suggestions of overall structures and significant generalisations. He seeks system, simplicity, scope; and when satisfied on these scores he tailors truth to fit. He as much decrees as discovers the laws he sets forth, as much designs as discerns the patterns he delineates.[24]

Metaphor participates in making versions of worlds. It is essential to human understanding, and it is a mechanism for creating new meaning. Language structures what we perceive, how we get around in the world and how we relate to other people. Language plays an important role in defining our everyday realities. Our conceptual system, in terms of which we both think and act, is fundamentally metaphorical by nature. Metaphor is, thus, not about transposing an unusual name, as a commonsense understanding of metaphor suggests. The essence of metaphor is, rather, 'understanding and experiencing one kind of thing in terms of another'.[25] Since metaphor is vital for understanding, it cannot be avoided in speaking 'objectively' or 'scientifically'.[26]

Such views of metaphor and 'world making' clearly challenge an extreme objectivist picture of the world. The extreme objectivist position claims that there is an objective reality, and that we can say things that are objectively, absolutely and unconditionally true or false about it. Science not only provides us with a methodology that allows us to rise above our subjective limitations and to achieve understanding from a universally valid and unbiased point of view but will, in the course of its development, give us also a correct and general account of reality. According to the objectivist view, to describe reality correctly we need words whose meanings are fixed, clear and precise. The ideas of metaphor and 'worldversions' challenge, on the other hand, an extreme subjectivist image of the world too. The extreme subjectivist position does not recognise the existence of intersubjective and socially conditioned frames of reference. The notions of metaphor and 'world making' allow a position which holds that the intersubjective frame of reference constrains the imaginative understanding of the individual as well as his or her power to 'create worlds' and produce new meaning.[27]

What, then, is looked for in interpretation? There are several answers. It is suggested that what is ultimately 'appropriated' in interpretation is the world the text proposes.[28] It is also thought that interpretative hermeneutics is a dialogue with past ways of understanding the world.[29] The anthropologist Clifford Geertz assumes that the interpretative analysis of culture is an attempt to search for meaning.[30] It is a search for meaning by sorting out the structures of signification of the social actors and by determining their social ground and import. The double task of the interpretative analysis is to uncover the conceptual structures that inform actors in a social world and to provide a vocabulary in which what symbolic action has to say about itself can be expressed. 'Critical hermeneutics',[31] on the other hand, suspects the claims to truth contained in the text or in the tradition one is inhabiting. It assumes the existence of 'ideological structures' which produce 'false consciousness' and aims at criticising – by employing critical interpretation – the misunderstandings of self and the reality that gives rise to them.

The aim of interpretation in this book is 'moderate'. The purpose is not to uncover the deep structures of a tradition. Nor is the book conceived as a conversation with past understandings for the truth they contain. The aim is, rather, to study the logic and underlying assumptions of Burton's texts. The analysis of metaphors is considered to be one means of actualising this type of research orientation. Interpretation means also linking the texts with wider theoretical discussions. These are assumed both to locate Burton's work in traditions of thinking and to open up new perspectives. The interpretative approach used to understand the texts of phenomenologists and social constructionists is more instrumental. Indeed, it includes interpretation, but it is employed in order to construct a conceptual framework which is an alternative to the framework suggested by Burton.[32]

The object of this book is to develop a non-totalist understanding of international conflict resolution in general, and of problem-solving conflict resolution in particular. It seeks a non-totalist understanding by studying conflict and conflict resolution in the light of constructionist ideas of the social world. It assumes that cultural patters are constitutive of conflict and conflict resolution. The study takes as its starting-point a totalist theory of international conflict resolution, namely Burton's sociobiologically-oriented conflict theory, and demonstrates the logic of argument and the denial of culture underlying his problem-solving theory.

An overview of the mediation literature is given in chapter 2 in order to locate problem-solving workshop conflict resolution within the context of peaceful third-party involvement. Pilot international problem-solving conflict resolution approaches are compared and their underlying theoretical assumptions studied in the chapter too. Chapter 3 analyses human needs thinking and examines the similarities between it and Burton's thinking. The aim of the chapter is also to examine the logic of Burton's argument by means of metaphor analysis, by analysing the metaphors which can be found in his human needs theory. The fourth chapter studies further Burton's views of action and rationality. In other words, it asks what mode of behaviour and forms of rationality Burton assumes when he explains conflict and conflict resolution.

Chapter 5 moves into phenomenology and social constructionism. Schutz's philosophy is studied in order to develop an alternative ontological basis and conceptual framework for the study of conflict and conflict resolution. Burton's biologically based ontology is challenged by discussing the social construction of reality, needs and identity. An account is given of culture such that it can be placed at the centre of the study of conflict and conflict resolution. The sixth chapter presents a phenomenological understanding of conflict and problem-solving conflict resolution. It argues that problem-solving workshop conflict resolution can be best understood as an attempt to find a shared reality between the parties in conflict. In order to justify the claim, the discussion started in the previous chapter on relevance structures, typifications and discursive rationality is continued. Attention is also paid to the role of the facilitator, and a new metaphor for describing his or her role in the workshop context is suggested. The conclusion comes up with practical suggestions for international problem-solving conflict resolution.

NOTES

1 M. Benvenisti, *Conflicts and Contradictions* (New York, Villard Books/Random House, 1986), pp. 118–19. Quoted from K. Avruch, 'Introduction: Culture and Conflict Resolution', in K. Avruch, P. Black and J. Scimecca (eds), *Conflict Resolution: Cross-cultural Perspectives* (New York, Westport CT and London, Greenwood Press, 1991), p. 2.
2 J. Burton, *Conflict: Resolution and Provention* (London, Macmillan, 1990), p. 208.
3 For non-totalist theories see K. Avruch, *Culture and Conflict Resolution* (Washington DC, United States Institute of Peace Press, 1998). K. Avruch and P. Black, 'Ideas of Human Nature in Contemporary Conflict Resolution Theory', *Negotiation Journal*, 6: 3 (1990), 221–8. K. Avruch and P. Black, 'The Culture Question and Conflict Resolution', *Peace and Change*, 16: 1 (1991), 22–45. K. Avruch and P. Black 'Conflict Resolution in Intercultural Settings: Problems and Prospects', in D. Sandole and H. van der Merwe (eds), *Conflict*

Resolution Theory and Practice: Integration and Application (Manchester and New York, Manchester University Press, 1993), pp. 131–45. K. Avruch, P. Black and J. Scimecca (eds), *Conflict Resolution: Cross-cultural Perspectives* (New York, Westport CT and London, Greenwood Press, 1991). P. Black and K. Avruch 'Some Issues in Thinking about Culture and the Resolution of Conflict', *Humanity and Society*, 13: 2 (1989), 184–95. C. Greenhouse, 'Cultural Perspectives on War', in R. Väyrynen (ed.), *The Quest for Peace* (London, Sage, 1987), pp. 32–47. For human needs approaches see J. Burton, *Violence Explained* (Manchester and New York, Manchester University Press, 1997). Burton, *Conflict: Resolution*. J. Burton (ed.), *Conflict: Human Needs Theory* (London, Macmillan, 1990). R. Coate and J. Rosati (eds), *The Power of Human Needs in World Society* (Boulder CO and London, Lynne Rienner, 1988).

4 Avruch and Black, 'The Culture Question'.

5 M. Ross, *The Culture of Conflict: Interpretations and Interests in Comparative Perspective* (New Haven CT and London, Yale University Press, 1993), p. 22.

6 *Ibid.* M. Ross, *The Management of Conflict: Interpretations and Interests in Comparative Perspective* (New Haven CT and London, Yale University Press, 1993).

7 L. Nader, 'Some Notes on John Burton's Papers on "Resolution of Conflict"', *International Studies Quarterly*, 16: 1 (1972), 54. See also L. Nader, 'Harmony Models and the Construction of Law', in K. Avruch, P. Black and J. Scimecca (eds), *Conflict Resolution: Cross-cultural Perspectives* (New York, Westport CT and London, Greenwood Press, 1991), pp. 41–59. S. Merry, 'Disputing without Culture', *Harvard Law Review*, 100: 8 (1987), 2057–73. S. Merry and S. Silbey, 'What do Plaintiffs want? Reexamining the concept of dispute', *Justice System Journal*, 9: 2 (1984), 151–78.

8 See J. B. Elshtain, *Women and War* (Brighton, Harvester Press, 1987). C. Nordstrom, *A Different Kind of War Story* (Pennsylvania PA, University of Pennsylvania Press, 1997). J. J. Pettman, 'Nationalism and After', *Review of International Studies*, 24: 4 (1998), 149–64.

9 A. de Reuck, 'A Theory of Conflict Resolution by Problem-solving', in J. Burton and F. Dukes (eds), *Conflict: Readings in Management and Resolution* (London, Macmillan, 1990), pp. 186–98.

10 B. Broome, 'Managing Differences in Conflict Resolution: the Role of Relational Empathy', in D. Sandole and H. van der Merwe (eds), *Conflict Resolution Theory and Practice: Integration and Application* (Manchester and New York, Manchester University Press, 1993), p. 97.

11 *Ibid.*, pp. 98–101.

12 D. Kolb, 'To be a Mediator: Expressive Tactics in Mediation', *Journal of Social Issues*, 41: 2 (1985), 23.

13 S. Cobb and J. Rifkin, 'Practice and Paradox: Deconstructing Neutrality in Mediation', *Law and Social Inquiry*, 16: 1 (1991), 37–8.

14 *Ibid.* See also V. Jabri, *Discourses on Violence: Conflict Analysis Reconsidered* (Manchester and New York, Manchester University Press, 1996).

15 For descriptions of problem-solving workshops see E. Azar, 'The Analysis and Management of Protracted Conflict', in V. Volkan, J. Montville and D. Julius (eds), *The Psychodynamics of International Relationships* II (Lexington MA, Lexington Books, 1991), pp. 93–116. J. Burton, 'Three Qualities of a Secure Nation', in M. Macy (ed.), *Solutions for a Troubled World* (Boulder CO, Earthview Press, 1987), pp. 239–48. R. Fisher, 'Third Party Consultation as a Method of Intergroup Conflict Resolution', *Journal of Conflict Resolution*, 27: 2 (1983), 301–34.

16 Discursive rationality will be discussed in more detail later in the book. For the conception see J. Dryzek, *Discursive Democracy: Politics, Policy and Political Science* (Cambridge, Cambridge University Press, 1990).

17 W. Connolly, *Identity/Difference: Democratic Negotiations of Political Paradox* (Ithaca NY and London, Cornell University Press, 1991), pp. 56–7.

13

18 For interpretative approaches see M. Neufeld, 'Interpretation and the "Science" of International Relations', *Review of International Studies*, 19: 1 (1993), 39–61. M. Hollis and S. Smith, *Explaining and Understanding in International Relations* (Oxford, Clarendon Press, 1991). R. Price, 'Interpretation and Disciplinary Orthodoxy in International Relations', *Review of International Studies*, 20: 2 (1994), 201–4.

19 H.-G. Gadamer, *Truth and Method*, second edition (London, Sheed & Ward, 1979), p. 230.

20 *Ibid.*, pp. 230–40 and 261.

21 P. Ricoeur, *Hermeneutics and the Human Sciences*, ed. J. Thompson (Cambridge, Cambridge University Press, and Paris, Editions de la Maison des sciences de l'homme, 1981), pp. 131–40. J. Thompson, 'Editor's Introduction', in P. Ricoeur, *Hermeneutics and the Human Sciences* (Cambridge, Cambridge University Press, and Paris, Editions de la Maison des sciences de l'homme, 1981), pp. 1–26.

22 Gadamer, *Truth and Method*, pp. 273 and 326–31. Ricoeur, *Hermeneutics and the Human Sciences*, pp. 142–4 and 182–93.

23 N. Goodman, *Ways of Worldmaking* (Indianapolis IN, Hackett, 1978), pp. 1–19 and 130–40.

24 *Ibid.*, p. 18.

25 G. Lakoff and M. Johnson, *Metaphors We Live By* (Chicago and London, University of Chicago Press, 1980), p. 5.

26 See also R. Dirven and W. Paporotté, 'Introduction', in R. Dirven and W. Paporotté (eds), *The Ubiquity of Metaphor* (Amsterdam PA, Benjamins, 1985), pp. vii–xix.

27 For the objectivist and subjectivist views see Lakoff and Johnson, *Metaphors We Live By*, pp. 185–228.

28 Ricoeur, *Hermeneutics and the Human Sciences*, p. 143.

29 Gadamer, *Truth and Method*, pp. 431–47.

30 C. Geertz, *The Interpretation of Cultures: Selected Essays* (London, Fontana Press, 1993), pp. 3–30.

31 J. Bleicher, *Contemporary Hermeneutics: Hermeneutics as Method, Philosophy and Critique* (London and New York, Routledge, 1980), pp. 143–74.

32 There are also other ways of conducting interpretative research. 'Biographical reconstruction' aims at understanding the intended meaning of the author, 'what the author said and meant', by constructing the biographical and historical details of the author in relation to his or her texts. 'Contextual reconstruction' sees the precondition for understanding to be in an intellectual and social context within which the text should be placed: past ideas should be studied in their historical context, in the context of the circumstances in which they were written. 'Critical reconstruction' identifies the discursive practices that turn a historical problematic into a ideological given, and offers ways to criticise these givens.

2

Peaceful third-party intervention and Burtonian problem-solving conflict resolution

P ROBLEM-SOLVING WORKSHOP conflict resolution is a form of peaceful third-party intervention. The approach argues that it differs from the traditional approaches to mediation in many respects. It assumes, for example, that conflicts can be best resolved in small-group discussions which are guided by facilitators. The role of the facilitator is to assist the parties to communicate rather than to suggest solutions. Conflict resolution – the term preferred by the workshop approach, and especially by Burton – is about dealing with the root causes of conflicts, not about negotiating on interests.

In general, there are two orientations to conflict resolution: competitive and cooperative. The orientations form a continuum, with the competitive orientation at one end and the cooperative at the other. Within the continuum there are such modes of conflict resolution as the use of deadly force (actual or threatened), litigation, adjudication, arbitration, conciliation, traditional mediation, facilitated problem solving and unfacilitated problem solving. The continuum can also be conceptualised by claiming that there are three procedures for dealing with opposing preferences, namely struggle, mediation and negotiation.[1]

The underlying theory of conflict sets the framework for the orientations to conflict resolution as well as for the conflict resolution theories. The 'subjectivistic' understanding of conflict defines conflict resolution as a process which deals with subjective elements, i.e. perceptions, attitudes and images. In this view, conflict resolution is about handling these subjective elements, and third-party roles are justified by third-party activities which aim at perceptual and attitudinal changes. The 'objectivist' definition of conflict, on the other hand, generates an idea of structural changes as a precondition for the termination of violent conflict. For example, the empowerment of a weaker party, which may take place in the process of mediation, is seen to provide a means of creating such preconditions.[2] It is also maintained that both psychocultural (subjective) and structural (objective) factors are critical in shaping the level of conflict and violence and in

15

defining who the opponents will be. Thus a successful conflict resolution process needs to address both aspects.[3]

Assumptions about the nature of international systems contextualise the means of conflict resolution. There are views which assume that conflicts which derive from great ideological forces and which aim, for example, at the creation of nations and states cannot be settled 'through the technical quick fixes of mediators and conciliators'.[4] The reality of power politics in international relations is, according to the argument, forgotten in attempts to resolve conflicts by the help of peaceful third-party interventions. The paradigm of power politics needs to be evoked as a legitimate general framework for the study of conflict resolution. The opposing approach, represented for example by Burton, maintains that strategies of conflict settlement inherent in power politics merely treat symptoms of conflict rather than the sources. Facilitation and assisted conflict resolution overcome the zero-sum negotiation structure embedded in power politics, and deal with the real root causes of conflicts.[5]

The aim of this chapter is to examine the cooperative end of the conflict resolution continuum and, more precisely, the modes of international conflict resolution which include third-party intermediary activities. The scope is further narrowed down to traditional mediation and facilitated problem solving. The objective is to place the Burtonian problem-solving conflict resolution approach within a wider context of mediation approaches. The chapter compares traditional mediation with problem-solving facilitation. Three pilot problem-solving workshop approaches, among them Burton's 'London school', are studied and their underlying theoretical assumptions pointed out.

Traditional third-party intermediary intervention

Third-party activity has traditionally been theorised in three ways. The focus has been on 'intermediary activities', 'general conflict theory' or the 'negotiation system'. The fourth main approach to third-party intermediary activities is found in problem-solving conflict resolution. Its roots are largely in social psychology, which emphasises the relationships and interactions between individuals, small groups and societies. The 'third-party consultation model', as problem-solving conflict resolution is also called, aims at offering an alternative to the traditional approaches. It seeks to create an alternative theoretical discourse on conflict resolution.

The traditional view which emphasises mainly intermediary activities studies third-party tactics and identities. Intermediary intervention is defined as 'any action taken by an actor that is not directly party to the crisis, that is designed to reduce or remove one or more of the problems of the bargaining relationship and, therefore, to facilitate the termination of the crisis itself'.[6] The definition and the questions related to the strategies and identities employed by third parties dominate the theoretical discussion about mediation. The theorising which takes as its starting point conflict theory in general, on the other hand, places pacific third-party activities among other forms of conflict resolution. Third-party intervention is one form of conflict resolution among legal regulation, the deterrence model and bargaining and negotiation. In a version of the theorising, psychological settlements are distinguished from material solutions. Conciliation deals primarily with subjective elements of conflict and leads to psychological settlement, whereas bargaining is needed for material settlement. In some theories the purpose of pacific third-party intervention is in the realm of conflict abatement or war avoidance rather than conflict resolution.[7]

Peaceful third-party interventions are also placed among negotiation processes. Negotiation is seen as a 'process in which explicit proposals are put forward ostensibly for the purpose of reaching agreement on an exchange or on the realisation of a common interest where conflicting interests are present'.[8] It is argued that mediation is simply an extension of the negotiation process. It is a 'variation on negotiation in which one or more outsiders ("third parties") assist the parties in their discussion'[9] or it 'is the continuation of negotiations by other means'.[10] Effective mediators rely on the same tools as effective negotiators, namely the creation and maintenance of doubt.[11] Mediators transform the bargaining structure from a dyad into a triad by promoting their own interests. In the negotiation triad the mediator is accepted by the parties not because of his or her neutrality but because of his or her ability to produce an acceptable outcome.[12] A subgroup of the negotiation approach is a 'cognitive' approach in which the perceptions and information-processing procedures of negotiators are studied. The cognitive approach examines, for example, the importance of positive sentiments and enhanced understanding for willingness to compromise in facilitated problem-solving workshops. It pays attention to the conditions that lead to cooperation or competition and their relation to the outcomes of mediation processes.[13]

The traditional approaches to third-party intermediary intervention discuss third-party roles, functions, qualities and resources. The theorising is influenced by the system-functional type of analysis. The parties in conflict and the third party are considered to form a system where the third-party functions are understood as the activities of an agent accomplishing a purpose within the system. Third-party roles represent the behaviour expected of the occupant of a given position or status in the system. They are characterised by certain qualities and activities, and they change according to changes in the system. Roles and functions vary from active to passive. The third party can become involved in conflict actively by using deadly force, whereas the third-party facilitative role in the problem-solving workshop is seen to be passive. Although the dichotomy of active and passive third-party roles is entertained by many theorists, a simple postulation of the continuum is highly problematic. It does not take into account the situational elements of third-party activities. For example, in a stalemate situation, the good offices of a third party are extremely 'active' action.

The distinction between active and passive action implicitly forms a basis for many categorisations of third-party roles. Third parties which impose a settlement on the original parties are distinguished from intermediaries which facilitate a settlement.[14] Similarly, it is suggested that there are five third-party roles, namely activist, advocate, mediator, researcher and enforcer. The roles are founded predominantly on the base and credibility of the intervener. Thus such questions as who the intervenor works for, who pays him or her, and consequently what are the structured expectations of the intervener's behaviour in that role are vital in evaluating intermediary actions. The role of an activist is characterised by his or her organisational base and relationship with at least one of the parties. The activist works extremely closely with the parties and becomes almost one of them. The role of an advocate, on the other hand, is based on the advocacy of certain values and parties within the organisation. The role of a mediator derives from the advocacy of processes and interactions, rather than from any of the parties *per se* or from any particular outcomes. The category of researcher includes such professionals as journalists and social science researchers. At the active end of the continuum, the enforcer has the formal power to sanction either or all of the parties.[15]

Third-party functions include the facilitation of communication between the parties and influencing them towards changing their position in order to make agreement possible. By clarifying the issues in conflict, by helping the parties to withdraw from commitments, by reducing the cost of concessions and by offering compromise formulas and substantive proposals, the intermediary provides a framework within which concessions become possible.[16] When the third party's involvement is seen from the point of view of a negotiation process which changes a negotiation dyad into a triad, such additional third-party functions as bargaining and making concessions emerge.

A part of the theorising concludes that the qualities of the third party imply the acceptability of intermediary activities. The third party has to have two basic qualities: impartiality and independence. Both are defined as perceived qualities. An intermediary is independent when he or she is perceived to be free from attachment to or dependence on a political entity that has a stake in the outcome of the crisis at hand.[17] The question of impartiality as it relates to the issue of acceptance is contested by some theorists. It is argued that the 'theory of the impartial intermediary seems to be incompatible with historical evidence of intermediaries who were considered "biased" by at least one of the parties, but were nevertheless accepted'.[18] The observation has expanded the area of theorising from the roles, functions and qualities of the intermediary to motivations, interests and three-cornered bargaining processes.[19] The third party is assumed also to have certain attributes and characteristics. For example, he or she should

18

possess such attributes as patience, sincerity, friendliness, sensitivity, compassion, tact, the ability to accept others, the ability to be non-judgemental and to control self. In a similar vein, salient third-party qualities are thought to include a high degree of professionalism and personal expertise, a high level of independence from the case of conflict being considered, and a lack of any formal, recognised political position.[20]

The model of third-party consultation

The fourth approach to third-party intermediary activities can be found in problem-solving conflict resolution, which Burton's theory exemplifies. The model relies on the cooperative tradition in the study of peace and war and, thus, rejects the power tradition.[21] Although many problem-solving approaches challenge the legal-normative approach to conflict resolution, a strong normative element can be found in them. Their normativity does not arise from international law and its rule-oriented ethics; rather, it arises from the commitment to peace. This commitment to peace – which is analogous to the commitment of the medical profession to the value of health – leads to an instrumental and pragmatic relation to knowledge. It is thought that knowledge drawn from all social sciences should be fully utilised to deal with the intractable problems of the contemporary world. Knowledge and theory are seen to have an intimate as well as instrumental connection with reality.

Social scientists are assumed to represent instrumental knowledge and rationality *par excellence*. With their knowledge they are supposed to be capable of social engineering within a problem-solving framework. In practice, they engage in social engineering by manipulating the setting and structure of the workshop, by choosing the participants, by acting themselves as intermediaries, and by controlling the conceptualisations of the conflict. There is an implicit assumption in the problem-solving model that the control of an environment – that is, managing inevitable changes at all levels of the physical and social world – for example, in the form of problem-solving workshops, is an integral part of human rationality. The Enlightenment idea of the universal human being who is essentially rational and who, because of that rationality, is determined to control the social as well as the natural environment is, thus, fundamental to problem-solving ideology.

Social engineering and instrumental rationality coincide with the principles of (neo)behaviouralism. Behaviouralism is concerned with the underutilisation of the social and behavioural sciences in practical affairs. It is based on uncritical trust in the existence of objective scientific facts and in their value in solving practical problems. Universalising tendencies in the spirit of behaviouralism can be found in the traditional view of problem solving. The conception of universal rationality leads problem-solving workshop approaches to assume that the methods used in workshops are suited to all cultural contexts. The approaches consist also of an element of emancipatory interest. The emancipatory interest manifests itself in a wish to create non-distorted and reciprocal communication which generates emancipation from domination and, finally, helps human beings to achieve rational autonomy. It is assumed that the process of emancipation is forwarded by the 'therapeutic' methods employed in the workshop.

Despite the attempt to create an alternative discourse on intermediary intervention, the third-party consultation model overlaps with the traditional mediation approaches introduced earlier, namely the 'intermediary actions', 'general conflict theory' and 'negotiation system' approaches. The 'intermediary actions' approach generates studies of third-party tactics and identity, which are also central themes in the third-party consultation model. Seen from the point of view of the 'general conflict theory' approach, problem-solving approaches aim at developing a general conflict and conflict resolution theory. Points of departure from the 'general conflict theory' approach are pointed out, for example, by clarifying the terminology. The third-party consultation model claims that the terms 'settlement', 'management' and 'regulation' refer to short-term solutions. These processes may be appropriate to those cases in which authoritative determinations are required in order to preserve social norms, whereas resolution processes are appropriate when any in-depth analysis of behaviour and relationships is required.[22]

Nor does the third-party consultation model accept the idea of a three-cornered negotiation system as an adequate means of conflict resolution. It is argued that negotiation processes and outcomes reflect the relative power of the parties and, therefore, while there may be a settlement, it is likely to be short-lived, as it relies on power relations remaining static. Similarly, the legal-normative approach is rejected, because it is seen to be based on historical and elite norms which do not reflect norms based on the real needs of the individual.[23] The third-party consultation model discusses widely, however, third-party roles, functions and qualities. In terms of third-party roles, problem-solving approaches support passive roles. They use the terms 'facilitator' and 'consultant' to refer to a panel which 'seeks to help the parties arrive at a common definition of their relationship, define their separate goals clearly, and through facilitated analysis, discover options which meet the needs of all'.[24] Some theorists also emphasise the capacity of the facilitator to act as a trainer who assists conflicting parties to learn to analyse their views about the conflict and conflict resolution.

The facilitator is seen to have four basic functions. One of the most important is simply to induce initially, and then sustain, a sufficiently high level of positive motivation from both parties to confront their conflict with a problem-solving attitude. Having established a sufficient level of motivation to participate in a consultative programme, the next function is the improvement of communication between adversaries. The third key function is to regulate in some manner the interaction between the participants. The final function, which in all consultative techniques is regarded as a central third-party activity, is helping the participants to diagnose their conflict. Third-party qualities, on the other hand, are summarised by claiming that the third party has to have professional and personal expertise, professional knowledge regarding conflict, moderate knowledge regarding the parties and their relationship, little power over the parties, control over the situation, and impartiality.[25] These qualities clearly differ from the qualities of the biased mediator in the mediated negotiation system. In the negotiation system the mediator has something at stake in the negotiation process and is, therefore, inclined to use power to control the situation. Moreover, the mediator in the negotiation triad is not, and does not necessarily need to be seen as, impartial.

History of problem-solving conflict resolution

The idea of problem-solving workshops was developed in the early 1960s, when there was an increase in interdisciplinary research in the social sciences in general, and in International Relations in particular, as argued in the introductory chapter. More precisely, such concepts as 'image', 'misperception', 'interaction', 'cultural understanding' and 'communication' became a more common usage of scholars in International Relations. Psychological attempts to explain the perceptions and belief systems of decision makers became one of the most important areas of empirical analysis in the field. A growing interest was in identifying the points at which psychological factors – in the form of images and interaction processes – enter into international relations. Given this interest, problem-solving workshops were seen to be one way to operationalise the factors.

Bringing psychological and social-psychological research into International Relations was meant to be an alternative to the dominant power-politics approach. The impact of social psychology began to undercut the hold of the realist paradigm on at least a part of the field in the late 1970s. The new approach challenged the realist paradigm by claiming that it may be possible to have a single theory of interpersonal, inter-group and inter-state behaviour, and that the view of international relations as a struggle for power may be incorrect. Power politics was considered to be simply an image of reality, not reality itself. Consequently, nation states were no longer the main focus of the research.[26]

In addition to these trends in International Relations theorising, the idea of problem-solving workshops as a form of international conflict resolution was influenced by the development of practical social casework techniques and the conciliation procedures employed in handling industrial and communal conflicts in the 1960s. It was thought that these methods have in common the absence of enforcement and the encouragement of processes of self-adjustment, and, therefore, it was assumed that they might be suitable for international conflict resolution too.[27] Three problem-solving conflict resolution schools emerged, namely, the London, Yale and Harvard schools, which employed International Relations theorising and practical techniques differently.

The London school's leader, John Burton, organised one-week-long problem-solving workshops in 1965 and 1966 which paved the way to other practical attempts. In 1965 there was a meeting between nominees of the governments of Malaysia, Singapore and Indonesia during the violent Borneo dispute. Similarly, there was a meeting in 1966 between nominees of the Greek President and the Turkish Vice-president of Cyprus. Both workshops were guided by a group of scholars facilitating face-to-face interaction between the parties. They were followed by Leonard Doob's two-week-long Fermeda workshop in 1970, which consisted of academics and civil servants from Ethiopia, Somalia and Kenya. Two pilot workshops were also held at Harvard University in 1971 and 1972. In the first, Palestinians and Israelis met over a weekend with a team of social scientists to discuss the conflict in the Middle East. The second workshop focused on the conflict between India, Pakistan and Bangladesh. The Stirling workshop, which brought together fifty-six Catholic and Protestant citizens of Belfast in 1972, was conducted by Doob's Yale team.[28]

An empirical comparison of the workshops is difficult, for pragmatic, contextual and theoretical reasons. Very few empirical data are available on workshops. The principle of confidentiality does not allow the facilitators to publish any detailed descriptions of the work. For example, the London school follows the principle of confidentiality strictly. A simple empirical comparisons of different workshops and their outcomes might also undermine the complexity of historical, societal, economical and cultural factors influencing them. Furthermore, the 'theoretical incompatibility' of the workshop approaches makes comparative studies difficult. The empirical case studies available on problem-solving workshops interpret and construct data according to certain theoretical frameworks. Observations of the behaviour of the participants, of the inputs of the facilitators and especially the evaluations of the outcomes of the workshops are always filtered through different theoretical frameworks whose incompatibility is obvious.

Despite these difficulties in comparing and studying actual workshops, there seems to be a consensus among facilitators and scholars on many practical arrangements and objectives.[29] The goals of the workshop approaches can be partly derived from the general objectives of action research. By creating a framework within which conflicting parties can generate ideas for creative conflict resolution, researchers become involved in an action programme which offers them the opportunity to make observations of continuing processes of conflict and conflict resolution. Opinions vary as to what is the ultimate goal of third-party consultation. According to Burton, the goal is conflict resolution. Kelman, on the other hand, emphasises that the workshop is designed to promote analytical communication which can be fed back and contributes to the resolution of conflict in a negotiation process.[30] In some accounts problem-solving workshops are seen as parallel to official diplomacy, and they are also called 'track-two diplomacy'. Second-track diplomacy is seen to support official diplomacy by offering a framework for the innovative search for solutions; solutions which lay stress on social-psychological factors of conflict.[31]

Misunderstandings and misperceptions characterise conflicts and form substantial barriers to their resolution. Since subjective elements play an important part in conflicts, manipulation of the psychological and physical environments of the problem-solving workshop is thought to be necessary. The manipulation of the psychological environment is done through psychological techniques as well as through managing the physical environment. Important physical arrangements range from the shape of the table to the location of the workshop. The manipulation is justified by claiming that none of the third-party functions or supportive activities can actually be carried out unless the essential physical and social arrangements are present. It is assumed that, when the parties are freed from their official and norm-oriented roles by the unofficial, neutral and relatively isolated setting of the workshop, they will engage in new thinking and behaviour. It is also noted that the creation of a 'cultural island' with an illusory atmosphere of friendship in which participants are encouraged to forget that they represent communities engaged in a bitter conflict can be negative for the purposes of conflict resolution. The participants should not be allowed to forget the reality of their conflict at any stage of the workshop.

The principle of symmetry should apply to all the arrangements of the workshop. Symmetrical arrangements, in an ideal case, imply equality in the number of participants, their institutional links, their manner of recruitment, the conditions they are allowed to impose on their participation, the distances they have to travel, and so on. Although it is not always possible to carry out the principle fully, it can be seen to be actualised satisfactorily when the workshop achieves and maintains credibility in the minds of the participants and the groups they represent. It is emphasised that the identification of the participants is one of the most important and demanding tasks of the facilitator. The task is vital, because the selection is an implicit statement about the parties in and the nature of a conflict. In addition, the selection of participants is essential because analytical problem solving is considered to include intensive work at the level of the perceptions, interactions and behaviour of individuals. Since the problem-solving workshop is often both process- and content-oriented, the ability of the participants to provide it with reasonable process and content inputs is important. How close should the participants be to the decision-making process? Burton and Kelman maintain that representatives have to be in a relationship with their principals because that enables the transmission of alterations in perceptions to decision-making structures. Contrary to Kelman's and Burton's views, Doob's Fermeda workshop consisted of academics and civil servants who worked in areas unrelated to foreign policy. Similarly, the Stirling workshop, organised by Doob and Foltz, consisted of participants who were not major political figures.

The mediating body is a panel of professionally qualified and experienced persons who are not committed to any particular settlement of the conflict, but are 'committed to the search for peaceful and just approaches to conflict resolution'.[32] According to Burton, it is preferable that those who comprise the facilitating party do not have specialist knowledge of the area or the parties involved in the dispute. Kelman and Cohen challenge Burton's view. They maintain that more extensive knowledge is necessary if the consultant is to grasp the nuances of the analysis and to develop credibility with the participants.[33] The third party facilitates communication between the parties, and draws upon social-scientific knowledge in interpreting communication, in analysing underlying attitudes and issues, and in injecting new concepts and ideas into the problem-solving process. The facilitative, non-judgemental and diagnostic third party is supposed to create an atmosphere where the discussion can be raised to a higher system level, from which it can flow back into constructive channels to the dispute in question. In terms of third-party identity, there is a consensus about the necessity of third-party impartiality and neutrality.

Comparison of pilot problem-solving workshop approaches

A comparison of three problem-solving approaches reveals that the Harvard group led by Kelman emphasises that international conflicts are not simply the product of misunderstanding and misperception. Real conflicts of interest or competing definitions of national interests are often, according to Kelman, at the centre of disputes. Although conflicts are not caused solely by subjective factors, face-to-face communication in problem-solving workshops is important because it is a preparation for diplomatic and political negotiations where a conflict can be resolved. In other words, the workshop approach can have a significant impact at those points in the policy process at which individual perceptions and attitudes play a determining role. Since most conflicts involve real clashes of interests, ideologies and structural commitments, the problem of transferring personal changes to the policy processes remains critical.[34]

According to Doob's Yale group, when a problem-solving workshop obliges participants to 'look within themselves and their own experiences to understand their reactions to pressure and conflict', such understanding will facilitate changes in behaviour back home.[35] Problem-solving workshops are expected to produce perceptional, attitudinal and behavioural changes through the development of self-awareness and awareness of others. The underlying assumption is that knowledge of self and circumstances can be applied to bring more control. Control, in turn, is thought to generate conflict management and cooperation in real-life situations. However, Doob and Foltz doubt the possibilities of conflict resolution through the workshop approach. They note about the Stirling workshop that 'we never dreamed that any workshop involving persons from Northern Ireland could ultimately resolve the destructive conflict there'.[36]

Two distinct phases of development are perceptible in the Burtonian approach: communication and human needs frameworks.[37] The communication framework includes a 'triangular conflict theory' which postulates three interrelated causes of conflict. It assumes that, in a society where the demands of individuals are not fulfilled, the situation is perceived to be unjust. Perceived injustice and misperceptions may lead to ineffective communication and, finally, to conflict. Conflicts occur first at a domestic level and, then, spill over to the international sphere. In this view, all three elements of conflict – needs, perceptions and communication – have to be dealt with in conflict resolution processes. The Burtonian needs theory holds the origin of conflict to lie in such human needs as participation, identity and security which will be pursued by individuals regardless of the consequences to self or system. If the institutions obstruct the fulfilment of needs, conflict will result. In other words, international conflicts arise from the failure of domestic systems to provide for the needs of people. Conflict resolution within the problem-solving framework, therefore, involves differentiating interests from needs by identifying universal needs, improving communication and deducing alterations in structures and institutions in order to fulfil the needs identified in the process.[38]

All methods employed by problem-solving workshop approaches are based on theoretical and philosophical premises, including an image of human 'being' and human behaviour. These premises are transferred to problem-solving workshops, to practices, by utilising different techniques. The methods imply what is seen to be conflict resolution. For example, if the method used focuses on learning, the techniques chosen by the facilitator encourage the participants to conceptualise the workshop situation in terms of learning: what is considered to be the resolution of conflict is something which involves learning. On the other hand, if a content-oriented technique, for example through theoretical inputs, encourages the participants to see the conflict situation in the light of universal human needs, the settlement is supposed to tackle those basic needs. In short, the methods set the framework within which the settlement can take place – the techniques are not neutral.

Laboratory methods, from which the workshop techniques mainly derive, are influenced by system theory and, especially, by its notion of feedback. A workshop group is considered to form a system where transactions take place: participants get feedback from other participants and from facilitators, and this feedback can serve to steer subsequent behaviour. Feedback is, thus, considered to be a stimulus which is responded to by a participant. There is an idea of open systems in the type of system theories which form a basis for group therapy and laboratory methods. Structures, within a group or in an environment, are seen to be 'continuously opened and restructured by the problem-solving behaviour of the individuals experiencing and responding to concrete situations'.[39]

The relation between individual and society is at the theoretical centre of some problem-solving approaches. The founders of laboratory methods saw the group as the link between the individual person and the larger social structure. The group was assumed to facilitate change in the larger social structure upon which individual lives depend. The emphasis was neither psychological nor sociological, neither the individual nor the social group, but their interplay.[40] Kelman states clearly the importance of this interplay. According to him, workshop groups are designed to produce change in individuals as a vehicle for change in the policies and actions of the political system.[41]

The Yale group mainly uses two methods which can be subsumed under the categories 'National Training Laboratory' (NTL) approach and 'Tavistock approach'. They are both experimental methods enabling participants to learn about psychological processes. In T-groups (T for training), which are a sub-method of NTL, participants are expected to mobilise problem-solving behaviour. The task of a trainer (facilitator) is to arrange the environment of groups in such a way that learning can take place in a collaborative growth-oriented environment which differs from the everyday competitive, survival-oriented environment the participants face back home. In T-groups members can learn about themselves, interpersonal relations, groups and social systems. The often repeated phrase is that they can 'learn how to learn'.[42] More precisely, at the Fermeda workshop the Yale group utilised a sensitivity training technique, which consisted of a series of small T-group sessions. In these the focus was on relatively free expression of feelings and interaction.[43] The Stirling workshop, on the other hand, used a combination of Tavistock and NTL training. The Tavistock approach is concerned not only with the 'here and now' events but also with the 'there and then' regressive forces which constantly obtrude into the otherwise productive functioning of the group. Learning in the Tavistock approach highlights such issues as authority, power and leadership. The Yale group argues that self-knowledge concerning these issues could be the initial step towards discovering ways through which communities might conceivably live together.[44]

Compared with the methods used at the Fermeda workshop by the Yale team, the Harvard group employs the laboratory method, but does not use solely T-groups or sensitivity training techniques. Since the Harvard school emphasises inter-group processes, it claims to require some additional methods and techniques. The techniques the team utilises in its 'interactional analysis' include structured group-oriented interventions, such as role reversal. Workshop participants are also divided into smaller groups that can work separately, and they are encouraged to engage in conflict fractionation exercises. Although the methods are not pure training methods, they involve participants in learning processes. Kelman and Cohen argue that learning, for example, a common language and symbol system can foster a vocabulary of de-escalation.[45]

The method used by the Burtonian approach can be traced back to two origins, namely the T-group and social casework methods. Casework techniques in social work, with their underlying psychoanalytic origin, consist of a wide range of activities.[46] Their ultimate goal is to develop in the individual the fullest possible capacity for self-maintenance in a social group. The Burtonian approach does not claim that states are maladjusted individuals with whom a facilitator works. Rather, the London school is interested in the supportive approach of the case worker and the professional relationships between the participants and the consultant involved in psychoanalysis, psychotherapy and group therapy.[47]

The pilot problem-solving schools are founded upon the idea of analytical learning in an atmosphere where the participants can be set free from their everyday roles. However, the teams disagree what should be learned and at what level. At the workshops of the Harvard and London groups, learning is oriented also towards content, whereas at the Yale group workshops it is mainly oriented towards group processes. The Yale group uses such concepts as 'emotions' and 'feelings', whereas the other two schools avoid that kind of discourse. The Yale group maintains that the expression of personal emotions is an integral part of conflict resolution in the workshop. The London and Harvard schools do not consider it important, because they want to emphasise the inter-group nature of conflicts. In particular, the Harvard group focuses on the inter-group level and, therefore, criticises the focus of the Yale group on the interpersonal aspects.

The Burtonian approach differs from the other problem-solving workshop schools in its emphasis on human needs. Burton's theory locates sociobiologically based needs at the centre of all violent political conflict. Neither perceptions nor structural factors have the importance of basic human needs. It follows that conflict resolution is highly dependent on the ability of the workshop to deal with needs. As argued, Burton bases his needs theory on sociobiology, which is one of the most influential branches of needs thinking. The next chapter moves into needs theories and discusses different version of them, and especially the variant of theory Burton represents.

NOTES

1 See M. Deutsch, 'Conflict and its Resolution', in C. Smith (ed.), *Conflict Resolution: Contributions of the Behavioral Sciences* (London, University of Notre Dame Press, 1971), pp. 39–49. P. Carnevale and D. Pruitt, 'Negotiation and Mediation', *Annual Review of Psychology*, 43 (1992), 532. D. Sandole, 'Introduction', in D. Sandole and I. Sandole-Staroste (eds), *Conflict Management and Problem Solving: From Interpersonal to International Applications* (London, Pinter, 1987), p. 3.

2 For the subjectivistic and objectivistic definitions of conflict see C. R. Mitchell, *Peacemaking and the Consultant's Role* (Westmead, Gower, 1981), pp. 12–42. K. Webb, 'Structural Violence and Definition of Conflict', in *World Encyclopaedia of Peace* II (Oxford, Pergamon Press, 1986), pp. 431–4. For a strong objectivist argument see H. Schmidt, 'Peace Research and Politics', *Journal of Peace Research*, 5: 3 (1968), 217–32. For a discussion about empowerment see A. J. R. Groom and K. Webb, 'Injustice, Empowerment, and Facilitation in Conflict', *International Interactions*, 13: 3 (1987), 263–80.

3 See M. Ross, *The Management of Conflict: Interpretations and Interests in Comparative Perspective* (New Haven CT and London, Yale University Press, 1993), pp. ix and 116.

4 K. J. Holsti, 'Paths to Peace? Theories of Conflict Resolution and Realities in International Politics', in R. Thakur (ed.), *International Conflict Resolution* (Boulder CO and London, Westview Press, 1988), p. 114. See also I. W. Zartman and S. Touval, 'International Mediation: Conflict Resolution and Power Politics', *Journal of Social Issues*, 41: 2 (1985), 27–45.

5 See J. Burton and F. Dukes, *Conflict: Practices in Management, Settlement and Resolution* (London, Macmillan, 1990). J. Burton, 'Functionalism and the Resolution of Conflict', in A. J. R. Groom and P. Taylor (eds), *Functionalism: Theory and Practice in International Relations* (London, University of London Press, 1975), pp. 238–49.

6 O. Young, *The Intermediaries: Third Parties in International Crisis* (Princeton NJ, Princeton University Press, 1967), p. 34. See also O. Young, 'Intermediaries: Additional Thoughts', *Journal of Conflict Resolution*, 16: 1 (1972), 51–65.

7 Holsti, 'Paths to Peace?', pp. 111 and 114. A. Curle, *Making Peace* (London, Tavistock Publications, 1971). P. Wehr, *Conflict Regulation* (Boulder CO, Westview Press, 1979).

8 F. Iklé, How Nations Negotiate (New York, Harper & Row, 1964), pp. 3–4.

9 P. Carnevale and D. Pruitt, 'Negotiation and Mediation', *Annual Review of Psychology*, 42 (1992), 532.

10 J. Bercovitch, 'The Structure and Diversity of Mediation in International Relations', in J. Bercovitch and J. Rubin (eds), *Mediation in International Relations: Multiple Approaches to Conflict Management* (Basingstoke and London, Macmillan, 1992), p. 3.

11 See T. Colosi, 'A Model for Negotiation and Mediation', in D. Bendahmane and J. McDonald, Jr (eds), *International Negotiation: Art and Science* (Center for the Study of Foreign Affairs, Foreign Service Institute, US Department of State, Washington DC, 1984), p. 25. D. Druckman, 'Four Cases of Conflict Management: Lessons Learned', in D. Bendahmane and J. McDonald, Jr (eds), *Perspectives on Negotiation: Four Case Studies and Interpretations* (Center for the Study of Foreign Affairs, Foreign Service Institute, US Department of State, Washington DC, 1986), pp. 263–88.

12 S. Touval and I. W. Zartman, 'Introduction: Mediation in Theory', in S. Touval and I. W. Zartman (eds), *International Mediation in Theory and Practice* (Boulder CO and London, Westview Press, 1985), p. 10. I. W. Zartman, and S. Touval, 'Conclusion: Mediation in Theory and Practice', in S. Touval and I. W. Zartman (eds), *International Mediation in Theory and Practice* (Boulder CO and London, Westview Press, 1985), pp. 255–6.

13 Druckman, 'Four Cases', pp. 263–88. D. Druckman, 'An Analytical Research Agenda for Conflict and Conflict Resolution', in D. Sandole and H. van der Merwe (eds), *Conflict Resolution Theory and Practice: Integration and Application* (Manchester and New York, Manchester University Press, 1993), pp. 25–42. D. Druckman, and B. Broome, 'Value Differences and Conflict Resolution, Familiarity or Liking?', *Journal of Conflict Resolution*, 35: 4 (1991), 571–93.

14 See Young, 'Intermediaries', p. 52. S. Touval, 'Biased Intermediaries: Theoretical and Historical Considerations', *Jerusalem Journal of International Relations*, 1: 1 (1975), 52.

15 J. Laue, 'The Emergence and Institutionalisation of Third Party Roles in Conflict', in

D. Sandole and I. Sandole-Staroste (eds), *Conflict Management and Problem Solving: Interpersonal to International Applications* (London, Pinter, 1987), pp. 26–8.

16 V. Jabri, *Mediating Conflict: Decision Making and Western Intervention in Namibia* (Manchester, Manchester University Press, 1990), p. 8.

17 Young, *The Intermediaries*, pp. 81–3.

18 Touval, 'Biased Intermediaries', p. 51.

19 For an expanded research agenda see C. R. Mitchell and K. Webb (eds), *New Approaches to International Mediation* (Westport CT, Greenwood Press, 1988).

20 See J. Bercovitch, *Social Conflicts and Third Parties: Strategies of Conflict Resolution* (Boulder CO, Westview Press, 1984), p. 53. Mitchell, *Peacemaking and the Consultant's Role*, p. 120.

21 See P. Lawler, 'Peace Research and International Relations: From Divergence to Convergence', *Millennium: Journal of International Studies*, 15: 3 (1986), 367–90. S. Smith, 'Paradigm Dominance in International Relations: the Development of International Relations as a Social Science', *Millennium: Journal of International Studies*, 16: 2 (1987), 189–206.

22 See Burton and Dukes, *Conflict: Practices in Management*, p. 4.

23 See J. Burton, *Conflict: Resolution and Provention* (London, Macmillan, 1990), p. 191. H. Kelman, 'Informal Mediation by the Scholar/Practitioner', in J. Bercovitch and J. Rubin (eds), *Mediation in International Relations: Multiple Approaches to Conflict Management* (Basingstoke and London, Macmillan, 1992), pp. 67–8.

24 J. Burton, *Resolving Deep-rooted Conflict: A Handbook* (London and New York, University Press of America, 1987), p. 7.

25 See Mitchell, *Peacemaking and the Consultant's Role*, pp. 122–8. R. Fisher, 'Third Party Consultation: a Method for the Study and Resolution of Conflict', *Journal of Conflict Resolution*, 16: 1 (1972), 73.

26 J. Vasquez, *The Power of Power Politics: A Critique* (New Brunswick NJ, Rutgers University Press, 1983), pp. 52 and 75.

27 For industrial conflicts see R. Blake, Robert H. Shepard and J. Mouton, *Managing Intergroup Conflict in Industry* (Houston, Gulf Publishing, 1964). For a summary of studies on inter-group conflict resolution see R. Fisher, 'Third Party Consultation as a Method of Intergroup Conflict Resolution', *Journal of Conflict Resolution*, 27: 2 (1983), 308–11. On communal conflict resolution and Quaker conciliation see C. Yarrow, *Quaker Experiences in International Conciliation* (New Haven CT and London, Yale University Press, 1978).

28 J. Burton, *Global Conflict: The Domestic Sources of International Crisis* (Brighton, Wheatsheaf, 1984), p. 160. J. Burton, 'Three Qualities of a Secure Nation', in M. Macy (ed.), *Solutions for a Troubled World* (Boulder CO, Earthview Press, 1987), pp. 243–7. L. Doob (ed.), *Resolving Conflict in Africa: The Fermeda Workshop* (New Haven CT and London, Yale University Press, 1970). S. Cohen *et al.*, 'Evolving Intergroup Techniques for Conflict Resolution: an Israeli–Palestinian Pilot Workshop', *Journal of Social Issues*, 33: 1 (1977), 166. H. Kelman and S. Cohen, 'Reduction of International Conflict: an Interactional Approach', in W. G. Austin and S. Worchel (eds), *The Social Psychology of Intergroup Relations* (Monterey, Brooks/Cole, 1979), p. 291. L. Doob and W. Foltz, 'The Belfast Workshop: an Application of Group Techniques to a Destructive Conflict', *Journal of Conflict Resolution*, 17: 3 (1973), 489.

29 For the general features of problem-solving workshops see Bercovitch, *Social Conflicts and Third Parties*. Burton and Dukes, *Conflict: Practices in Management*. A. de Reuck, 'Controlled Communication: Rationale and Dynamics', *The Human Context*, 11: 1 (1974), 64–80. *UNITAR Research Reports*, 'Social Psychological Techniques and the Peaceful Settlement of International Disputes', L. Doob (ed.), No. 1 (New York, 1979). Fisher, 'Third Party Consultation as a Method'. R. Fisher, 'Third Party Consultation: a Method for the Study and

Resolution of Conflict', *Journal of Conflict Resolution*, 16: 1 (1972), 67–94. R. Fisher, 'Developing the Field of Interactive Conflict Resolution: Issues in Training, Funding and Institutionalization', paper presented at the fourteenth annual scientific meeting of the International Society of Political Psychology, Helsinki, 1–5 July 1991. B. Hill, 'An Analysis of Conflict Resolution Techniques: From Problem-solving Workshops to Theory', *Journal of Conflict Resolution*, 26: 1 (1982), 109–38. H. Kelman, 'The Problem-solving Workshop in Conflict Resolution', in R. Merritt (ed.), *Communication in International Politics* (Chicago, University of Illinois Press, 1972), pp. 168–204. H. Kelman, 'Interactive Problem-solving: a Social-psychological Approach to Conflict Resolution', in J. Burton and F. Dukes (eds), *Conflict: Readings in Management and Resolution* (London, Macmillan, 1990), pp. 199–215. H. Kelman and S. Cohen, 'The Problem-solving Workshop: a Social-psychological Contribution to the Resolution of International Conflicts', *Journal of Peace Research*, 13: 2 (1976), 79–90. Mitchell, *Peacemaking and the Consultant's Role*. This part of the chapter derives from these sources. The ideas which can be particularly identified with an author are footnoted.

30 J. Burton, *World Society* (Lanham MD, University Press of America, 1987), p. 162. H. Kelman, 'Informal Mediation by the Scholar/Practitioner', in J. Bercovitch and J. Rubin (eds), *Mediation in International Relations: Multiple Approaches to Conflict Management* (Basingstoke and London, Macmillan, 1992), pp. 64–9.

31 D. Bendahmane and J. McDonald, Jr (eds), *Perspectives on Negotiations: Four Case Studies and Interpretations* (Center for the Study of Foreign Affairs, Foreign Service Institute, US Department of State, Washington DC, 1986). J. McDonald, Jr, and D. Bendahmane (eds), *Conflict Resolution: Track Two Diplomacy* (Center for the Study of Foreign Affairs, Foreign Service Institute, US Department of State, Washington DC, 1987).

32 Kelman and Cohen, 'Reduction of International Conflict', p. 300.

33 Burton, *World Society*, pp. 159–60. Kelman and Cohen, 'The Problem-solving Workshop', p. 81.

34 Kelman, 'The Problem-solving Workshop', p. 169. Kelman and Cohen, 'The Problem-solving Workshop', p. 79. Kelman and Cohen, 'Reduction of International Conflict', p. 301.

35 L. Doob and W. Foltz, 'The Belfast Workshop: an Application of Group Techniques to a Destructive Conflict', *Journal of Conflict Resolution*, 17: 3 (1973), 493–7. L. Doob, 'A Cyprus Workshop: an Exercise in Intervention Methodology', *Journal of Social Psychology*, 94 (1975), 161–78.

36 Doob and Foltz, 'The Belfast Workshop', p. 492.

37 A. J. R. Groom and C. R. Mitchell, who have worked closely with Burton, have developed the needs theory in a non-deterministic and non-biological direction. See A. J. R. Groom, 'No Compromise: Problem-solving in a Theoretical Perspective', *International Social Science Journal*, 63: 1 (1991), 77–86. C. R. Mitchell, 'Necessitous Man and Conflict Resolution: More Basic Questions about Basic Human Needs Theory', in J. Burton (ed.), *Conflict: Human Needs Theory* (London, Macmillan, 1990), pp. 149–76.

38 J. Burton, *Conflict and Communication: The Use of Controlled Communication in International Relations* (London, Macmillan, 1969). J. Burton, *Deviance, Terrorism and War* (New York, St Martin's Press, 1979). J. Burton, *Violence Explained* (Manchester and New York, Manchester University Press, 1997).

39 P. B. de Maré, *Perspectives in Group Psychotherapy: A Theoretical Background* (London: Allen & Unwin, 1972), p. 142. See also K. Benne, L. Bradford and R. Lippitt, 'The Laboratory Method', in L. Bradford, J. Gibb and K. Benne (eds), *T-group Theory and Laboratory Method* (New York, Wiley, 1964), pp. 15–44. M. Lakin, *Experiential Groups: The Uses of Interpersonal Encounter, Psychotherapy Groups, and Sensitivity Training* (Morristown NJ, General Learning Press, 1972).

40 de Maré, *Perspectives in Group Psychotherapy*, p. 21. L. Bradford, J. Gibb and K. Benne, 'Two Educational Innovations', in L. Bradford, J. Gibb and K. Benne (eds), *T-group Theory and Laboratory Method* (New York, Wiley, 1964), p. 5.

41 Kelman, 'Informal Mediation', p. 86.

42 See D. Appley and A. Winder, *T-groups and Therapy Groups in a Changing Society* (London and San Francisco, Jossey-Bass, 1973). L. Bradford, J. Gibb and K. Benne, 'Preface', in L. Bradford, J. Gibb and K. Benne (eds), *T-group Theory and Laboratory Method* (New York, Wiley, 1964), pp. vii–x.

43 The Fermeda workshop used T-groups in its first phase. In its second phase the general assembly was formed with the aim of achieving a joint solution. Doob, *Resolving Conflict in Africa*, pp. 9–11 and 119–24. W. Foltz, 'Two Forms of Unofficial Conflict Intervention: the Problem-solving and the Process-promoting Workshops', in M. Berman and J. Johnson (eds), *Unofficial Diplomats* (New York, Columbia University Press, 1977), pp. 204–8. See also a critique of the method as it was used in the Fermeda workshop, A. Eshete, 'Appraisal by an Ethiopian', in L. Doob (ed.), *Resolving Conflict in Africa* (New Haven CT and London, Yale University Press, 1970), pp. 85–103.

44 Doob and Foltz, 'The Belfast Workshop', pp. 500–2. D. Alevy *et al.*, 'Rationale, Research, and Role Relations in the Stirling Workshop', *Journal of Conflict Resolution*, 18: 2 (1974), 276–84. Foltz, 'Two Forms of Unofficial', pp. 201–21. The Tavistock design has been criticised, because participants are put through what is essentially group psychoanalysis. A group of persons who were involved in organising the Stirling workshop writes about the method: 'For some individuals, there can be no denying, this can be a very illuminating process, but inevitably involving the kind of punishing self-analysis which is the basis of psychoanalysis. The value of introducing psychoanalytic techniques into a foreign culture and unfamiliar situation is at the very least questionable.' G. H. Boehringer *et al.*, 'Stirling: the Destructive Application of Group Techniques to a Conflict', *Journal of Conflict Resolution*, 18: 2 (1974), 266.

45 Kelman, 'The Problem-solving Workshop', p. 194. Kelman and Cohen, 'Reduction of International Conflict', pp. 291–5.

46 On social casework see E. Younghusband (ed.), *New Developments in Casework: Readings in Social Work* II (London, Allen & Unwin, 1966).

47 Burton, *Conflict and Communication*, pp. ix and 66–9.

31

3

Burton's human needs theory and the denial of culture in conflict resolution

URTON'S PROBLEM-SOLVING conflict resolution includes a version of human needs thinking. What is particular to the version – as argued in the previous chapter – is that it forms the very core of his conflict and conflict resolution theory. Furthermore, his human needs theory rejects the importance of culture in international conflict resolution. This chapter aims at studying Burton's needs theory and locating his version of theory in a wider tradition of thinking. Both points of convergence and departure between needs theories and Burton's version are pointed out. The study is mainly conducted by employing an analysis of metaphors: Burton's theory is treated as a narrative whose power is based on metaphors. Also the assumptive basis of needs thinking as it relates to the analysis of behaviour and motives is examined in this chapter in order to lay the foundations for an understanding of the rationale of Burton's workshop theory.

There is a long tradition of human needs thinking in Western philosophy and the social sciences. A starting-point for many theories is biology; needs are assumed to arise from man's biological nature. It is also argued that, since needs are biological, they are universal. Theorists have tried to identify the most funda-mental needs and have produced lists which have often only added to the number of needs considered essential. There are clearly two categories of needs which theorists have deduced: 'physiological' needs which are seen to be vital for living organisms to survive and 'psychological' needs which are assumed to contribute to general human welfare.

All these issues are challenged in a needs debate. It is claimed that all lists intended to identify needs are subjective, and potentially endless. Since there is no empirical evidence to support needs thinking, the lists are bound to remain subjective. Moreover, there cannot ever be any empirical evidence, because the concept of need cannot be operationalised. Since it cannot be operationalised, needs theories cannot be verified, or, as Popper would point out, the concept is not falsifiable. It is also asked whether we know according to any objective criteria when needs are satisfied; there may be different degrees of needs satisfaction. The differentiation of needs from their satisfiers is also unclear, it is said, in many needs theories. Although needs are assumed to be universal, the satisfiers could still be seen as culturally constituted.

Examples of the political use of needs theory

Although there is a vast literature on human needs, there is no consistent research programme. In other words, several versions of human needs theory exist. Common to most of them is the postulation of certain universal needs rooted in the biological conditions of being human. The idea of human needs provides a foundation for certain types of assumptions about human nature and the role of culture in human affairs. The approach is thus ideological, as are all social scientific constructs. Two intellectual traditions in Western thinking have explicitly adopted the human needs approach to understand political phenomena. First, the concept of human needs receives considerable attention in the area of political theory. Human needs are a central concept in the language of Stoicism, classical tragedy, Augustinian Christianity, Enlightenment discourse and Marxism. More recently, development studies discuss the notion of needs. There are efforts to identify minimal standards of basic human needs, to determine levels of human needs deprivation, and to recommend how such needs can be satisfied.[1]

For Abraham Maslow, whose version of needs theory is widely employed in social science, the theory of human needs is a theory of the ends and ultimate values of an organism. In short, needs are organisers of behaviour. Maslow's hierarchy of needs includes such needs as physiological needs, safety needs, belongingness and love needs, esteem needs, and a need for self-actualisation.[2] He claims that, when the physiological needs are satisfied, higher needs emerge. An often forgotten element in Maslow's theory is that the hierarchy is by no means meant to be rigid, because it allows a range of variations in needs satisfaction. Maslow's views have some direct relevance to conflict analysis. He writes: 'If it is easy to accept basic needs frustration as one determinant of hostility, it is quite easy to accept the opposite of frustration (i.e. basic need gratification) as an *a priori* determinant of the opposite of hostility (i.e. friendliness).'[3]

Human needs are also related to social control. In Paul Sites's view, individuals attempt to control the physical world in order to gratify their biological needs. He lists eight basic needs: a need for response, a need for security, a need for recognition, a need for stimulation, a need for distributive justice, a need for meaning, a need to be seen as rational and rationality itself and a need to control. Needs are essential in becoming a human being, since the primordial priority of needs stems from primary emotions which are prerequisites of the survival of the physiological organism and psychological self. Given this essentiality of needs, the influence of needs is many times stronger than the influence of the social and cultural forces which play upon human beings. Sites's theory consists of an element of political theory too. He argues that the satisfaction and deprivation of individual human needs are the key sources of societal order and change. People will fight and die to protect values related to needs gratification.[4] Similarly, James MacGregor Burns studies the significance of needs gratification for political processes. According to him, the need for food, security, sex and the higher needs suggested by Maslow have to be gratified if a society is to be harmonious. Burns considers needs as 'wellsprings of political leadership'. Leadership arises from the capacity of a leader to induce followers to act for certain goals that represent the values and the motivations – the wants and needs, the aspirations and expectations – of both leaders and followers.[5]

These three writers illuminate some typical trends in a political branch of needs thinking. They all reduce the origin of human needs to biology. Since needs are seen to derive from the biological nature of the human being, they are also considered to be the primary motivations of human behaviour, and to relate to the social world. The value given to needs satisfaction is assumed to provide a foundation for either social stability or disorder. A linkage between needs satisfaction and social harmony is established in the theories.[6] Human needs thinking postulates also an idea of 'metaphysical originality'. According to the idea, there is something given in the human condition, for example, subconscious, emotions or human needs. The given is considered to be something original and authentic, and human nature is seen to have its main ground on this originality. The original human condition, characterised by human needs in needs theories, is claimed to have priority over other conditioning factors of man's 'being-in-the-world'. Metaphysical originality is also used as a point of reference in scientific explanations concerning human beings. For example, human behaviour is derived from human needs by interpreting human needs as motivations of behaviour.

Burton's functionalist theory of human needs

Burton's needs theory has several similarities to the needs theories introduced above. Burton also reduces the origin of needs to biology. He considers human beings to be determined to satisfy their needs, and postulates a linkage between needs satisfaction and social harmony. In his *World Society*[7] the notion of sociobiological values is developed. Burton's claim is that 'people of all races and creeds have some common values and similar objectives'.[8] The common denominator in different branches of social sciences and the common explanatory factor for human behaviour at different levels can be found in universal sociobiological values. According to Burton, sociobiological values are the preferences of people, the drives that finally underpin or destroy institutions. These values are closely related to, if not direct expressions of, biological drives and motivations.[9]

A fully developed universalistic and biologically based human needs theory is presented in Burton's and Sandole's 'generic theory of human needs'. According to them, a generic theory implies an explanation that transcends observable differences in human behaviour. It is a theory which is universal and applies to all social levels. Burton's and Sandole's theory states that there are fundamental drives and motivations that cannot be repressed. The drives and motivations are based on universal and genetic basic needs – such as the drive for identity, for development, for meaning and for consistency in response – and they direct human behaviour. There can be no long-lasting and authentic social stability unless the basic needs satisfaction of individuals is met.[10] Burton establishes his generic theory of needs by employing the methodological principle of abduction. For him, abduction implies a trust in an original personal hypothesis from which deductions flow. He maintains that abduction is vital, because rarely can there be realistic testing in politics. As the idea of abduction suggests, the emphasis on improving theory is more important than the processes of verification and falsification.[11]

A logic of functional analysis can be found in Burton's version of needs theory. Burton assumes that human needs will be pursued regardless of the consequences. In every society there are, however, elite groups which gain most through the maintenance of the *status quo* and, therefore, resist the demands of the needs satisfaction of other groups in society. Burton calls the phenomenon of resistance 'role defence'. He assumes that if the institutional values, which often reflect the interests of elites, do not fully allow the satisfaction of human needs of all groups in the society, conflict will emerge. Conflict may cause structural changes which weaken the elite positions.[12] Thus, it is maintained, unless elite groups or authorities allow the satisfaction of needs, they are not functional for the society, i.e. they do not contribute to its survival, because human needs satisfaction is the ultimate prerequisite for the stability of society. According to the logic, the functionality of authorities is dependent on the functionality of human needs fulfilment. This functional and instrumental view of society implies that if social forms do not satisfy individual needs, they must be changed. As Ramashray Roy points out, the underlying typically liberal views maintain that the individual is prior to society, society is created by individuals and society exists to serve individual purposes.[13] Although functionalist theories tend to stress the fulfilment of needs as leading to harmony and Burton stresses the non-fulfilment of needs as leading to conflict, the logic of a functional type of explanation prevails in Burton's needs theory.

Similarly, problem-solving conflict resolution is seen in Burton's theory as a steering mechanism whose ultimate function is to contribute to the survival of society. The survival is brought about through controlling and managing change, i.e. through non-cataclysmic change. According to Burton, problem-solving processes help parties in a conflict to cost accurately the consequences of change and the resistance to change. For Burton 'the processes of facilitated conflict resolution are designed to cut down the delays and upheavals that occur in change and to speed up the evolutionary process toward greater fulfilment of societal needs'.[14] Steering of a society takes place within the framework set by the satisfaction of human needs. If there is a tension between human needs and institutions, it is change in institutions that is necessary. The focus in Burton's needs as well as conflict theory is on the individual unit: the needs of the unit determine the effective operation of the social system of which it is a part.

Medical metaphor and a thesis of alienation

For Burton, human needs as such do not lead to conflict. Rather, conflict emerges from the frustration caused by unfulfilled needs. Human needs are something original and constructive in the sense that they include a potential for harmonious society. Institutional arrangements of a society may temporarily destroy the originality, and conflict arises. Deviance and dysfunctional violent conflicts are symptoms of deeper problems in the society, manifestations of conflicts between human needs and structures. In short, conflicts are political manifestations of system failures, the failures of a domestic system to provide the needs of people.

The implicit medical metaphor in Burton's theory insinuates that dysfunctional conflicts and deviant behaviour are signs, like physical symptoms, of something else, of disease. Conflict, as a symptom of a disease, is not as such malign, since it is merely a sign of system failings. In order to understand how conflict can be a symptom, two things have to be noted. First, conflict is endemic, and, second, functional conflicts can be differentiated from dysfunctional ones, or, at least, the functional value of conflict can be differentiated from its dysfunctional consequences. Conflict can have, for example, group-binding, group-preserving and internal cohesion increasing functions. Since conflicts are endemic, the aim is to retain conflict which has functional value and 'to control it so as to avoid perversions which are destructive of human enjoyment and widely held social interests'.[15]

The medical metaphor and analogy included in Burton's theory are firmly rooted in Western thinking. A general medical analogy of society and statesman can be found, for example, in Plato's *Statesman*.[16] According to Plato, the doctor cannot be challenged so long as he acts for the physical welfare of his patients, and by analogy the statesman cannot be challenged so long as he acts for the common social welfare of the citizens he governs. Plato considers the statesman as a specialist who practises an art upon a whole community of non-specialists. Plato seems to suggest that the statesman can have expertise in values. A true statesman has an insight into the nature of reality which, in turn, gives him the moral strength to govern.[17] The medical metaphor of conflict, on the other hand, has its roots in Talcott Parsons's sociology. He considers conflict to be primarily a disease. Conflict appears to Parsons as a partly avoidable, partly inevitable and endemic form of sickness in the body social. Similarly, Lewis Coser's idea of conflict relies on the metaphor. In his discussion of the civil rights movement among Afro-Americans in the United States in the 1960s Coser notes that the riots in Los Angeles 'indicate a sickness in the body social which demands immediate remedy if it is not to undermine social order altogether'.[18]

Johan Galtung, a founding father of Scandinavian peace research, emphasises the professional nature of the field by drawing an analogy between peace research and medical science. As Peter Lawler summarises, Galtung portrayed peace research 'as on a par with the physician's craft: an admixture of social scientific skills applied in accordance with a Hippocratic ethical obligation to improve the health of the emergent world community and not any of its constituent elements (states, nations, classes, races, and so on)'.[19] Galtung emphasises also the ability of the peace researcher to deliver diagnosis, cure and prognosis for the ills of the body politic. Like a medical doctor, a peace researcher can take an objective stance towards social ills and promote the health of the world community.

The medical metaphor can be found in Maslow's texts too. He, like Burton, entertains the idea that the deviance of an individual can be caused by society. Although Maslow does not explicitly relate unfulfilled needs to conflict, the medical metaphor in his text is powerful. It creates an image of a sick society which is capable of producing defeated and alienated individuals. Maslow writes:

> If we were to use the word *sick* in this way, we should then also have to face squarely the relation of people to their society. One clear implication of our definition would be that (1) since a person is to be called sick who is basically thwarted, and (2) since such basic thwarting is made possible ultimately only by forces outside the individual, then (3) sickness in the individual must come ultimately from a sickness in the society. The good society would then be defined as one that permitted people's highest purposes to emerge by satisfying all their basic needs.[20]

If conflict is a sign, what is the disease? The disease in the body social is alienation. The notion of alienation also has a long tradition in Western thinking.[21] The term can best be understood through its negative connotations. The theological use of alienation established a meaning by speaking of the isolation of the human from God. Kant took a first step towards building a link between alienation and reification. The link imputes a negative value judgement on the objectifying process of economic transfers. Durkheim's description of *anomie*, which can be interpreted as alienation, brings in social norms. For Durkheim *anomie* is a situation in which the social norms regulating individual conduct have broken down or are no longer effective as rules of behaviour.[22]

The human needs narrative of Burton postulates a version of the alienation thesis. The thesis consists of the idea of human needs as something original which cannot be suppressed. Values imposed by institutions may try to alienate individuals from their human values, separate people from their needs and the metaphysical originality constituted by needs. As Burton explicitly argues, 'alienation occurs in any system if, in practice, participation and identity are denied'.[23] Institutional values may cause alienation, whose symptom is deviant behaviour and dysfunctional conflict. The result is a sick society which is characterised by a further denial of human needs satisfaction. Moreover, in the pathological society the major constraints of human behaviour, namely values attached to relationships, do not work and, as a consequence, authorities lose their legitimacy. Burton writes:

> We arrive at the position that the individual in society will pursue his needs and desires (some of which may be programmed genetically and may include some elements of altruism) to the extent that he finds this possible within the confines of his environment, his experience and knowledge of options and all other capabilities and constraints; he will use the norms common within society and push against them to the extent necessary to ensure that they work in his interests; but if the norms of the society inhibit and frustrate to the degree that he decides they are no longer useful, then, subject to values he attaches to social relationships, he will employ methods outside the norms, outside the codes he would in other circumstances wish to apply to his behaviour. In doing so he will be labelled deviant by society; but this is the cost he is prepared to pay to fulfil his needs.[24]

In the sick body social there is 'generally an erosion of authority and defensive responses by authorities'.[25] Decision-makers are not, according to Burton, perceived as being concerned with the common good, and this gives rise to revolutionary, and often violent, changes in leadership. Revolutionary attempts, in turn, lead to even more coercion and an endeavour to enforce law and order by the leaders who want to preserve old structures and institutions.

Social contract and sociality

There is a link between needs fulfilment and sociality in Burton's texts. The medical metaphor and the alienation thesis suggest how an individual becomes antisocial. Burton argues also that if the society offers relationships cherished by the individual, he or she will not challenge them by antisocietal behaviour. Once the basic human needs of the individual are fully satisfied, individuality will merge into and become identical with sociality. By the same token, if basic human needs are fully developed, the individual will be a fully moral person. According to Burton, needs theory 'draws attention to means of promoting harmonious behaviour within a legitimised authority structure'.[26] Unless the needs of individuals and groups are fulfilled, the social and political order cannot be harmonious. Burton notes that the more secure the identity of, for example, a minority ethnic group the more likely it is to accord recognition to others, and to cooperate with wider social and political systems. Individuality becomes sociality, because needs provide objective and rational criteria for policy making and, as a result, a type of society emerges which is acceptable to everyone.[27]

By assuming that there is a natural compatibility between needs fulfilment and sociality, Burton brings forth the old problematique of the relationship between individuality and sociality. The question why authorities have to fulfil needs or offer possibilities for human needs satisfaction sheds some light on the problem. Human needs fulfilment is a source of power in Burton's theory: authorities have legitimacy and can maintain power in a society which enables needs to be satisfied. It is assumed that legitimisation does not derive from force. Rather, its source is in human needs, which cannot be suppressed in the long run. Burton notes the reciprocal gains attained from the legitimised relationship. He writes: 'Legitimisation, on the other hand, stresses the reciprocal nature of relations with authorities, the support given because of the services they render, and respect for legal norms when these are legitimised norms.'[28]

Burton's notion of legitimisation implies a theory of social contract which is seen to suffice to explain the sources of sociality. Traditional social contract theories define certain mutual obligations that generally link rulers and ruled, those in authority and those subject to authority.[29] Burton's theory, on the other hand, does not strictly define any tasks based on mutual obligations. It, rather, provides criteria for legitimised changes in political institutions and social structures in general. According to the tradition of social contract theory set by Rousseau, the obligations of the ruler are protection, the maintenance of peace and order, and the guarantee of material security. In Burton's theory the obligation of the authorities is the general promotion of social conditions such that human needs fulfilment becomes possible. Peace and order, sociality and social harmony, are assumed to follow automatically. The social contract is seen in contract theories to serve to regulate inherent and unavoidable conflict among (1) the demands and requirements of the individual worker or household for food, clothing, shelter and a share in the amenities and pleasures of life, (2) the needs of the society as a whole and (3) the demands and requirements of the dominant individuals or groups.[30] According to Burton (1) and (2) are functionally related in the sense that individual needs satisfaction is supposed to benefit the whole society. However, there can be conflict between the individual and the elite groups or, rather, reified institutional values imposed by the elite groups. The social contract serves to regulate the conflict by offering criteria for legitimate changes when institutional values undermine human values. Social contract theories accept reciprocal obligations by free and rational human agents. Contractual obligations postulated by contract theorists are often founded on natural law or the natural rights of human beings. Natural law is assumed to consist of a body of rules prescribing rights and duties that are considered to be 'natural' in the sense that they pertain to human nature.[31] In Burton's theory the ultimate source of natural law is in needs. As Burton argues, the 'natural law is in this case a set of needs of the individual that must be satisfied if he is to be an effective unit in a harmonious society'.[32]

The form of rationality suggested by the Burtonian type of human needs thinking is mainly instrumental. Since natural law is seen to be based on needs, the mode of human rationality which follows is a rationality of man who tries to maximise his or her needs and continuously reorganises priorities according to respective opportunity costs. This understanding of rationality does not undermine the idea of a social contract. On the contrary, it supports the view by interpreting the contract as a way to guarantee mutual benefits for both the individual and the authority.

Purification through professional cure

Since the problems are 'sick societies' and 'alienated people' a professional cure is needed. When a conflict occurs, the authority of the traditional mediator is, however, undesirable, because it is often based on power and coercion as a means of dealing with conflicts. Given the fundamental tension in many conflicts between the preservation of institutions in the interests of social stability and the satisfaction of the needs of individuals, problem-solving conflict resolution offers a way to take into account and cost conflicting interests and strategies. The professional facilitator needed in the problem-solving workshop feeds back to the participants knowledge about common patterns of behaviour in similar circumstances.[33]

In Burton's view the authority of the third party has to derive from the recognition by the parties of his or her professional expertise. 'The third party is an observer in a scientific role' is an often repeated phrase of Burton's.[34] The third party is considered to be in a scientific role when he or she makes no assessments, judgements or value interventions, and adopts a neutral position. The expertise of the facilitator arises from his or her superior knowledge of the 'natural law based on needs' and common patterns of human behaviour.[35] The ideal behaviour of the facilitator suggested by Burton can be traced back to the principles of the positivist natural sciences. According to them, the scientist was to remain an outside observer of the processes of nature. This idea was already being challenged in the 1920s, for example by atomic physicists. Heisenberg claimed then that even in science the object of research is no longer nature itself but man's investigation of nature. His argument disputed the hypothetical distinction between the researcher and the research object prevailing in the natural sciences at that time.[36]

Burton does relax the requirements of the ideal facilitator by employing the metaphor of a doctor. Like Galtung, he maintains that the study of conflict and its resolution and prevention is a profession in the same way that medicine and engineering are professions. They are all universal professions in the sense that the basics of their fields do not vary across cultures. As with any other profession, the profession of facilitator needs an ethical code which guides behaviour. Burton derives three general rules from the medical profession: professionalism, secrecy and perceived neutrality. The rules imply that the creation of a relationship of trust with a client is vital if a professional relation is to emerge.[37] The facilitator, like the doctor, has the expertise to recognise the symptoms of the sick body social. Since the disease is alienation, he or she helps the individuals themselves to overcome the malady. The professional help is needed because individuals and groups are often so deeply involved in their conflict (symptoms) that they do not know how to get the resolution (healing) process started.

The types of skills needed in conflict resolution are, according to Burton, not those possessed by a general practitioner. They are, rather, therapeutic skills. The connection between psychotherapy and needs gratification can be found already in Maslow's texts. He saw therapy as a way to satisfy needs on an interpersonal basis.[38] Similarly, the techniques used in the problem-solving workshops which derive from T-group experiments and social casework have a psychoanalytic origin. The medical analogy has limits. The participants in the Burtonian type of problem-solving workshop are not considered to be 'sick' or 'alienated' individuals, nor are the techniques employed aimed at working at an individual level. Despite the limits, the doctor metaphor justifies certain types of facilitative techniques. The techniques employed in the workshop differ from the techniques used by the traditional mediator, because they are thought to deal with the real causes of conflict, not with symptoms.

A filter metaphor creates an image of the relationship between the facilitator and the participants in the problem-solving workshop. In a problem-solving workshop the facilitator provides a 'filter' and helps the participants to screen out false assumptions and implications from existing knowledge, cultural and ideological orientations and personal prejudices. The main contribution of the facilitator to a conflict resolution process is in checking the preconceptions of the participants and observing and testing their images of reality. Through the filtering processes purification from prejudices, cultural elements and ideologies is assumed to be achieved, and the metaphysical originality – defined now as knowledge of real human needs – is expected to be gained back. Purification is achieved by means of a negative and a positive process. The negative process is the filtering process, where all preconceptions about the existing state of affairs are removed. The positive side is the replacement of conflict-laden theories and information with alternatives that do not lead to conflict. Disclosure is, from the point of view of the participants, the method of filtering. As the psychoanalyst helps the patient to reveal his or her inner feelings, so the facilitator helps the parties to disclose, first, their stereotypes and prejudices and, later, their fundamental and real needs. The vacuum left by the filtering process is filled with 'perfect knowledge' which is assumed to eliminate false consciousness about original human conditions.[39]

The filter metaphor suggests that the problem-solving procedures are not relative to culture and, moreover, that the aim of the workshop is actually to filter away cultural factors. The view clearly denies culture its constitutive role in conflict and conflict resolution. The denial leads to the assumption that there are culture-free techniques of conflict resolution. The underlying notion of an acultural human being derives from Burton's version of needs theory in which needs are rooted in biology and considered to be universal, ahistorical and acultural.

The 'organic cell' and functional cooperation

How is it possible to maintain the healthy situation achieved in the problem-solving workshop that provides society with the preconditions for permanent, but dynamic, harmony? Functional cooperation is the answer for Burton. He maintains that conflict resolution must be based on functional arrangements which are designed to meet a specific set of social, economic or technical needs. Legitimate functional arrangements establish a control mechanism by building up and maintaining valued relationships in society.[40]

David Mitrany's account of the New Deal's political strategy reveals the basic tenets of functional cooperation. He writes:

> Each and every action was tackled as a practical issue in itself. No attempt was made to relate it to a general theory or system of government. Every function was left to generate others gradually, like the functional subdivision of organic cells; and in every case the appropriate authority was left to develop its functions and powers out of actual performance.[41]

The metaphor of the 'organic cell' and its biological analogy are the very core of the functionalist approach suggested by Mitrany. The metaphor creates an image of evolutionary and teleological processes in which cells – as well as societies or even world society – develop internally towards more sophisticated specialisation and subdivisions. Specialisation occurs according to tasks or functions. As a cell responds to its environment, is sensitive to it, so will a society through functional arrangements become more sensitive to changes in its environment and develop new ways of adaptation.

The approach is pragmatic in the sense that there is no need, according to Mitrany, to refer to general theory when tackling practical problems: praxis guides theory. In Mitrany's words, functionalism 'knows only one logic, the logic of problem'.[42] Problems should be dealt with in an incremental manner, because reality is in constant flux where no fixed plans can be applied. The view is liberal and believes in human rationality. The argument is that people can work together most easily on functional, occupational and technical matters, and that by working together in these roles they begin to know and understand each other in other roles. Rewarding common activity, growing gradually as a result of the learning experience of previous success, changes the attitude of rational people towards each other.[43]

Mitrany maintains that the state is unable to guarantee such basic needs as security and the maximisation of welfare. Functional institutions are needed because in them problems are dealt with in an open participatory way by the relevant experts. Gradually a sense of community will arise out of interests held in common. Shared interests will further emerge through task expansion and spillover in which cooperation deepens in existing areas and spreads to new domains. States will lose their salience, and loyalties are transformed from states to functional bodies. The greater the number and diversity of ties the less likely is war to occur. Mitrany recommends two types of actions: actions which take as many issues as possible out of the field of political competition and actions which develop a web of common activities. The network of activities which serves all people will gradually build up foundations for a 'living international society', for a 'working peace system'.[44]

Burton follows Mitrany and applies the idea of functional cooperation to conflict resolution. He maintains that resolution can be assisted by this type of cooperation. In order to tackle human needs, conflict resolution processes must be concerned with finding the political structures which promote the full development of the individual. According to Burton, such structural arrangements might include the development of decentralised systems and forms of functional cooperation. Consequently, functional cooperation would work against elite power and reduce the danger of dysfunctional conflicts.[45]

More important, the logic of Mitrany's functional cooperation can be found in the notion of problem-solving workshop conflict resolution as suggested by Burton. As in a functional institution, problems in the problem-solving workshop are assumed to be dealt with in an open, participatory manner. They are seen to be dealt with not solely by experts, but with their help. Gradually a sense of community is expected to evolve, bringing the participants together more and more in a positive manner to resolve, or at least to discuss, problems which are perceived to be held in common. Problem-solving processes are seen to be learning processes where participants learn about themselves and others. Pragmatism prevails in the workshop in the sense that the participants are also encouraged to discuss practical issues, given that they reflect their real needs. The workshop is thought to be an 'exercise in reason' in which the liberal faith in human rationality is realised.[46]

Mitrany's functionalist approach is in accordance with some views of human needs thinking, because also 'functionalists hold that violence has its roots in the social and economic circumstances of people, and that if we give them a moderate sufficiency of what they want and ought to have they will keep in peace'.[47] As demonstrated earlier, in the Burtonian version of needs theory violence is partly a product of social circumstances. When social structures hinder needs satisfaction, and violence emerges, the individual is not to be blamed. Social circumstances and their relation to social harmony as well as the 'common needs of people' as a foundation for cooperation are, thus, emphasised in both approaches.

Functionalist ideology offers a further justification of trust in the expertise of the facilitator. Functionalism implies that benefits will accrue and spread widely in society when specialists concentrate on a particular task, service or function. The specialists can consider problems of a technical nature, and minimise the role of 'ideology'. As a consequence, effective control and effective management are obtained.[48] This view of expertise supports the notion of acultural problem-solving conflict resolution in which the aim is to limit the power of ideological and cultural factors. The expert facilitator with the capacity to treat problems in a 'technical' manner can best fulfil the limiting function.

There are inherent contradictions in Burton's human needs narrative. The ideas of voluntarism, learning and pragmatism which are rooted in Mitrany's functionalism are opposed by an element of determinism arising from human needs thinking. Since, in the Burtonian version of needs thinking, needs are derived from biology and interpreted as motivations, to an extent they determine human behaviour. At the same time, human beings are seen to be capable of learning and their behaviour is considered to be based on free will. Similarly, the liberal trust in universal reason, which is assumed to actualise in the workshop context, opposes the notion of individual and instrumental rationality found in Burton's needs theory.

Needs as an explanation of human behaviour

The aim of this part is to study the assumptive basis of needs thinking as it relates to the analysis of human behaviour. The purpose is to examine needs theories – especially John Burton's version of needs theory – as one class of explanation of motives. Motive is understood in a following manner: if a human being has a motive, he or she must have a goal of some sort, however weak its influence or however obvious or attainable it may be. There are four types of motive explanations: (1) explanations which deal with the reason of the actor (2) explanations which postulate *the* reason (3) causal explanations and (4) end-state explanations.[49]

Needs theories are one type of end-state explanation of human behaviour. An end-state explanation explains behaviour by reference to requirements of the organism which serve to organise and motivate behaviour. In this view, needs can be interpreted as a construct, a fiction or hypothetical concept, which stands, for example, for a force in the region of the brain. Furthermore, needs can be assumed to have substantial impact on the perception and organisation of reality as well as on behavioural activities within it.[50]

Seen from another point of view, there is a 'psychologist's use of needs'. That is, needs are seen as hidden causes, whose discovery is made possible by the special technique of the psychologist. Three senses can be noted in the 'psychologist's use of needs'. First, need is used in the sense of conditions for survival, whether of the individual or of the species. In the second sense it is not merely survival that is at stake but quality of survival. The third sense identifies need with homeostatic processes of a physiological nature in which certain kinds of activities restore an independently defined equilibrium.[51]

As suggested earlier where the idea of metaphysical originality in needs thinking was identified, the concepts 'force' and 'hidden causes' are vital for needs theories. If we assume, according to the logic of metaphysical originality, that there is a fundamental stratum of the person which acts as the 'engine' that motivates behaviour, we need to further specify what is the 'engine', or force. It is not sufficient to state that needs as such act as a motivational force, because the questions 'why' and 'how' remain unanswered. As Patricia Springborg notes, almost all subsequent versions of needs theory agree that an explanation of human motivation and conduct is to be sought not in the metaphysical realm of the soul, divine will, or spirit, but in certain instincts, drives, propensities or powers of man as a physical being.[52] Thus one way to specify the 'engine' is to claim that needs correspond with drives,[53] whose demands seek immediate satisfaction at any cost, subject only to the higher cognitive and moral constraints of ego and superego, or, as Burton would claim, of values attached to relationships.

Early attempts to specify human needs proceeded on the assumption that behind every behaviour one could find a corresponding drive. These attempts proved to be problematic, because it was assumed implicitly that every object and situation for which an organism aims must be accompanied by a characteristic drive for the object. Such instincts as an instinct for 'social behaviour' and an instinct 'to avoid eating apples in one's own orchard' became postulated by needs theorists. Lists of needs (needs understood as drives), on the other hand, present difficulties of operationalisation and data gathering.[54] In sum, the problem of how to conceptualise the complexity and diversity of human motives in a way that permits empirical enquiry has not been solved by the conception of 'needs as drives'.

Although teleological (goal-oriented) forms of explanation are employed by many needs theorists, the concept of stimulus and its causal form of explanation can also be found in several theories. Causality enters into a needs explanation if drive is identified with the energy potentially available for behaviour, and it is asked what triggers that potential. It can be answered, as stimulus–response behaviourism does, that an aspect of the environment perceived by an organism acts as a stimulus and triggers behaviour. Some writers have expressed an extreme view by claiming that the use of the drive concept 'reflects an ignorance of the stimulus: if more were known about the stimuli associated with each specific drive, one could dispense with a general non-specific drive factor'.[55]

To sum up, needs theories form a class of prescriptive end-state explanations of human behaviour. Often a reference to needs implies a standard pattern of prescribed goals, but it does not really explain actions by reference to them.[56] Therefore it is necessary, in order to establish a plausible explanation, for needs theories to postulate the idea of drives as the engine of behaviour. Yet the problems of using the notion of drive illuminate the unsatisfactory capacity of needs theories to explain behaviour.[57] The claim for the empirical and objective definition of needs can be understood in the light of these problems. If we could specify a particular set of empirical needs, we would be able to explain at least a part of human behaviour by referring to them. As a consequence, we could repudiate prescriptive explanations based on a normative needs concept.

Needs as an explanation of behaviour raise the question of human nature and, closely related to it, the question of the ontological foundation of needs. As Springborg points out in her study of Western human needs thinking, a long line of philosophers, from Aristotle to Hegel, and the existentialists, have emphasised the concept of desire. It has been assumed that desire is in some way symptomatic of the human condition. Desire is seen to be expressive of human beings' freedom, because it indicates mankind's own role in fulfilling its needs and in reinforcing its identity and development. On the other hand, the concept of needs can be used to argue a quite different case: one can establish a strong connection between human nature and needs by claiming that needs are embedded in human beings' biological structure.[58] For example, Maslow and Burton argue that needs are biologically founded, genetically implanted. Maslow discusses the 'instinctlike nature of basic needs'. Similarly, Burton's and Sandole's generic theory, which assumes that we are dealing with universal patterns of behaviour and, moreover, with the explanation that transcends observable differences of human behaviour, is founded on belief in the biogenetic origin of needs.[59]

Burton's biologically oriented needs theory exemplifies the idea of universal human nature. The logic of universalistic needs thinking assumes that what is true of human nature must – because universality is one of its facets – be true of all individuals in all cultures. Needs represent a set of objective data that conform to this requirement. The recourse to the universality of needs offers a potent way to defuse contextualism. Moreover, it is concluded by many needs theorists that what is universal, by virtue of its universality, can be accorded greater significance than any local variation: the universal is thought to be more basic than the parochial.[60] Discussions about needs may also include implicit statements about the sociality of needs. As demonstrated in the previous sections, in many needs theories there is a tendency to postulate the compatibility between individuality and sociality. As a result, it is supposed that human nature as such is good. Even the

idea of biologically founded needs can include the axiom. The principle characterises in particular the humanist psychology advocated, for example, by Maslow.[61]

Burton's engines of behaviour

In *Deviance, Terrorism and War* Burton unconventionally differentiates action
from behaviour by claiming that 'the distinction between action and behaviour
is important in this context. Action is observable. Behaviour is the motivation,
the reason for action. It cannot be observed. Observing behaviour is interpretation of action and, as such, may not coincide with the actual motivation leading
to action.'[62] The definition suggests that behaviour is something more original
and deeper than action: it is the reason for action. Action as such is a surface
under which it is possible to find a more fundamental stratum of causes.

The hidden sources of action can be found in human needs, argues Burton.
He claims that 'there are human needs more compelling in directing behaviours
than any possible external influences'.[63] He defines needs as underlying and basic
motivations that cannot be bargained away. Therefore, according to Burton,
needs can be used to explain, for example, dissidence, deviant behaviour and role
defence. Burton's way of using the concept of motivation can be classified as a
'psychologist's conception' in which the motive is seen to be the reason that is
actually operative. As R. S. Peters points out, 'the logical force of the term
"motive" has often been interpreted causally by postulating a particular sort of
causal connection between pursuing the goal and some inner spring of action'.[64]
Burton's interpretation of motive is in accordance with Peters's observation,
because Burton postulates a causal connection between needs as reasons for
action and pursuing the goal of needs satisfaction. His discussion of drives, on the
other hand, can be seen as an attempt to reinforce the causal connection, because
drives clearly establish causal conditions which initiate goal-directed behaviour.

In *Conflict: Resolution and Provention* Burton states explicitly that human
beings have drives. He writes that 'human beings, however, appear to have
certain inherent drives that are not within their ability to control, and which cer-
tainly cannot be suppressed by external socialisation, threats and coercion'.[65]
Moreover, Burton identifies needs with drives by claiming that 'needs, in particular, are inherent drives for survival and development, including identity and
recognition'.[66] He uses here a typical end-state explanation by explaining
human behaviour by reference to requirements of the organism which serve to
organise and motivate it. In addition to establishing causal conditions which initiate behaviour, Burton's explanation relies on teleology in the sense that it postulates a striving or motivation towards something. The concept of drive – or
'needs as drives' – lends itself to be understood, thus, also as a goal-oriented
requirement in his version of needs theory.

In Burton's needs theory, needs act as motives. Since needs are drives, drives are considered as ultimate motives for behaviour. The terms 'motive' and 'drive' become almost synonymous. Needs are assumed to be also goals. Burton writes that 'needs relate to those goals that are universal' and the 'claim for territory could be a tactic in the pursuit of the goal of security'.[67] This use of 'motive' implies that whenever one explains an action by reference to a motive one assigns both a goal and a cause. Burton employs both causal explanation, assigning a cause for behaviour, and teleological explanation, using goals as an explanatory factor. His list of needs, however, limits the scope of causes and goals. He is not arguing that behind every action we can find a corresponding drive. Rather, he claims that there is a certain set of needs (drives), and the ultimate goal of an individual is the satisfaction of those particular needs.

Nor does Burton claim that he is explaining all behaviour. He states that he aims to explain conflictual behaviour and study the behavioural reasons that lead to conflict. Therefore the notion of frustrated and denied needs – or needs satisfaction and obstruction of needs maximisation[68] – is fundamental to his theory: it helps to explain behaviour that is inconsistent with normal behaviour. In the Burtonian explanation of frustrated needs the classic Freudian mechanism is at work. It is assumed that if frustrated in their original purpose the drives must seek substitute outlets and, as such, may turn up in the disguise of opposites.[69] Burton assumes that, for example, the need for identity, if blocked, may end up taking the form of a territorial claim. The territorial claim, in turn, may be perceived and conceptualised by the actors in terms of conflicting interests.

Despite the aim of explaining mainly 'deviant' behaviour, Burton's needs theory does imply a general theory of behaviour. It is not logical to argue that deviant and conflictual behaviour is motivated by certain drives and normal behaviour by something else. If we postulate a theory based on drives, that inevitably, to a certain extent, explains all types of behaviour. However, it is not to say that there may not be other causes that give rise to behaviour.

As noted earlier, Burton's needs theory relies on the idea of metaphysical originality by equating needs with drives, and by giving drives the status of a motivational force. Drives do not act in a vacuum; they need a trigger to be activated. For Burton, environment plays an important role both as a trigger and as a constraint. He writes:

> All behaviour is a response by an actor – an individual or a group – to the environment. Behaviour cannot be analysed without reference to the personality of the actor. Nor can behaviour be analysed in isolation from the physical setting, the institutional structures and the legal and social rules of the society in which it occurs. It is the result of interaction between the needs and interests of actors and environmental constraints (including the needs and interests of other actors).[70]

The idea of biologically founded human nature is closely related to the notion of drive. In *Deviance, Terrorism and War* Burton postpones the explicit discussion of the bases of human nature. He states that 'for the purposes of this study it is not necessary to enter into any argument whether such needs are genetic or environmentally induced'.[71] On the other hand, while studying nationalism, he concludes that 'these manifestations of nationalism have biological origins and protective functions'.[72] Later, in Olson's and Groom's words, he 'comes down heavily in favour of nature'.[73] He writes, for example, that 'in ontological terms the individual is conditioned by biology' and that needs are 'goals that are ontological or universal in the human species, and which are probably genetic, and which, therefore, are not subject to change even in changed conditions'.[74]

The idea of universal and biologically founded human nature forms the ontological core of Burton's needs theory. The idea of universal human nature is, however, inherently problematic. As Springborg argues, it is not necessarily the case that the common denominator to which we refer in explaining uniform phenomena is necessarily a real entity as such, a simple or discrete thing. She continues: 'This is the problem posed by the theory of universals, raised first by Plato. It is not necessarily the case that the existence of tables in all shapes and forms must be explained in reference to a blueprint or archetypal table which represents their essence; no more is this the case with man.'[75]

All notions of human nature denote 'models of human being'. The medical metaphor discussed earlier insinuates the model of well functioning, healthy individuals whose temporary alienation is caused by the sick society. In the model, pathologies – or deviant behaviour, as Burton calls them – are considered as an effect of dysfunction. This type of image points to a hidden prejudice in favour of the homeostatic model of human being, and favours an account of behaviour as causally determined rather than intentional (goal-oriented).

Values, interests and culture

Burton maintains that 'there are drives and motivations toward human goals that cannot be repressed; for instance, drives for identity, development, meaning, consistency in response (which implies distributive justice), and other ontological needs stated earlier'.[76] The use of both words, 'drive' and 'motivation', implies that there are other motivations than drives. This brings up the traditional distinction between needs and interests and between needs and wants.[77] Burton differentiates needs from interests and values. His argument is that human motivations include 'some that are required for the development of the human species, some that are culturally specific, and some that are of a transitory nature'.[78] For Burton, needs are universal in the human species, values are cultural and interests are transitory.

Values are characteristic of particular social communities, and may alter over periods of time, argues Burton. They are acquired, not genetic. Values motivate behaviour in the sense that preservation of values may lead individuals to defensive and aggressive behaviours. It is the pursuit of needs that is the reason, for example, for the formation of identity groups, but it is values attached to identity groups, and the defence of these values from which aggressive behaviour arises. Interests, on the other hand, refer to the occupational, social, political and economical aspirations of the individual and identity group. They are typically related to material goods, and, therefore, are transitory, negotiable and competitive. Interests are not in any way an inherent part of the individual as are needs and, moreover, they may conflict with needs. Interests motivate behaviour too, but only in a very limited sense: they motivate behaviour which is mainly aimed at an occupational, social, political or economical gain.[79]

Burton's theory consists of an 'onion model' of human beings. The very essence of human being can be found in universal and ontological needs which resist cultural influences. The second layer of the onion is values, which are, to a certain extent, influenced by culture, and, therefore, are relative to societies. Since individuals attach values to needs, values impinge upon needs. The uppermost layer is interests, which are limited in scope and largely under the influence of culture. Interests are related mainly to material gains. All these layers motivate behaviour, but they do it differently: their scope and force vary. The ultimate motivation arises from needs. They are seen to be the engine of behaviour. Values attached to needs have a narrow motivational power. Similarly, utilitarian interests motivate in limited fields.

The layer metaphor raises the question of culture. What is the role of culture in motivating human behaviour? Burton makes his view on culture clear by arguing that culture and needs must be differentiated. Although culture is of the vital importance – it is a satisfier, and many deep-rooted conflicts have an intercultural dimension – 'culture as such, however, we must conclude, is not an important consideration in a facilitated analytical problem-solving conflict resolution process'.[80] Burton recognises the role of culture, but it does not and should not, according to him, intrude into problem-solving processes, as the filter metaphor also indicates. Culture is reasonably deep in Burton's theory, in the layer of values, but it is far from fundamental. Culture is interpreted in Burton's theory in a thoroughly individualistic and instrumentalist manner, existing so far as it can be identified with an instrumental needs satisfier. If human needs are innately prescribed in a needs theory, as they are in Burton's version, it puts a 'heavy burden on culture for which the theory in general makes no room'.[81]

Burton's way of differentiating values and interests from needs does not shift the image of a biologically bounded human being in a social constructionist direction. Since cultural elements brought in by the notions of values and interest do not penetrate to the 'core of the onion', to the level of needs, these conceptions do not elicit discussions on the possibility of culturally and socially founded human existence. Nor does the distinction significantly extend the scope of motives, because the onion model gives priority to needs by placing them in the deepest motivational stratum.

Another way to differentiate needs from interests – and to introduce cultural elements into the theory – would be to claim that the basic division is between artificially (culturally) produced wants and objective needs.[82] In that case, it could be argued, conflicts are caused by the discrepancy between needs and wants, and that the aim of the problem-solving workshop is to overcome the difference by making the participants aware of their true needs. Even this distinction is problematic. It means returning to the Marxist division between real and artificial, between true and false needs.[83] The notion of false needs (or rather wants) evokes easily the notion of 'false consciousness', that is, that human beings under the influence of some forms of society or modes of production (e.g. capitalist) do not get to know their true needs. The problem is that the conception of 'false consciousness' presupposes a 'correct' diagnosis of needs and wants, which is likely to be a dogmatic diagnosis.[84] A 'correct', often also called 'objective', diagnosis of needs, by viewing real needs as independent of the perceptions, concepts and frames of reference of actors in the social world, tends to produce an authoritarian definition of needs which dictates what the real needs should be.

Burton does not use the terminology, but there is an element of this discussion in his theory. It is an aspect that can be found particularly in his conflict resolution theory, where he supposes that many conflictual claims can be reduced to needs. For example, a claim to territory can be interpreted as a need for identity. The logic of the statement is that there is something more original underlying artificial wants. The idea of false consciousness enters into the argument because it is implicitly assumed that the conflicting parties do not know their real needs, and therefore they operate at the level of false wants. The role of the facilitator becomes, according to the logic, justified with reference to a need to raise the level of the participants' consciousness.

Human needs and determinism

Human needs thinking often includes a form of biological determinism. In particular, if needs are referred to as drives, we have little choice but to conform. If needs are considered to constitute a natural law similar to physical natural laws, as Burton considers them to, their determining force cannot be avoided.[85] The notion of determinism as it relates to the explanation of human behaviour is complex. Determinism can be seen to imply a framework which sets certain limits on behaviour, and a form of determinism is implicitly included in the idea of genetically implanted needs.

A simple causal explanation, favoured by a part of sociobiology which claims that everything can be explained in terms of genes, involves biological determinism. Since determinism is the thesis that every event has a cause, belief in determinism often embraces the claim that all human behaviour is causally explicable.[86] Burton's explanation of conflictual behaviour relies on both the causal and the teleological modes of explanation, as demonstrated earlier. He does not claim that everything can be explained in terms of genes. In other words, he does not reduce all behaviour to biology. In this sense his determinism is different from that which can be found in some versions of sociobiology.

There are different degrees of determinism. It is vital to discriminate between such notions as biology 'determines', 'guides', 'sets constraints on' or 'sets a framework for' human being and behaviour. Burton's statement that the 'individual is conditioned by biology' seems to suggest the extreme degree of determinism.[87] However, the sentence can be given another interpretation: the term 'conditioned' can be understood to refer to a set of biological conditions which establishes a framework for behaviour. The degree of determinism in this interpretation is less than in the view suggested, for example, by Kevin Avruch and Peter Black. They argue that Burton's conflict theory is based on biogenetic determinism.[88]

Whichever interpretation we choose, human nature is defined as a given, as a constraint, as a limit by Burton. Humans as humans are seen to have a limited range of options open to them, and that what is taken as a given sets the limits of action. The limited range of possibilities implies that there is a constancy and predictability about what humans will do in specific situations, and 'what is taken as a given maps out a conceptual space' within which theorising on human being takes place.[89]

There are several ways to relax determinism in needs thinking. For example, the study of needs satisfiers, as undertaken by the conflict theorist Christopher Mitchell, assumes that there are culturally and historically relative means to satisfy needs. Marxist theory, on the other hand, supposes that human being is infinitely malleable, because of the possibility of self-creation through praxis. Needs in a human being are considered to be expressive of an ability to transcend the limits of material existence. Humans are self-conscious subjects who know the area of their dependence on the material world, and, therefore, understand the boundaries of freedom. Furthermore, a way to relax biological determinism is to take into account the complicated effects of social learning. Social learning theory can be employed in needs theories by claiming that needs cannot be directly translated into human motives, but, rather, they acquire motive status through social learning.[90] Similarly, different socialisation processes can be seen to shape human being to the extent that it overcomes biological conditions. Burton does not, however, agree with these arguments. He does not discuss praxis as a means to transcend human beings' limitations. Nor does he agree with social learning theories. On the contrary, he claims that the scope of socialisation is limited, and human being is conditioned more by needs than by society.[91]

What type of rationality, then, is included in the Burtonian needs thinking,

52

given his determinism? Avruch and Black claim that in Burton rational behaviour (costing) masks an underlying fundamental irrationality, the at-any-cost fulfilment of basic human needs.[92] The conclusion needs modifying. Since Avruch and Black identify needs in Burton's theory with Freudian irrational Id, they arrive at the conclusion that behaviour is not controlled by reason, that is, it is irrational. Burton's needs theory can be seen, however, from a biological angle. In that view, rationality denotes the survival value of the organism. Parsons calls views which advocate the explanation of action in terms of the ultimate non-subjective conditions such as heredity and environment 'radical anti-intellectualistic positivism'. One form of radical positivism is instinct theory, which, according to Parsons, always refers to the concept of survival value.[93] Similarly, Burton's needs theory refers to the survival of a 'human organism' and sees behaviour in terms of non-subjective conditions such as drives.[94] Given the idea of survival value, behaviour, even at the form of 'at any cost fulfilment of basic human needs', is rational – or at least functional – from the point of view of a biological organism. Behaviour is rational, because it contributes to survival.

NOTES

1 On the traditions of Liberalism, Marxism and Gandhism see R. Roy, 'Three Visions of Needs and the Future: Liberalism, Marxism, and Gandhism', in R. Coate and J. Rosati (eds), *Power of Human Needs in World Society* (Boulder CO and London, Lynne Rienner, 1988), pp. 59–76. R. Coate and J. Rosati, 'Human Needs in World Society', in R. Coate and J. Rosati (eds), *Power of Human Needs in World Society* (Boulder CO and London, Lynne Rienner, 1988), pp. 1–20. P. Springborg, *The Problem of Human Needs and the Critique of Civilization* (London, Allen & Unwin, 1981). On development studies see P. Ghosh (ed.), *Third World Development: A Basic Needs Approach* (Westport CT, Greenwood Press, 1984). F. Lisk, 'Conventional Development Strategies and Basic Needs Fulfilment', *International Labour Review*, 115: 2 (1977), 175–91. P. Streeten, 'From Growth to Basic Needs', *Finance and Development*, 16: 3 (1979), 28–31. P. Streeten and S. Burki, 'Basic Needs: Some Issues', *World Development*, 6: 3 (1978), 411–21. B. van Weigel, 'The Basic Needs Approach: Overcoming the Poverty of *Homo Oeconomicus*', *World Development*, 14: 12 (1986), 1423–34.

2 Maslow's list is a foundation for many accounts of needs in the current needs debate. For example, Johan Galtung mentions security needs, welfare needs, identity needs and freedom needs. Oscar Nudler assumes the need for identity, the need for growth and the need to transcend to be fundamental. Joseph Scimecca reduces all needs to the needs of self-reflectivity and freedom. J. Galtung, 'The Basic Needs Approach', in K. Lederer (ed.), *Basic Needs: A Contribution to the Current Debate* (Cambridge MA, Oelgeschlager Gunn & Hain, 1980), p. 66. O. Nudler, 'Human Needs: a Sophisticated Holistic Approach', in K. Lederer (ed.), *Basic Needs: A Contribution to the Current Debate* (Cambridge MA, Oelgeschlager Gunn & Hain, 1980), pp. 143–7. J. Scimecca, 'Self-reflectivity and Freedom: Toward a Prescriptive Theory of Conflict Resolution', in J. Burton (ed.), *Conflict: Human Needs Theory* (London, Macmillan, 1990), pp. 205–18.

3 A. Maslow, *Motivation and Personality* (New York, Harper & Row, 1970), p. 36.

4 P. Sites, 'Legitimacy and Human Needs', in J. Burton and F. Dukes (eds), *Conflict: Readings in Management and Resolution* (London, Macmillan, 1990), pp. 117–44. P. Sites, 'Needs as

Analogues of Emotions', in J. Burton (ed.), *Conflict: Human Needs Theory* (London, Macmillan, 1990), pp. 7–33.

5 J. M. Burns, 'Wellsprings of Political Leadership', *American Political Science Review*, 71: 1 (1977), 266–75.

6 See R. Roy, 'Social Conflicts and Needs Theories', in J. Burton (ed.), *Conflict: Human Needs Theory* (London, Macmillan, 1990), p. 126.

7 J. Burton, *World Society* (Lanham MD, University Press of America, 1987).

8 *Ibid.*, p. 124. Burton lists such sociobiological values as freedom, self-determination, group integrity, equal opportunities in education and employment, and the preservation of cultures and identity.

9 *Ibid.*, pp. 123–36.

10 J. Burton and D. Sandole, 'Generic Theory: the Basis of Conflict Resolution', *Negotiation Journal*, 2: 4 (1986), 333–44.

11 See J. Burton, *Conflict: Resolution and Prevention* (London, Macmillan, 1990), pp. 19–20 and 256. The term 'abduction' as it is originally used by C. S. Peirce suggests that 'while Induction is the inference of the Rule from a Case and a Result, Hypothesis [abduction] is the inference of the Case from a Rule and a Result'. U. Eco, 'Horns, Hooves, Insteps: Some Hypotheses on Three Types of Abduction', in U. Eco and T. Sebeok (eds), *The Sign of Three: Dupin, Holmes, Peirce* (Bloomington IN, Indiana University Press, 1983), p. 203.

12 J. Burton, 'Theory and Reality', *Millennium: Journal of International Studies*, 4: 3 (1975), 258–9. J. Burton, 'The Dynamics of Change in World Society', *Millennium: Journal of International Studies*, 5: 1 (1976), 75–7. J. Burton, *Deviance, Terrorism and War* (New York, St Martin's Press, 1979), pp. 140–50. J. Burton, *Global Conflict: The Domestic Sources of International Crisis* (Brighton, Wheatsheaf, 1984), p. 19. J. Burton, 'The History of International Conflict Resolution', in E. Azar and J. Burton (eds), *International Conflict Resolution: Theory and Practice* (Brighton, Wheatsheaf, 1986), p. 53. J. Burton, *Resolving Deep-rooted Conflict: A Handbook* (London and New York, University Press of America, 1987), p. 19. J. Burton, 'Conflict Resolution as a Function of Human Needs', R. Coate and J. Rosati (eds), *Power of Human Needs in World Society* (Boulder CO and London, Lynne Rienner, 1988), p. 203. Burton, *Conflict: Resolution and Prevention*, pp. 55–7.

13 Roy, 'Three Visions of Needs', p. 74.

14 Burton, 'Conflict Resolution as a Function', p. 203.

15 Burton, *World Society*, p. 138. See also J. Burton, *Violence Explained* (Manchester and New York, Manchester University Press, 1997), p. 38.

16 Plato, *Statesman*, trans. J. B. Skemp (London, Routledge, 1952).

17 *Ibid.*, § 293b–e, pp. 194–5. J. B. Skemp, 'Introduction', in Plato, *Statesman*, trans. J. B. Skemp (London, Routledge, 1952), pp. 40–51.

18 L. Coser, *Continuities in the Study of Social Conflict* (New York, Free Press, 1956), p. 87.

19 P. Lawler, *A Question of Values: Johan Galtung's Peace Research* (Boulder CO and London, Lynne Rienner, 1995), p. 224.

20 Maslow, *Motivation and Personality*, p. 31.

21 On the notion of alienation see H. Barakat, 'Alienation: a Process of Encounter between Utopia and Reality', *British Journal of Sociology*, 20 (1969), 1–10. J. Israel, *Alienation: From Marx to Modern Sociology* (Boston MA, Allyn & Bacon, 1971). E. Mizruchi, 'An Introduction to the Notion of Alienation', in F. Johnson (ed.), *Alienation: Concept, Term, and Meanings* (New York and London, Seminar Press, 1973), pp. 111–24. R. Schacht, *Alienation* (London, Allen & Unwin, 1971). On criticism of the alienation thesis see T. Denise, 'The Concept of Alienation: Some Critical Notices', in F. Johnson (ed.), *Alienation: Concept, Term, and Meanings* (New York and London, Seminar Press, 1973), pp. 141–60. For seminal accounts of alienation see T. Hobbes, *Leviathan*, ed. M. Oakeshott (Oxford, Blackwell,

[1651] 1955), chapter XIV. J.-J. Rousseau, 'A Discourse on the Origin of Inequality', in J.-J. Rousseau, *The Social Contract and Discourses*, trans. G. D. H. Cole (London, Dent, [1755] 1973), pp. 66–75. J.-J. Rousseau, *The Social Contract*, ed. M. Cranston (London, Penguin Books, [1762] 1968), Book I.

22 J. Der Derian, *On Diplomacy: A Genealogy of Western Estrangement* (Oxford, Blackwell, 1987), pp. 15–20. F. Johnson, 'Alienation: Overview and Introduction', in F. Johnson (ed.), *Alienation: Concept, Term, and Meanings* (New York and London, Seminar Press, 1973), pp. 6–7. M. Seeman, 'On the Meaning of Alienation', *American Sociological Review*, 24: 6 (1959), 787.

23 Burton, *Conflict: Resolution and Provention*, p. 94.

24 Burton, *Deviance, Terrorism and War*, pp. 78–9.

25 Burton, *Global Conflict*, p. 39.

26 Burton, *Deviance, Terrorism and War*, p. 213.

27 *Ibid.*, p. 63. J. Burton, *Dear Survivors* (Boulder CO, Westview Press, 1982), p. 26. Burton, *Global Conflict*, pp. 147–8. Burton, *Conflict: Resolution and Provention*, pp. 21 and 106. On the linkage between individuality and sociality see Roy, 'Social Conflicts and Needs Theories'.

28 Burton, *Conflict: Resolution and Provention*, p. 127.

29 They are mutual obligations in the sense that each of the parties is subject to a moral obligation to carry out certain tasks as its part of the implicit social contract and that failure by either party to meet the obligation constitutes grounds for the other to refuse the execution of its task. B. Moore, Jr, *Injustice: The Social Bases of Obedience and Revolt* (New York, Sharpe, 1978), p. 20.

30 *Ibid.*, p. 32.

31 On the connection between natural law and human needs thinking see R. Rubenstein, 'Basic Human Needs Theory: Beyond Natural Law', in J. Burton (ed.), *Conflict: Human Needs Theory* (London, Macmillan, 1990), pp. 336–55.

32 J. Burton, 'The Rôle of Authorities in World Society', *Millennium: Journal of International Studies*, 8: 1 (1979), 78.

33 Burton, *Conflict: Resolution and Provention*, pp. 202–28.

34 See Burton, *Deviance, Terrorism and War*, p. 37. Burton, *Dear Survivors*, p. 121. Burton, *Conflict: Resolution and Provention*, p. 204.

35 J. Burton, 'Resolution of Conflict', *International Studies Quarterly*, 16: 1 (1972), 6. Burton, *World Society*, p. 153.

36 See R. North and M. Willard, 'The Post-behavioural Debate: Indeterminism, Probabilism and the Interaction of Data and Theory', in M. Banks (ed.), *Conflict in World Society: A New Perspective on International Relations* (Brighton, Wheatsheaf, 1984), p. 33.

37 Burton, *Global Conflict*, pp. 149 and 162–3. Burton, 'The History', p. 41. Burton, *Resolving Deep-rooted Conflict*, pp. 27–9. Burton, *Conflict: Resolution and Provention*, pp. 214–16 and 228. Burton and Dukes, *Conflict: Practices in Management*, pp. 186–8.

38 Maslow, *Motivation and Personality*, pp. 92–110.

39 Burton, *Conflict: Resolution and Provention*, p. 208.

40 Burton, 'Functionalism and the Resolution of Conflict', p. 238. Burton, *Deviance, Terrorism and War*, pp. 166–7.

41 D. Mitrany, *The Functional Theory of Politics* (London, Martin Robertson, 1975), p. 163.

42 *Ibid.*, p. 258. See also D. Mitrany, *A Working Peace System* (Chicago, Quadrangle Books, 1966), p. 56.

43 Burton, *World Society*, p. 110. P. Taylor, 'Introduction', in D. Mitrany, *The Functional Theory of Politics* (London, Martin Robertson, 1975), p. xxi.

44 Mitrany, *A Working Peace System*. Mitrany, *The Functional Theory of Politics*, p. 225.

45 J. Burton, 'Regionalism, Functionalism, and the United Nations', *Australian Outlook*, 15: 1 (1961), p. 79. Burton, *Conflict and Communication*, pp. 88–94. Burton, 'Resolution of Conflict', p. 19. Burton, 'The Rôle of Authorities', pp. 76–7. Burton, 'Conflict Resolution as a Function', p. 196. J. Burton, 'Unfinished Business in Conflict Resolution', in J. Burton and F. Dukes (eds), *Conflict: Readings in Management and Resolution* (London, Macmillan, 1990), p. 329.

46 See also K. Avruch and B. Black, 'Ideas of Human Nature in Contemporary Conflict Resolution Theory', *Negotiation Journal*, 6: 3 (1990), 225.

47 Taylor, 'Introduction', p. xi.

48 P. Taylor, 'Functionalism: the Approach of David Mitrany', in A. J. R. Groom and P. Taylor (eds), *Frameworks for International Co-operation* (London, Pinter, 1990), pp. 128–9.

49 R. S. Peters, *The Concept of Motivation* (London, Routledge, New York, Humanities Press, 1958), pp. 27–51.

50 S. Renshon, 'Human Needs and Political Analysis: an Examination of a Framework', in R. Fitzgerald (ed.), *Human Needs and Politics* (Oxford and New York, Pergamon Press, 1977), pp. 53–4.

51 A. R. Louch, *Explanation and Human Action* (Berkeley CA and Los Angeles, University of California Press, 1966).

52 Springborg, *The Problem of Human Needs*, p. 4.

53 'Drive' is understood here as an explanatory concept referring to goal-oriented behaviour. See P. Young, 'Physiological Drives', *International Encyclopaedia of the Social Sciences*, 4 (1968), p. 275. R. Bolles, *Theory of Motivation* (New York, Evanston IL and London, Harper & Row, 1967), chapter 5.

54 Renshon, 'Human Needs and Political Analysis', pp. 56–7.

55 Quoted from Young, who refers to R. Bolles. Young, 'Physiological Drives', p. 276.

56 See Peters, *The Concept of Motivation*, p. 18.

57 See further, on the difficulties needs theories have in explaining behaviour, Louch, *Explanation and Human Action*, pp. 70–9. Renshon, 'Human Needs and Political Analysis'. Springborg, *The Problem of Human Needs*, pp. 252–74.

58 Springborg, *The Problem of Human Needs*, p. 252. It is important to note the difference between needs regarded as a human condition and needs regarded as the very essence of human nature.

59 Maslow, *Motivation and Personality*, p. 54. Burton and Sandole, 'Generic Theory', pp. 333–44.

60 C. Berry, *Human Nature* (London, Macmillan, 1986), pp. 82–5.

61 Springborg, *The Problem of Human Needs*, p. 186. Maslow argues that the gratification of basic needs leads to consequences that may be called 'desirable', 'good', 'healthy' and 'self-actualising'.

62 Burton, *Deviance, Terrorism and War*, p. 32. Burton's differentiation between action and its hidden sources leads him to claim that traditional International Relations theory has missed 'hidden behavioural data', which explains why conflicts persist. Burton, 'World Society and Human Needs', p. 47. The distinction between action and behaviour as it is suggested by Burton is not used in this book. Rather, action is identified with behaviour and the Burtonian notion of behaviour is identified with the motives of behaviour.

63 Burton, *Conflict: Resolution and Provention*, p. 33. See also Burton, *Deviance, Terrorism and War*, pp. 59 and 73. Burton, *Dear Survivors*, p. 75. Burton, *Resolving Deep-rooted Conflict*, p. 23. J. Burton and H. Ramsden, 'Order and Change', in A. J. R. Groom and C. R. Mitchell (eds), *International Relations: A Bibliography* (London, Pinter), 1978, p. 132. Burton claims in *World Society* (p. 126) that sociobiological values (needs) are 'closely related to, if not direct expressions of, biological drives and motivations'. Thus 'they are a fundamental particle of human behaviour'.

64 Peters, *The Concept of Motivation*, pp. 38–9.

65 Burton, *Conflict: Resolution and Provention*, p. 32.

66 *Ibid.*, p. 39. See also Burton, 'The Dynamics of Change', pp. 66–7. Burton, *Global Conflict*, p. 138. Burton and Sandole, 'Generic Theory', p. 338.

67 J. Burton, 'About Winning', *International Interactions*, 12: 1 (1985), 74–5.

68 The terms 'needs maximisation' and 'goal maximisation' refer in this context to the tendency of human beings to satisfy their needs at any cost. Burton, 'The Dynamics of Change', p. 75. Burton, *Dear Survivors*, p. 15. Burton, 'About Winning', p. 88.

69 For the Freudian model see Springborg, *The Problem of Human Needs*, pp. 190–1.

70 Burton, *Deviance, Terrorism and War*, p. 183. See also Burton, 'The Dynamics of Change', p. 70.

71 Burton, *Deviance, Terrorism and War*, p. 75. See also Burton, *Violence Explained*, p. 37.

72 Burton, *Deviance, Terrorism and War*, p. 80. See also Burton, 'The Dynamics of Change', pp. 66–7.

73 W. Olson and A. J. R. Groom, *International Relations Then and Now: Origins and Trends in Interpretation* (London, HarperCollins, 1991), p. 212.

74 Burton, *Conflict: Resolution and Provention*, pp. 36 and 212. In his earlier work Burton saw human being as more malleable, and made more room for society. In *Dear Survivors* (p. 130) he claims that although drives are biologically based, part of them may be acquired, that is, they are generated by the experience of living within a society.

75 Springborg, *The Problem of Human Needs*, p. 191.

76 Burton and Sandole, 'Generic Theory', p. 338. See also Burton, *Violence Explained*, p. 37.

77 Already the Stoics made the disjunction between subjective desires and objective needs. The relation of needs and wants was also much discussed by the Epicureans. The utilitarians, unlike the Stoics and the Epicureans, removed the dichotomy between subjective desires and objective needs. In more recent needs theories Maslow considered instinctoid needs good, and claimed that culture has the power to induce false or artificial needs. Springborg, *The Problem of Human Needs*, pp. 13–14 and 187.

78 Burton, *Conflict: Resolution and Provention*, p. 36.

79 Burton, *Global Conflict*, pp. 145–8. Burton, 'About Winning', pp. 74–75. Burton, 'The Means to Agreement', p. 234. J. Burton, 'World Society and Human Needs', in M. Light and A. J. R. Groom (eds), *International Relations: A Handbook of Current Theory* (London, Pinter, 1985), p. 50. J. Burton, 'The Facilitation of International Conflict Resolution', in L. Kriesberg (ed.), *Research in Social Movements: Conflict and Change* VIII (London and Greenwich CT, Jai Press, 1985), p. 37. J. Burton, 'The Procedures of Conflict Resolution', in E. Azar and J. Burton (eds), *International Conflict Resolution, Theory and Practice* (Sussex, Wheatsheaf; Boulder CO, Lynne Rienner, 1986), p. 96. J. Burton, 'The Theory of Conflict Resolution', *Current Research on Peace and Violence*, 9: 3 (1986), 128. Burton, *Resolving Deep-rooted Conflict*, p. 16. Burton, 'Conflict Resolution as a Function', p. 194. Burton, *Conflict: Resolution and Provention*, pp. 37–9. Burton and Sandole, 'Generic Theory', p. 337.

80 Burton, *Conflict: Resolution and Provention*, p. 215.

81 Springborg, *The Problem of Human Needs*, p. 188. See also Avruch and Black, 'Ideas of Human Nature', p. 227; Burton, *Conflict: Resolution and Provention*, p. 211.

82 For example, Christian Bay bases his theory of human needs on the idea of artificially produced wants (synonymous desires) and underlying needs. According to him, wants do not always coincide with needs. His thesis is that 'whenever superficial wants are fulfilled but underlying needs remain frustrated, pathological behaviour is likely to ensue'. C. Bay, 'Politics and Pseudopolitics: a Critical Evaluation of some Behavioral Literature', *American Political Science Review*, 59: 1 (1965), 48. See also C. Bay, 'Taking the Universality of Human Needs Seriously', in J. Burton (ed.), *Conflict: Human Needs Theory* (London, Macmillan, 1990), pp. 235–56.

83 Such writers as Herbert Marcuse, Wilhelm Reich, Erich Fromm and Jean-Paul Sartre have tried to trace the doctrine of true and false needs back to Marx. To put it simply, the recent Marxist tradition of needs thinking has argued that capitalist society has forced people to consume greater and greater quantities of commodities that no individual really needs. Exploitation in this context, then, consists not in the failure to meet basic needs so much as in the creation of false needs. Springborg, *The Problem of Human Needs*, pp. 1–18.

84 B. M. Smith, 'Metapsychology, Politics, and Human Needs', in R. Fitzgerald (ed.), *Human Needs and Politics* (Oxford and New York, Pergamon Press, 1977), p. 132.

85 See Burton, 'The Rôle of Authorities', p. 78. Burton, 'International Conflict Resolution and Problem Solving', p. 255.

86 R. Trigg, *Understanding Social Science* (Oxford, Blackwell, 1985), pp. 171–2. For detailed definitions of biological determinism and reductionism see S. Rose, R. C. Lewontin and L. Kamin, *Not in our Genes: Biology, Ideology and Human Nature* (Harmondsworth, Penguin Books, 1985), pp. 5–7. For biological explanations of aggression and violence see K. Webb, 'Science, Biology, and Conflict', *Paradigms*, 6: 1 (1992), 65–96.

87 Burton, *Conflict: Resolution and Provention*, p. 36. Burton states also that 'this biological approach is resisted by many who label it determinism. But if there are universal human needs their final description will be made possible through biology'. Burton, *Global Conflict*, p. 142. He argues also that 'needs theory is not biological determinism' (personal communication).

88 Acruch and Black, 'Ideas of Human Nature', p. 222.

89 Berry, *Human Nature*, p. 104.

90 C. Mitchell, 'Necessitous Man and Conflict Resolution: More Basic Questions about Basic Human Needs Theory', in J. Burton (ed.), *Conflict: Human Needs Theory* (London, Macmillan, 1990), pp. 149–76. Springborg, *The Problem of Human Needs*, pp. 10 and 99. Renshon, 'Human Needs and Political Analysis', p. 60.

91 See Burton, *Conflict: Resolution and Provention*, pp. 33 and 70.

92 Avruch and Black, 'Ideas of Human Nature', p. 227.

93 T. Parsons, *The Structure of Social Action* (New York, Free Press, 1967), pp. 67 and 115–16.

94 Burton states that 'needs are inherent drives for survival and development'. Burton, *Conflict: Resolution and Provention*, p. 39. See also Burton, 'World Society and Human Needs', p. 52.

4

The rationale of
Burton's totalist theory

THE FACILITATOR HAS an important role to play in organising the problem-solving workshop. The facilitator manipulates the workshop in the sense that he or she chooses the participants, organises the setting and chairs discussions. However, that does not explain why conflicting parties decide to enter into the workshop, i.e. choose to search for a problem-solving solution. Nor does it explain how they behave in the workshop situation. For analytical purposes the Burtonian approach is divided into three in this chapter: the entry decision, behaviour within the workshop structure and the behaviour of the facilitator. At every stage it is asked 'What is the mode of behaviour Burton assumes while explaining action?' and 'What is the form of rationality related to the assumed form of behaviour?' The aim of the first part is to study how Burton's theory explains the entry moment, and what kind of reasoning process the participants are assumed to go through. It is tentatively supposed that Burton bases his explanation of entry on rational choice theory or, more generally, on a model of strategic action. The second part of the chapter studies the same issues from the point of view of workshop behaviour, and the third studies it from that of the facilitator. Jürgen Habermas's notion of the teleological and strategic models of action, which offers, at least, conceptual tools for the analysis of Burton, will be studied first. The chapter also discusses the assumptive basis of Burton's explanations. The study of presuppositions leads us to ask such questions as 'What is the ultimate motivational force underlying behaviour?' and 'What kind of suppositions are made about human being and culture?'

Strategic action and rational choice

Since Aristotle the concept of teleological action has been at the centre of the philosophical theory of action. Habermas means by teleological action a situation where the 'actor attains an end or brings about the occurrence of a desired state by choosing means that have promise of being successful in the given situation and applying them in a suitable manner'.[1] The emphasis is on a decision between alternative courses of action.

Habermas defines a strategic model:

> The teleological model of action is expanded to a strategic model when there can enter into the agent's calculation of success the anticipation of decisions on the part of at least one additional goal-directed actor. This model is often interpreted in utilitarian terms; the actor is supposed to choose and calculate means and ends from the standpoint of maximising utility or expectations of utility. It is this model of action that lies behind decision-theoretic and game-theoretic approaches in economics, sociology, and social-psychology.[2]

Habermas discusses the assumptions underlying the teleological model of action. He claims that the teleological concept of action can be viewed under the aspect of purposive-rationality. It is assumed in the model that there are actors who achieve their ends by way of an orientation to, and influence on, the decisions of other actors. Success in action is dependent on other actors, each of whom is oriented to his or her own success and behaves cooperatively only to the degree that fits his or her egocentric calculus of utility.[3]

The Habermasian definition of strategic action draws attention to fundamental questions which can be asked when studying Burton's explanation of the entry stage. First, does an actor calculate means and ends from the point of view of utility when he or she makes a decision to enter a workshop? Second, and more generally, how is an actor assumed to make a rational choice? Third, what is the mode of rationality which is included in Burton's notion of behaviour at this stage of conflict resolution behaviour? The model of strategic action is essentially individualistic, but that does not contradict the Burtonian idea of actor, because for Burton the most important actor is the individual.

Before studying Burton in more detail, the theory of rational choice – or the rational choice paradigm, as it is also called – needs to be examined further. The rational choice approach can be seen to be a subgroup of Habermas's teleological model. The approach proposes to analyse human choice behaviour on the assumption that actors are rational in the sense that they tend to maximise the satisfaction of their preferences or expected utility.[4] It offers a model of optimising behaviour, or, as psychologists see it, the rational choice paradigm is a heuristic device for interpreting behaviour. There are several versions of this theory, including utility theory, decision-making theory, game theory and exchange theory, but they all focus on studying human choice behaviour. In the social sciences the rational choice paradigm has found the most sympathetic response among economists. In general the paradigm is appealing because it is seen to offer a way to model behaviour. As a model, especially as it is employed by economists, the paradigm tells us what we ought to do in order to achieve our aims as far as possible. Unlike moral theory, rational choice theory emphasises conditional imperatives, pertaining to means rather than ends.[5]

Burton's explanation of the decision to enter into the workshop starts with needs maximisation. He states that 'parties to a conflict are responding to the situation in the ways that appear most beneficial to them in light of the knowledge that they have of the motivations of others and the options open'.[6] Actors in conflict 'seek to maximise their satisfactions in the best way they know within the structural conditions existing and within the limits of their knowledge of options'.[7] Human beings, according to Burton, tend to maximise their satisfactions of needs in a way that appears beneficial to them: the Burtonian actor is motivated by the possibility of maximising his or her needs turned into utilities.[8]

This form of needs satisfaction is different from the form discussed earlier, for two reasons. First, it is assumed that the actor takes into account and anticipates other actors and their decisions. That is not the case in the 'everyday' type of needs satisfaction which aims at needs fulfilment at any cost. Second, the actor calculates means and ends and tries to end up with the best maximisation of utility. In 'everyday' needs satisfaction the actor does not calculate, because he or she is 'conditioned' to gain the fundamental goal, that is, to achieve needs satisfaction. The needs explanations are, thus, used by Burton in two separate ways and in two situations. Needs are employed to explain the behaviour of individuals in general, and, on the other hand, needs are used to explain behaviour in a conflict situation and in decision making in conflict. Consequently, the meaning of the notions of 'needs satisfaction' and 'needs maximising' varies according to the context.

The main assumption in Burton's theory as it relates to the decision to enter the workshop is that humans maximise their needs, utilities or gains. (Burton's own terminology varies here.) The maximisation takes place by responding to the environment, and that, in turn, produces behaviour. There are limitations, according to Burton, on utility maximising in terms of the knowledge available and in terms of the motivations of other actors. This implies that the 'Burtonian rational choice model' is not burdened with the game-theoretic assumption that the parties have perfect knowledge of such parameters as the rules of game and the ways to calculate utilities or probabilities. In brief, Burton assumes that human beings are capable of rational behaviour and taking into account the motivations of others and the options available. Burton's theory conforms to the Habermasian notion of strategic action.

The conclusion that Burton employs the strategic model can be elaborated further by asking why the parties choose to enter the workshop when other options may be available to them. Burton studies the issue, and asks whether it is realistic to expect conflicting parties to pursue the seemingly complex processes of problem-solving conflict resolution. He gives two sets of answers. According to the first, since parties cannot afford to have a decision forced on them on important matters of values, they prefer conflict resolution rather than settlement. It is in the interests of participants that conflict is resolved analytically so that stability is the outcome. Moreover, Burton argues, traditional mediation processes have failed because they have not been able to offer a framework in which parties could meet without prejudicing their power and bargaining positions in some way, without attracting charges of appeasement and without making it appear that they are too readily seeking a peaceful solution. Given the failure of traditional mediation processes, parties seek alternative procedures. On the other hand, parties may not be aware of these and perceive no options, and, therefore, perpetuate conflict.[9] These descriptions do not yet explain anything. They simply assume that parties have certain interests, and that, given the option of the problem-solving workshop type of conflict resolution and the failure of traditional means, parties will rely on problem-solving procedures.

The other set of explanations refers to costs and benefits and the capacity of actors to analyse them. For Burton the crucial question is whether resolution processes will be preferred to the cost of conflict. The question dictates the mode of answer, which states that the longer-term costs of conflict will be unacceptable in the absence of an agreement. Therefore, according to Burton, even the more powerful party is prepared to seek problem-solving solutions. Alternative conflict resolution procedures may have costs as well, but these are assumed to be significantly lower than the costs of social disruption in the future if the conflict continues. Burton states that 'whatever ultimate goals we seek to promote or preserve' they are 'most surely and most economically achieved by problem-solving procedures'.[10] What, then, leads Burton to think that actors want the 'most economical solution'? He bases his argument on the presupposition that 'all varieties of human species have abilities to think, and with or without help can follow a logical and analytical thought process'.[11] They are able to go through costing processes which help them to maximise their utilities.

The parties perceive the entry situation as a game, and the facilitator has a role to play at the entry stage. According to Burton, the conflict is perceived as a zero-sum game by the parties at this stage, and, therefore, the perception of other actors and the anticipation of their moves are important.[12] Since the parties are reasoning actors, the facilitator acts as a 'pull' factor: he or she pulls the actors towards the problem-solving procedures by setting out the workshop option. The long-term costs of the conflict act as a natural 'push' factor in the minds of the conflicting parties.

In sum, Burton assumes that the actors engage in calculations about the expected utility of various outcomes. He does not discuss in detail how the actors consider costs, benefits and probabilities, although he supposes that human beings are capable of rational choices, i.e. maximising the satisfaction of preferences (utilities). The prevailing mode of rationality derives from the ability to cost means to an end and to assess consequences of actions.

The entry mode of rationality

There are several elements in Burton's theory which suggest a human tendency to rational behaviour – contrary to Avruch and Black's claim that Burton's version of biogenetic determinism leads to irrationality of behaviour. The question is, what is the type of rationality which is postulated by Burton, and, more crucially, is that form of rationality appropriate to explaining human behaviour in the contexts of workshop entry and problem solving? A study of ontological views of Western rationality are needed to understand the concept of instrumental rationality which characterises the Burtonian entry stage.

Cognitive-instrumental rationality has marked the self-understanding of the modern era. This type of rationality, according to Habermas, 'carries with it connotations of successful self-maintenance made possible by informed disposition over, and intelligent adaptation to, conditions of a contingent environment'.[13] The *telos* inherent in the cognitive-instrumental mode of rationality is instrumental mastery. On this 'realistic' model, rational actions have the basic character of goal-directed, feedback-controlled interventions in the world of existing states of affairs.[14] Similarly, Michael Oakeshott discusses the modern 'Rationalist' whose reason is aimed at problem-solving and whose character is that of the engineer. The mind of the 'Rationalist' is controlled by the appropriate technique, and his or her attention is related to his or her specific intentions. According to Oakeshott, the view takes purpose as the distinctive mark of rational conduct: rational conduct is behaviour deliberately directed towards and governed solely by the achievement of a formulated purpose. In consequence, the view reduces mind to a neutral instrument, to a piece of apparatus in the service of purposes.[15]

Habermas's and Oakeshott's accounts of cognitive-instrumental rationality and the Rationalist come close to the Weberian notion of *Zweckrationalität*. *Zweckrational* (instrumental, means–ends rational) action is rational in the sense of employing appropriate means to a given end. It appears that a person acts rationally when his or her 'action is guided by considerations of ends, means and secondary consequences' and when, in acting, he or she 'rationally assesses means in relation to ends, ends in relation to secondary consequences, and, finally, the various possible ends in relation to each other'.[16] *Zweckrational* action presupposes conscious reasoning in terms of means and ends. This type of action can be defined subjectively and objectively. Subjectively defined, it refers to the expectations the actor has about the consequences of alternative ways of acting, and to his or her conscious efforts to bring about one or some of these expected consequences. There is also, on the other hand, an objectively rational correlate of *zweckrational* action in Weber's theory. The selection of means to a given end can be assessed in terms of objective rationality, since it is thought to be possible to discriminate objectively – for Weber, scientifically – between adequate and inadequate means.[17]

Weber's definitions of rationality refer to ideal types, and, moreover, they are not assumed to exist without other forms of rationality.[18] For the purposes of this study, Weber's definition of *Zweckrationalität* has to be relaxed. A useful definition is offered by John Dryzek, who uses the term 'instrumental rationality' and defines it in terms of the capacity to devise, select and effect good means to clarified ends. According to him, the ideas of instrumental rationality and analytical sensibility go hand in hand. Analytic sensibility implies that complex phenomena are assumed to be best understood through intelligent disaggregation into their component parts, and that those parts are then best apprehended in a piecemeal fashion.[19]

Since the problem faced by the Burtonian actor at the entry stage is to choose the combination of means and ends that will maximise his or her expected utility, Burton has to justify the basis of the choice. Rational choice theory often discusses at this point the issue of rational belief as it relates to probability.[20] According to Burton, however, the bases of a choice can be found simply in the costs. In his view, every actor engages in costing through instrumental reasoning; through reasoning which evaluates means, ends, means–ends relations and consequences. From the point of view of motivation, the actor is motivated[21] at this stage largely by the possibility of maximising utility.

Different criticisms are levelled at the rational choice paradigm and its notion of instrumental rationality. Several writers note that instrumental rationality has nothing to say about either the source or the rationality of the goal of the agent. It speaks only about the most effective means to given ends.[22] In Burton's case the rationality and source of goals can be ultimately derived from universal human needs: the goal is always needs satisfaction. A choice which satisfies a need maximises a utility, and, on the other hand, a maximised utility often satisfies a need.

The notion of interaction is also limited in the rational choice paradigm and in its view on rationality: interaction is thought to be the sum of choices made by each actor.[23] Although instrumental rationality offers insights neither into the rationality of goals nor into interaction apart from the sum of choices made by each actor, the narrative of the prisoners' dilemma can add to it – according to an unconventional interpretation by Norman Denzin – a form of cooperation. For Denzin the prisoners' dilemma is a narrative which principally produces an image of social actors. As he puts it:

> The story of 'The Prisoner's Dilemma' thus contains the rational actor within the prison-house of rationality. For the sake of the theory, and its own narrative structure, the story argues that the actor can get out of that prison only by cooperating with others. In this way, rational choice theorists make the egoistical actor a social being. Once he or she is placed within the game-theory context, all of the assumptions regarding rational choice are brought back into place. What was previously rewarding for individuals now becomes rewarding for groups. Groups will attempt to

induce members to accept and adhere to actions which maximise collective rewards.[24]

An actor has an opportunity of cooperation, but only in the form of game. Similarly, in Burton's theory the actor is basically self-interested, since he or she wants to maximise his or her personal utility, but by making the decision to enter the workshop he or she transcends personal interests and engages in a sphere of common goals.

In Burton's model we have the basic idea of rationality as an instrumental choice of what maximises expected utility. An important feature of this idea is that it makes the rational agent a bargain-hunter. He or she never pays more than he or she must and never gets less than he or she could at the price. Adding the notion of marginal utility to rational choice theory guarantees that the actor will reject inferior choices where it is unclear what his or her best choice is.[25] The rational choice model turns interests and needs into utilities, and reduces motivation to maximising those utilities. The paradigm postulates rational, calculating and maximising human nature. When the model is applied to conflict resolution the sociocultural context is taken as given and its relation to the dispute is treated as unproblematic.[26] In other words, the model has universalising tendencies, and it does not discuss the cultural context of utility maximising. By keeping silent about culturally bounded utilities it can neither explain nor understand choices made in a particular conflict situation.

Three modes of behaviour within the workshop structure

This section of the chapter studies the workshop situation and its modes of behaviour and rationality. Burton's method is to build upon his previous theories and explanations, namely needs theory and the strategic model of action. A pragmatic notion of human action is introduced by Burton at the stage of behaviour within the workshop structure, and the conception of rationality enriched by discursive elements.

Burton claims that needs relate to universal goals. Conflict, however, is never over these universal goals. It is the question of how best to achieve a goal that causes disputes.[27] Given that needs are goals which are sought by all persons, in all cultures and in all circumstances, their satisfaction is also the ultimate target of any problem-solving workshop. Actions are purposive in the workshop context, because they drive at need fulfilment. Purposive actions are explained by reference to their goals in Burton's theory. Those goals need not be attained, but they motivate behaviour and affect the way the agent behaves. In terms of the mode of explanation, Burton employs the form of teleological explanation which assumes a goal at work.

The needs explanation is not the only one employed by Burton. The problem-solving workshop is always a costing process; a costing process which involves changes in values and means. Burton argues that 'given a problem-solving forum, each party, in its own interests, will seek to find means of satisfying, not only its own needs and interests, but also those of others in order to avoid costly and dysfunctional conflicts'.[28] In other words, the parties are assumed to solve problems by finding outcomes that are positive-sum. The Burtonian actor chooses something by costing different options in terms of ends and means. The actor maximises his or her own interests in the problem-solving forum in a way that also maximises the interests of others, and simultaneously transforms the zero-sum relationship into a positive-sum relationship. For Burton, an option which satisfies the needs of all parties is the most beneficial to the participants. Burton, thus, employs the narrative of the prisoners' dilemma to explain sociality and cooperation. By cooperating with others the rational actor is thought to be able to get out of the 'prison-house of egoism'. Unlike the traditional interpretation of the prisoners' dilemma, Burton does not assume that cooperation arises from the second-best choice. He thinks that the most beneficial choice from the point of view of the individual participant includes the possibility of cooperation.

In addition to the needs explanation and the strategic model of action, Burton explains behaviour also by discussing the conceptualisation of the workshop in terms of common problems. The conception of a 'pragmatic mode of behaviour'[29] is appropriate for describing this element in Burton's explanation. The ontological assumption of the view is that reality, or at least parts of it, can be seen and interpreted in the light of problems to be solved.

Burton himself denies the role of pragmatism in problem solving. For him, pragmatism implies an 'absence of knowledge, of theory and of predictive capacity'.[30] He continues by defining pragmatism in relation to conflict resolution:

> In other words, pragmatism is the process of exploring alternatives almost at random, though intuition and experience may guide. If these alternatives prove useful or beneficial they should be followed, even in the absence of any reasoned or theoretical justifications which would throw light on longer-term consequences. If they fail others must be sought, again by pragmatic means. Faced with a problem or a specific conflict, the pragmatist employs intuition, unconsciously held theories, trial and error, innovation and expediency.[31]

Burton's view of pragmatism is restricted and based on limited aspects, and even these chosen elements are partly misinterpreted. To challenge Burton's view on pragmatism it is sufficient to summarise that although pragmatists deny the possibility of transhistorical knowledge, that implies neither rejection of reason nor trust in intuitive means.[32] Despite Burton's denial of pragmatism, it can be demonstrated how pragmatism opens up points of views to Burton's explanation of workshop activities.

In pragmatism a human being, in order to tackle practical problems and to bring change to an environment, has to be active. The notion of active experience is especially at the centre of John Dewey's thinking. He refuses to identify experience with a passive registry of the 'given'. Rather, the experiencing subject is seen to be active, a judging agent who takes what is presented to be such-and-such, selects and emphasises in arriving at a settled experience. This stress on the reconstructive function of experience means also blurring the edges of the traditional distinction between 'theoretical' and 'practical'. As John Smith notes, 'the older empiricism saw experience primarily as the ultimate basis of theoretical knowledge; Dewey envisaged experience as a means and ultimately method oriented to the future and aimed at the selective control of consequences and outcomes'.[33] Dewey's instrumentalism can be grasped by claiming that in his view 'ideas are not mirrors, they are weapons'.[34] The function of ideas is to prepare us to meet events. In short, the learning capacity of the human species, its ability to overcome obstacles that make for insecurity, are, for pragmatism and especially for Dewey, matters essentially related to the role performed by reflective intelligence in the course of experience.[35]

Burton argues that 'human decision making has, given appropriate concepts and insights into the nature of social problems and their future costs, capabilities that can and do influence future evolution'.[36] He assumes that the problem-solving workshop provides a context for this type of decision making, that is, decision making which uses concepts and insights as 'weapons' for influencing and transforming reality and problems. The facilitator provides the participants with a conceptual and theoretical 'armament', if they do not have it already. Decision making deals with the future in the sense that it evaluates future costs and tries to anticipate future obstacles to needs satisfaction. The human mind, within an appropriate framework, is for Burton an active instrument which constantly judges, selects and emphasises in order to avoid unpredicted and uncontrollable change and events.

Connotations that have become attached to the term 'experience' itself in its ordinary usage under the influence of pragmatism draw attention to some aspects of the workshop structure. The term 'experience' has the connotation of personally undergoing, living through or enduring situations and events. It suggests also the acquisition of skills enabling one to respond in an appropriate fashion to the way objects encountered will behave, persons will conduct themselves or systems will work. The term, thus, refers to active and transforming skills to achieve a certain aim or to resolve a problem arising. On both connotations experience means interactions and transactions, commerce between the experiencing subject and whatever is encountered or needs to be handled.[37]

Burton regards the workshop as a place where active and constructive encounters between the conflicting parties can take place. In the workshop the

participants can acquire 'skills' to resolve problems and to consider the consequences of their actions. The participants are encouraged to be analytical in
order to discover options that are acceptable in terms of their interests, and
which satisfy their needs. They are encouraged to develop skills which enable
them to respond to their environment in a more beneficial fashion in the future.
Burton's conception of 'conflict provention' can be interpreted also in this
light.[38] Conflict provention means, then, anticipating the future in order to
produce controlled and unconflictual changes in the society by employing skills
acquired in a problem-solving workshop.

There is a structural analogy between the Deweyian notion of knowing and
the Burtonian explanation of workshop experience. Dewey discriminates four
logical moments within a reflective experience. First, reflection arises when there
is a discrepancy or conflict, a felt difficulty within our experience. Second, a
careful formulation of the problem is essential if our inquiry is to be productive.
The third moment demands suggestions for a possible solution. The last step
involves reasoning of the consequences of suggestions, which can lead to testing
and confirming hypotheses.[39] According to Burton's explanation, the methods
used in the problem-solving workshop help the participants to conceptualise and
percieve their conflict in terms of problems to be solved. As in Dewey's reflective
experience, a problem has to be formulated in order to create a productive
problem-solving process. The formulation of a problem is not, however, enough.
Considerations of practical actions have to be produced and tested against
reality.[40]

Burton's needs theory offers the fundamental targets for the workshop. The
notion of needs can be given another interpretation. William James considers
needs as yardsticks of competing metaphysical (e.g. materialism and theism)
views. Smith summarises James's ideas:

> At this point, however, James introduced another and quite different consideration,
> namely human needs and the possibility of their fulfilment. Instead of two alterna-
> tives differing solely in their account of 'what's what' in regard to the future, their
> difference is now to be estimated with respect to their 'appeal' to the person called on
> to believe them and this means what each of the alternatives implies about the life
> and destiny of the person.[41]

The Burtonian notion of 'needs as navigation points' denotes needs as universal
yardsticks for the workshop: the participants can evaluate and reflect upon the
workshop procedures, the options open to them and their own behaviour and
others' behaviour from the point of view of needs. Burton's explanation of workshop behaviour does not suggest that using needs as navigation points should
take solely an abstract form, rather, needs allow the evaluations of the practical
consequences of the workshop too.

In particular, dealing with functional problems involves the parties in evaluating the practical consequences of their actions. As demonstrated earlier, Mitrany's functionalist approach has influenced the Burtonian notion of problem solving. In Mitrany's functionalism, as well as in pragmatism, there is planning, but problems are thought to be best dealt with in an incremental manner. Similarly, Burton assumes that the workshop participants are guided by a practical interest in solving functional problems. These problems are assumed to be dealt with in an incremental manner, since the solution is not a final end product. Rather, the solution 'is itself another set of relationships that contains its own sets of problems'.[42]

Dewey's account of control offers also an angle from which to study some practical elements of problem-solving workshops. Dewey defines the problematic situation in general as some form of maladjustment between the interest and the needs of the organism and the potentialities of the environment. Given the problem of maladjustment as it is defined by Dewey, the control of an environment with the help of technology, social planning and engineering is regarded as solving problems. By comparison, self-control or, more important, reorientation of the self with respect to personal values and ideas, did not receive a great deal of attention in Dewey's thinking. The types of problem where the organism 'becomes problematic to itself', and the problems consequent on that development, are not noted by Dewey. There are, however, problems which cannot be resolved solely in terms of controlling devices projected by an instrumental intelligence aiming at reshaping the environment.[43]

The Deweyian notion of control can be related to workshop activities by asking to what extent the behaviour of the participants is assumed to be motivated by the aim of control. The whole project of the problem-solving workshop can be seen in the light of social engineering which aims at controlling the environment, that is, managing inevitable changes at all levels of the social world by solving problems. Burton does not stop there; he goes further when he explains behaviour in the workshop. He introduces elements of discursive rationality which aim neither solely at controlling nor at purposive considerations of means to an end when resolving a conflict. Discursive rationality points strongly to reorientation and reinterpretation of the 'self' with respect to personal, as well as cultural, values and ideas. In other words, the aspect of control is important in Burton's explanation, but it is not, according to him, the only purpose the actors have within the problem-solving structure. The interactional nature and hermeneutical elements (actors' own interpretations of the situation) of the workshop suggested by Burton add, thus, a new layer to his explanation of workshop behaviour.[44]

The study of Burton's explanation of workshop activities reveals how he builds upon the notion of biologically conditioned human 'being'. The layer following needs theory assumes that human nature is rational in the sense that it is capable of costing and evaluating the consequences of actions. A human being is considered to be able to learn voluntarily, and to change and control its natural and social environments. Control of an environment is not always sufficient for resolving a conflict, and, therefore, Burton postulates an image of a person who engages himself or herself in self-reflective and interpretative behaviour.

Instrumental and discursive rationality

Since the workshop includes purposive cost–benefit analysis of means to an end for resolving the conflict at hand, the notion of instrumental rationality remains in Burton's explanation. The type of explanation referring to a pragmatic interest implies also instrumental rationality, because it assumes the finding of instrumentally solvable functional problems in the workshop. Solving problems is seen to be instrumental for more general and important aims, namely conflict resolution and needs satisfaction. The communicative aspect of the workshop structure, on the other hand, suggests the form of discursive rationality advocated, for example, by Dryzek.[45] Although Dryzek promotes partly uncritically discursive rationality, the concept as he develops it opens up an interesting insight into Burtonian problem solving. It describes fruitfully an aspect of workshop rationality which is hinted at, but not fully theorised, by Burton.

What does discursive rationality mean, and how does it appear in the Burtonian notion of workshop behaviour? Dryzek's views rely heavily on the notion of communicative rationality developed by Habermas. According to Dryzek, discursive rationality is rooted in the interaction of social life. Dryzek refers to Habermas and writes[46]:

> Communicative *action* is oriented toward intersubjective understanding, the coordination of action through decision, and the socialisation of members of the community . . . Communicative *rationality* is the extent to which this action is characterised by the reflective understanding of competent actors. This situation should be free from deception, self-deception, strategic behaviour, and domination through the exercise of power. Communicative rationality is a property of intersubjective discourse, not individual maximisation, and it can pertain to the generation of normative judgements and action principles rather than just to the selection of means to ends. However, communication is concerned in part with the coordination of actions, so communicative rationality cannot totally replace instrumental rationality; rather it can only restrict the latter to a subordinate domain.[47]

The proper home of communicative rationality, according to Habermas, is the life-world of social interaction, where individuals construct and interpret the identities of themselves and others. Communicative rationalisation, in its ideal form, is seen by Habermas to free the life-world from custom, myth and illusion on the one hand and from the domination of specialists and manipulators on the other. Dryzek claims that discursive rationality can contribute to the resolution of complex social problems, because it also allows for reasoned consensus on normative judgements that, if attained, could motivate actions. It makes understanding across different frames of reference possible, since it constitutes generalisable rather than particular interests.[48]

Dryzek discusses 'discursive designs' which are the institutional manifestations of discursive rationality. He uses such examples as alternative dispute resolution procedures and problem-solving workshops. These are discursive designs, according to Dryzek, since around them the expectations of a number of actors can converge; individuals participate in them as citizens, not as representatives of states or a hierarchical body; no concerned individuals are excluded; the collective and individual needs and interests of the individuals involved are included; they are oriented to the generation and coordination of solutions and actions situated within the context of a particular problem, and within the design there is no hierarchy or formal rules, though debate may be governed by informal canons of free discourse, and a decision rule of consensus obtains.[49] Following Dryzek's argument, it can be claimed that a third party is needed to facilitate communication within such a design, because he or she can help the parties to overcome instrumental rationality and to move into the sphere of discursive rationality.

If a problem-solving approach requires that all the actors involved scrutinise the nature of their relationships and analyse the ultimate roots of their differences in the interests of the extinction of the causes of conflict, it involves discursive rationality. Beyond the continued pursuit of instrumental rationality, the workshop as a discursive design can allow for the exercise of discursive reasons about normative judgements, interests, goals, values and problem definitions. Given this understanding of the problem-solving workshop, possible different cultural backgrounds of the participants become highlighted. As Dryzek states, cultural differences are not merely semantic; they involve lack of agreement on the very existence of certain objects. If an agreement is absent, participants can still reach consensus based on reasoned disagreement by striving to understand the cultural tradition and conceptual framework of the other participants.[50]

The Burtonian explanation of workshop behaviour lends itself to interpretation in the light of discursive design and discursive rationality. Burton's explanation fulfils many of Dryzek's criteria of discursive rationality: interaction and intersubjective understanding are taken into account; the individuals participate as citizens; all relevant parties are assumed to be included; there is a particular problem context which does not, however, exclude the scrutiny of mutual relationships; the workshop is structured in a non-hierarchical manner and discussions are informal and free to an extent. Moreover, the third party does not merely emphasise instrumental costing, he or she also guides the participants in the direction of the communicative possibilities of the workshop.

However, it would be a mistake to entirely identify the Burtonian account of workshop behaviour with Dryzek's idea of discursive design, because Burton does not refer solely to the discursive mode of rationality while explaining behaviour in the workshop. What are the main differences? First, the ontological roots of Burton's explanation are in universal and biologically founded needs, and, therefore, it contains a certain degree of determinism. Unlike Burton, Dryzek claims that needs, such as identity, become constituted in a discursive design, in communicative social interaction. All forms of biological determinism are lacking from Dryzek's view. Second, Dryzek opposes social engineering and sees discursive rationality as a weapon against tendencies which enable engineering. As described earlier, Burton's texts suggest a form of social engineering within the workshop. Third, unlike Dryzek, Burton puts a lot of emphasis on analytical reasoning and instrumental costing processes in order to guarantee a purposive account of the conflict at hand. As pointed out above, Dryzek explains workshop activities mainly in the light of discursive, non-purposive reasoning. Furthermore, Dryzek emphases dialectic interaction, whereas Burton's views on utility maximisation reduce the notion of interaction to a 'sum of choices made by each actor'. Fourth, unlike Burton, Dryzek considers culture as a main constitutive factor of human 'being'. In sum, Burton's man is more determined by biological conditions than Dryzek's socially constituted human. Burton's actor is strongly tied to utility maximisation and instrumental rationality, whereas Dryzek's actor is largely communicative, and therefore eager, through discursive designs, to modify his or her socially and culturally produced needs, values and goals.

Interaction

Until now the focus has been largely on the question of how Burton explains human behaviour. However, the workshop concept leads us also to the study of interaction, as the notion of discursive rationality clearly demonstrates. Although Burton does not fully theorise discursive rationality, we can examine how and to what extent he explains interaction while discussing the workshop context.[51]

There are three approaches to interaction as it relates to conflict resolution in the workshop context in Burton's texts. First, in *Conflict and Communication* (which does not yet present Burton's version of needs theory) there is an assumption that misperceptions, false interpretations, prejudice between national groups and unrealistic expectations about the policies of other states are elements, if not causes, of conflicts. It is argued that psychological factors play an important role in conflicts, and controlled communication is a means of tackling them. The virtue of controlled communication is that it is based on face-to-face discussions in which people have to present viewpoints as well as reassess and correct perceptions and interpretations. The improvement of communication, that is, making it effective, between the parties in conflict is thought to be important, because it makes corrections possible.[52]

Burton approaches interaction from the point of view of communication by arguing that the improvement of communication in an interactive problem-solving process is a precondition for conflict resolution. The picture of communication given by Burton is, however, narrow. He limits the discussion to the claim that communication needs to be effective: it needs to be effective in terms of the accuracy of conveying information and the exactness of interpretation. For Burton, 'information must be received as was transmitted' and it is vital that 'what was transmitted was sent deliberately and contained accurate information'.[53]

The second approach to interaction suggests that the facilitator heavily influences direct interaction between the participants. Burton notes that the 'seminar [Falklands/Malvinas workshop] format, including the third party panel of scholars, was designed to ensure an analytical and explanatory discussion that would reveal the hidden data of motivation and intention'.[54] Burton states also that the 'quality of the interaction and of the outcome depends almost entirely on the input from the facilitating panel'.[55] The facilitator is seen to be largely in charge of the analytical interaction between the participants. He or she creates an innovative atmosphere and facilitates qualitative interaction which consists of direct and effective communication. Positive interaction is, in this view, something which seldom exists in a conflict resolution situation without the facilitator.

Third, Burton discusses interactive decision-making models. In that mode of decision making decisions are made as a result of interaction among all parties concerned. Problem-solving workshops are a form of interactive decision making in which the participants are assisted to monitor communication. According to Burton, the 'system of interaction is an open one, that is, the parties are subject not merely to interaction among themselves, but to interaction with a wider environment over which there can be no control'.[56] His argument is the same as earlier, namely: positive interaction can be created in problem-solving conflict resolution processes, and analytical and effective communication advances it.

Since Burton only hints at the possibility of discursive rationality, interaction is an under-theorised and under-explained issue in his texts. He does state that in the intimate and analytical interaction of problem-solving conflict resolution 'the only reality which is relevant is that of the participants'.[57] The statement can be seen to point to interaction which relies on the creation of a shared reality and shared interpretations of the conflict and conflict resolution situation. Since the dominant mode of rationality is then discursive, priority is given to multiple interpretations of reality instead of biologically based needs. If the problem-solving workshop is explained in this way, there is no need to postulate the notion of universal human needs: there is no need to find the universal denominators of human being.

Burton does not accept the interpretation suggested above. He argues that the interactive procedures of conflict resolution are essentially the same for people of all cultures, because there is a 'universal culture' based on needs.[58] In other words, there is the common reality founded on needs of which it is possible to find a common definition. Different interpretations of reality are referred to in the problem-solving context only in order to find the seminal 'needs reality'. The workshop, which acts as a filter, filters out cultural influences, among them 'culturally bounded' interpretations of reality.

Burton's version of needs theory, which extends its internal logic to his conflict and conflict resolution theory, explains human behaviour mainly from the point of view of the solitary ego. It explains behaviour from the point of view of the needs-conditioned and utility-maximising individual. The internal logic of Burton's needs theory leads him to assume that common goals are achieved through utility-maximising behaviour and, therefore, there is no need to theorise interaction. The supposition is, however, problematic: it gives a narrow, biological, picture of human being, prioritises instrumental rationality over other rationalities, and dismisses culture.

The facilitator's pure mind

Needs as an 'engine', as a motivational force of facilitative behaviour, do not determine the facilitator. Burton gives lists of recommended behaviour, but does not explain explicitly why the facilitator acts.[59] Burton's starting-point for explaining the expertise of the facilitator can be found in his version of needs theory. When a need is theoretically established, it opens up a space for expertise, since the means of satisfying it may very well be in the domain of an expert.[60] Human needs can be discovered, if not satisfied, with the right kind of expert knowledge. On this argument, then, one person may know what another person needs better than he or she himself or herself. Needs can be generally spoken about also as realities to be studied disinterestedly by needs experts.

Why does Burton reject discussion of the needs of the facilitator? The 'primitiveness' of needs or, more precisely, the simplicity of drives explains the lack of study. The facilitator has, as Burton seems to suggest, overcome the state of simple needs satisfaction, because he or she is fully aware of his or her own needs. He or she is no longer conditioned entirely by biology, by biologically founded drives. The motivational force of a facilitator is derived not from drives but, rather, from self-awareness and self-reflection. The claim can be supported and illustrated by studying the double role of the facilitator suggested by Burton.

The 'third party is in an analytical, almost a teaching situation, drawing attention to false assumptions, and opening up possibilities of arriving at potentially realistic ones', argues Burton.[61] The third party is a full participant in the workshop, but what makes his or her participation special is superior knowledge of the reasons for behaviour and of the alternative options available to the participants. The knowledge is superior because it implies awareness of general theories of conflict and human behaviour. It enables the third party to be also an 'observer in a scientific role' who 'makes no assessments, judgements or value interventions'.[62] Since the facilitator is not greatly influenced by culturally dependent values or wants, he or she can act as a filter. Burton emphasises the capacity of the facilitator for reasoning, and sees his or her mind as an instrument capable of dealing with complex problems and putting general theories into practice. The mind of the facilitator is filled with expertise knowledge, and it does not consist of prejudices and is neutral in relation to the values of the participants.

The motivational force of the Burtonian facilitator can be found in the purposive, instrumental mind which aims at solving problems and theorising on the basis of experience. Oakeshott calls this type of mind which is assumed to be unprejudiced and open without dispositions a 'purified mind'. Behind the belief in the purified mind there is a conviction that mental disinterestedness and absence of prejudice are intellectual virtues. The notion arises from a desire for certainty and the conviction that certainty is possible only in respect of something we have been given, i.e. the capacity to employ the mind.[63]

If the instrumental mind is the ultimate basis of behaviour, in what kind of context is this mind assumed to work? Given Burton's thesis of alienation and the notion of professional cure (the medical metaphor) which is needed to overcome alienation, the mind of the expert facilitator is assumed to work in curative processes. A parallel to the principles of psychoanalytic therapy and problem solving helps us to understand these processes. According to Springborg, therapy 'puts a heavy emphasis, not on the causality of behaviour, since that is beyond the control of the individual to a certain extent, but on the ability of the individual to understand, adapt to, and monitor his own development and his relations to the external world'.[64] Although the analyst helps to interpret the psychic processes of the patient with reference to metapsychological principles, the form which therapy takes is that of the patient telling the analyst, rather than the analyst telling the patient. Psychoanalysis is concerned principally with the subject and his or her interpretations.

The workshop context created by the facilitator is aimed at increasing the ability of the participants to understand the development of a particular conflict and relationships as they relate to that conflict. The subject's own interpretation of a conflict situation is important, but the third party is needed to refer to human needs as 'navigation points', as ontological principles and fundamental goals of the workshop. Human needs are employed by the facilitator in the same way as metapsychological principles are used by the psychoanalyst. Needs are depth metaphors of which the facilitator is aware, but the participants are not. The facilitator can help the participants to interpret the situation by referring to these ontological principles. The facilitator is supposed to be able to fulfil the task, if his or her mind is free from the burden of 'cultural prejudices' which hinder the understanding of the universal principles of human behaviour.

There are, however, major differences between the ideas of psychoanalytical therapy and Burtonian problem-solving conflict resolution. For example, Freudian theory could never have engaged in postulating needs and drives in a behavioural manner; it never presumed to have a scientific knowledge of the causality of behaviour. Therefore, it rarely stepped outside the frame of reference that the patient himself or herself supplied.[65] Burton, on the other hand, postulates needs in a behavioural manner, giving them the status of a motivational force. Since needs are thought to be 'objectively' defined, they are employed as reference points outside the frames of reference of the participants. The facilitator uses them, for example, to conceptualise and interpret the commonalities between the participants although the participants themselves do not necessarily raise the question of common needs.

Although the Burtonian purified mind is abstract in the sense that it is free from prejudices and aims at certainty, it is not alienated from practices. As concluded earlier, the notion of action research is vital for problem-solving approaches. The term 'experience' in its ordinary use is in accordance with the idea of action research. To speak of medical, legal or business experience is to refer to the encounter of an individual and his or her familiarity with the materials, operations and transactions appropriate to one of these practices. The primary emphasis falls on being acquainted with, or actually having done, the operation in question. According to the second connotation, to speak of the experience is to point to the ability to perform effectively.[66] The Burtonian explanation of the behaviour of the facilitator does not arise solely from the notion of the purified mind, because it includes elements which emphasise the familiarity of the facilitator with workshop practices. Familiarity, in turn, implies effective behaviour.[67]

The rationality of the facilitator

The conception of rationality underlying the notion of a purified mind derives from Enlightenment rationality. The eighteenth-century writer Condorcet exemplifies this type of rationality. Enlightenment means in this framework a political concept for emancipation from prejudice through the diffusion of scientific knowledge with its many practical consequences. For Condorcet, perfection no longer means the realisation of a *telos* found in the nature of a thing; it signifies instead a process of improvement that has a direction but is not teleologically limited in advance. Condorcet advocates 'scientifically organising learning processes' which are based on scientific help in answering normative questions. He assumes that all problems to which religious and philosophical doctrines previously supplied answers can be largely transposed into scientifically manageable problems, and in this sense rationally resolved. He supposes that rationality that has broken through in the natural sciences does not merely reflect standards peculiar to Western civilisation but is inherent in the human mind in general.[68]

The idea of the rationalisation process found in Condorcet's thinking is summarised by Habermas:

> He [Condorcet] relies on an automatic efficacy of the mind, that is, on the belief that human intelligence is disposed to the accumulation of knowledge and brings about advances in civilisation through a diffusion of this knowledge *per se*. This automatism appears in two aspects, which stand in an inverse relation to one another. From the *practical* perspective of those involved, the civilising advances appear to be the results of a practice of disseminating knowledge, of the influence of philosophers on public opinion, of the reform of the schools, of popular education, and so on.

In addition to the practical perspective there is always a theoretical perspective of the scientist:

> From the *theoretical* perspective of the scientists, the civilising advances present themselves as phenomena that can be explained by laws of nature. Thus: from the practical perspective, rationalisation appears as a communicative practice carried on with will and consciousness; from the theoretical perspective, it appears as a cognitive process flowing along in a lawlike way.[69]

The Burtonian problem-solving project as a whole is characterised by Condorcetian rationality, and, moreover, the mode of rationality is embodied especially in the behaviour of the facilitator.[70] Three points from Burton's views support the claim. First, Burton's criticism of dogmatism and his attachment to 'scientific processes' reflect the Enlightenment tradition. Burton assumes that he rejects ideological constructs of humanity in favour of an advanced, scientific and non-ideological model.[71] Second, the Burtonian project is based on belief in the existence of natural-law-like needs. By assuming that a set of needs can be discovered scientifically (objectively) Burton trusts in scientific procedures in finding the essence of humanism. He supposes that, because we can define these needs objectively, they can work as guidelines for future decision making and policies. The problem-solving workshop is a 'scientific learning process' where science, based on knowledge of natural laws, helps in answering normative (value) questions. Third, the role of the Burtonian third party as a teacher is similar to that of Condorcet's Enlightener: both are assumed to contribute to the civilising process by diffusing knowledge.

Two other forms of rationality can be found in Burton's explanations of the behaviour of the facilitator. In addition to Enlightenment rationality, the facilitator is assumed to be capable of social engineering, which demands instrumental rationality. The facilitator selects the participants, organises the workshop setting and chairs discussion. All these activities require instrumental rationality which is based on the capacity to devise, select, and effect good means to clarified ends. The end is conflict resolution, and the workshop procedures and setting are means to that clear end. These are means which can be manipulated and engineered with the help of an instrumental mind. The workshop can, on the other hand, be considered to be a discursive design where the facilitator participates in and practises discursive rationality with the participants. The facilitator takes part in exercising discursive reasoning about normative judgements, staying, nevertheless, neutral in relation to the values the participants have.

The rationality debate as an epistemological question

The question of the rationality of the facilitator and his or her modes of behaviour cannot be detached from the continuing rationality debate in the social sciences. The debate is vital, since the Burtonian facilitator is assumed to be a scientist theorising on the basis of his or her practical workshop activities.[72] The discussion can be seen from many angles. It can, for example, be reduced to the question: what does it mean to understand or explain social actions? Habermas summarises the essence of the debate by arguing that 'different models of action presuppose different relations of actor to world; and these world-relations are constitutive not only for aspects of the rationality of action, but also for the rationality of interpretations of action by, say, social-scientific interpreters'.[73] Two issues are important: the views of common rationality or common-good reasons and of the access of a researcher to those reasons. In other words, do we have to postulate a certain form of common rationality to explain human action, and how does a researcher have an access to the domain of behaviour?

The rationality debate has been advanced by Peter Winch, who employs Wittgenstein's notion of a language game.[74] Winch considers social action as rule-following. His thesis is that 'our idea of what belongs to the realm of reality is given us in the language that we use'.[75] The concepts we have settle for us the form of the experience we have of the world. Language in some sense determines or constitutes what is perceived. The inevitable conclusion which follows from Winch's argument is that truth is relative to a language game or, rather, to a form of life from which a language game arises. In this view, reason becomes relativised: what counts as a reason is context-dependent. Martin Hollis and Steven Lukes clarify the difference between the rationalist and relativist positions:

> The crucial point is that the giving of reasons involves a claim that what is cited would, if true, be a good reason. In other words it has to be objectively true that one thing is good reason for another. Where the relativist sees only differences in these standards for rating reasons as good, the rationalist insists on ranking the standards.[76]

Winch represents the relativist end of the continuum. Similarly, for example, Ian Hacking claims that 'our discoveries are "objective", simply because the styles of reasoning that we employ determine what counts as objectivity'.[77] Candidates for truth or falsehood have no existence independent of the styles of reasoning that settle what it is to be true or false in the domain in question. We cannot reason as to whether alternative systems of reasoning are better or worse than ours, because the 'propositions to which we reason get their sense only from the method of reasoning employed'.[78] At the other pole, the argument goes that there is a 'strong core of human cognitive rationality common to the cultures of all places on earth and all times since the dawn of properly human social life'.[79]

Burton is closer to the rationalist view than to that of Winch. Burton's position is not, however, simple. If we accept Avruch and Black's interpretation of Burton's version of needs theory, needs lead inevitably to irrationality. We cannot, therefore, assume any common rationality or good reason which underlies behaviour. Unlike Avruch and Black's view, the interpretation of Burton's needs theory which refers to survival value presupposes a certain form of rationality. That is, behaviour is rational when it contributes to the survival of an organism. Nevertheless, it is not justifiable to speak about common-good reason underlying behaviour, because the notion of survival value does not necessarily imply any reasoning process. An organism may behave 'automatically', without reasoning, in a way that guarantees its survival.

Burton conceives, on the other hand, a person as calculating and cost–benefit-oriented in a conflict situation, as demonstrated earlier. He presupposes a common form of rationality and makes a claim to universality. Given these presuppositions, explaining human behaviour, even across different cultures, is possible, because people are seen to behave similarly (and maybe also predictably) on the basis of their instrumental rationality in all conflict situations. Discursive rationality, however, brings in an element of situational rationality which opposes universalising tendencies. A discursive design, from which discursive rationality arises, is sensitive to different language games, and therefore, does not necessarily denote a universal good reason. On that view, an explanation, or rather understanding, of behaviour is context-dependent.

The question about the access of the researcher to the domain of behaviour is here restricted to the question whether our explanation of behaviour, and especially behaviour in other cultures, is necessarily dependent on the rules of logic as we know and use them. Is our social inquiry inherently 'perspectival', that is, are the perspectives of actors and observers – sets of beliefs, attitudes and assumptions that specify how social reality is to be understood – different? 'Perspectivism' can be formulated in either a weak or a strong form. In a weak form, it asserts that interpretation and explanation must make reference to the perspectives of actors. In a strong form, it asserts that the perspective of an interpreter cannot be divorced from the account he or she gives. The strong form assumes that there can be no perspective-neutral interpretation and explana-tion.[80]

Even weak perspectivism is incompatible with theorising based on the notion of utility maximising. The strategic action model which relies on the notion does not investigate the beliefs and motivations of actors, but imputes them for predictive and explanatory purposes.[81] It is included in the notion of utility maximising that the 'concept of the objective world – in which the actor can intervene in a goal-directed manner – . . . must hold in the same way for the actor himself and for any other interpreter of his actions'.[82] Habermas discusses that assumption:

> An interpreter can go beyond this *subjectively* purposive-rational orientation and compare the actual course of action with the constructed case of a corresponding *objectively* purposive-rational course of action. The interpreter is able to construct this ideal-typical case in a nonarbitrary manner since the agent relates in a subjec-tively purposive-rational way to a world that is, for categorical reasons, identical for actor and observer, that is, cognitively and instrumentally accessible to both in the same way.[83]

By employing a rational choice framework Burton presupposes non-arbitrary access to the objective domain of behaviour on the part of the researcher. Although Burton does not rely on the rational choice paradigm in a strict sense,[84] by postulating the utility maximising actor he accepts implicitly many of the underlying assumptions of the paradigm. To put it simply, as far as rational choice theory is concerned, Burton rejects perspectivism in his explanation of behaviour. Burton's version of needs theory, which suggests the existence of needs independently of the perceptions of actors, i.e. 'objectively', presupposes that the researcher has unproblematic access to the objective domain of needs, of motivational forces. It is assumed by Burton that it is not necessary for the researcher while explaining the behaviour of an actor to refer either to the per-spective of the actor or to his or her own perspective.

There are two features in the Burtonian way of explaining behaviour which bring him close to the rationalist pole of the rationality debate. First, his version of needs theory gives needs the status of natural laws. Since they are seen to be objective laws, similar to those in the natural sciences, there is no need to make any reference beyond them when explaining human behaviour. Second, Burton's explanation of the entry stage postulates an image of the utility-max-imising human being. This view presupposes a purposive-rational actor whose world is accessible to an interpreter. The world is thought to be accessible both to an actor and to an interpreter in the same way.

The discursive and hermeneutical elements in Burton's explanations indi-cate relativism. He argues that the interpretations of the participants of their conflict are an important part of a workshop. It could logically follow – although

Burton does not go so far – that these interpretations form the very core of theorising. This view would shift the emphasis from the rationalist to the relativist pole. If the workshop was explained more explicitly by Burton from the point of view of discursive designs, as Dryzek suggests, the focus could be on culturally bounded communication and interactions without reference to any universal ontological basis (e.g. needs). By developing the discursive and hermeneutic elements of the workshop further, Burton could move from the realm of explanation to that of understanding.

Concluding remarks

Burton's explanation of human behaviour consists of different layers which imply different forms of rationality, namely instrumental, discursive and Enlightenment rationality. Which of Burton's explanatory layers has priority over other layers? Avruch and Black's answer is, as shown earlier, that, since Burton postulates biogenetic needs as an ontological basis, needs and their irrationality form the most important layer, in relation to which the other levels are inevitably of minor importance. This view can be widened further by claiming that the layers postulated by Burton are logically inconsistent. If we establish our explanations of behaviour on something irrational, on something which is not totally in our control (e.g. needs or irrational Id), it is logically incoherent to establish parallel explanations which rely on inherent human rationality (e.g. utility-maximising or communicative behaviour). It is, however, possible to relax the irrationality thesis of needs theory, and claim that needs are rational, because they relate to the survival of the organism. Since needs contribute to survival, they are fundamentally rational, given the foundational value of survival. In that case the assumption of the existence of different forms of rationality is plausible.

The way Burton establishes his explanatory models is complex. He builds up a model of a cost–benefit-oriented person whose aim is personal utility maximisation. On the other hand, he is in favour of discursive designs which aim at expanding communication, self-reflection and consensus. The role of the facilitator is crucial to bridge these two models: he or she, as a purified mind, transfers the parties from the first, cost–benefit, to the second, discursive, realm.

The next chapter of the book moves into phenomenology. The aim is through sociological phenomenology to emphasise discursive and hermeneutical elements of problem-solving workshop conflict resolution. By employing a phenomenological interpretation, an alternative ontological basis – which is lacking from many attempts to challenge the Burtonian approach – is developed. The following questions will be discussed: the constitution of human being (e.g. through needs or social interaction); the manner in which identities are produced in social interaction and through culture; the most fruitful way to understand human actions, if reference can no longer be made to universal needs; and an understanding of the double role of the facilitator without a reference to a purified mind.

NOTES

1 J. Habermas, *The Theory of Communicative Action: Reason and the Rationalization of Society* I (London, Heinemann, 1984), p. 85.
2 *Ibid.*, p. 85.
3 *Ibid.*, pp. 87–8.
4 C. R. Mitchell defines expected utility (EU): 'The essence of the EU approach is that those making a choice among options consciously calculate the overall value, or "utility" outcomes likely to result from such options. They then combine this utility with their estimated probability of particular outcomes and make a choice regarding the optimum course of action to achieve the outcome offering the highest Expected Utility. Expected Utility is obtained by combining three factors. First, there are the *benefits* to be obtained from a particular outcome. Secondly, there are the *costs* of pursuing and obtaining that outcome. Finally, there is the estimated *probability* that choosing a course of action will produce anticipated outcome, so that the benefits accrue while the costs are borne.' C. R. Mitchell, 'Ending Conflicts and Wars: Judgement, Rationality and Entrapment', *International Social Science Journal*, 127: 1 (1991), 38.
5 For a comparison of how economists and psychologists use the rational choice paradigm see R. Hogarth and M. Reder, 'Introduction: Perspectives from Economics and Psychology', in R. Hogarth and M. Reder (eds), *Rational Choice: The Contrast between Economics and Psychology* (Chicago and London, University of Chicago Press, 1987), pp. 1–23. Rational choice theorists themselves are well aware of the assumptions underlying the paradigm as well as of the critical readings aimed at disputing the assumptive basis. The tradition of critical readings of the rational choice paradigm is not new, and, moreover, the questions imposed have been partly answered by rational choice theorists. The level of critique adopted in this book is ontological. N. Denzin's question 'Is the postulate of rationality which structures this theory suitable for the analysis of the structures of rationality and emotionality that organise daily life, or is its utility limited only to the ideal norms which organise certain forms of economic action and the activities of certain kinds of scientific theorists?' is vital for this book too. N. Denzin, 'Reading Rational Choice Theory', *Rationality and Society*, 2: 2 (1990), 173. For an excellent introduction to the paradigm and to its criticism see J. Elster, 'Introduction', in J. Elster (ed.), *Rational Choice* (London, Blackwell, 1986), pp. 1–33. See also M. Hollis, *Models of Man: Philosophical Thoughts on Social Action* (Cambridge, Cambridge University Press, 1977), pp. 36–8. M. Hollis, *The Cunning of Reason* (Cambridge, Cambridge University Press, 1987), pp. 15–46. For discussions on the rational choice paradigm in the analysis of international conflict see B. Bueno de Mesquita, 'An Expected Utility Theory of International Conflict', *American Political Science Review*, 74 (1980), 917–31. W. Edwards, 'Utility, Subjective Probability, their Interaction and Variance Preferences', *Journal of Conflict Resolution*, 4: 1 (1962), 42–51. C. R. Mitchell and M. Nicholson, 'Rational Models and the Ending of Wars', *Journal of Conflict Resolution*, 27: 3 (1983), 495–520. M. Nicholson, *Rationality and the Analysis of International Conflict* (Cambridge: Cambridge University Press, 1992). D. Wittman, 'How a War Ends: a Rational Model Approach', *Journal of Conflict Resolution*, 24: 4 (1979), 743–63. For an example of a critical reading of the paradigm and an answer to it see N. Denzin, 'The Long Good-bye: Farewell to Rational Choice Theory', *Rationality and Society*, 2: 2 (1990), 504–7. P. Abell, 'Denzin on Rational Choice Theory', *Rationality and Society*, 2: 4 (1990), pp. 495–9.

6 J. Burton, *Deviance, Terrorism and War* (New York, St Martin's Press, 1979), p. 121.

7 *Ibid.*, p. 175. See also J. Burton, 'Resolution of Conflict', *International Studies Quarterly*, 16: 1 (1972), 8. J. Burton, 'Theory and Reality', *Millennium: Journal of International Studies*, 4: 3 (1975), 254. J. Burton, 'About Winning', *International Interactions*, 12: 1 (1985), pp. 88 and 91.

8 As K. Avruch and P. Black note, rational choice theory turns interests and needs into utilities. They write: 'They [people] strive to fulfil their needs. They try to maximise that which they find desirable. When we follow the logic of this, we see that we have turned interests and needs into utilities; human motivation, in its entirety, is thus reduced to maximising these utilities.' Benefits are thought of in the light of the rational choice paradigm as utilities that can be maximised and minimised, and the choices which produce the greatest benefit are claimed to maximise utility. K. Avruch and P. Black, 'Ideas of Human Nature in Contemporary Conflict Resolution Theory', *Negotiation Journal*, 6: 3 (1990), 226.

9 Burton, *Deviance, Terrorism and War*, p. 98. J. Burton, *Global Conflict: The Domestic Sources of International Crisis* (Brighton, Wheatsheaf, 1984), p. 89, pp. 100 and 117. Burton, 'About Winning', pp. 78–80. J. Burton, *Conflict: Resolution and Provention* (London, Macmillan, 1990), p. 217.

10 Burton, *Conflict: Resolution and Provention*, p. 120. See also J. Burton, *Violence Explained* (Manchester and New York, Manchester University Press, 1997), p. 47.

11 Burton, *Conflict: Resolution and Provention*, p. 214. See also Burton, *Violence Explained*, p. 47. J. Burton, *Dear Survivors* (Boulder CO, Westview Press, 1982), p. 131. Burton, *Conflict: Resolution and Provention*, pp. 47, 69, 120, 165, 202, 214 and 218. J. Burton, 'International Relations or World Society?' in J. Vasquez (ed.), *Classics in International Relations*, second edition (Englewood Cliffs NJ, Prentice Hall, 1990), p. 106. J. Burton, 'Unfinished Business in Conflict Resolution', in J. Burton and F. Dukes (eds), *Conflict: Readings in Management and Resolution* (London, Macmillan, 1990), pp. 330–1.

12 For Burton's notion of game see Burton, 'About Winning', pp. 71–3. J. Burton, 'The Procedures of Conflict Resolution', in E. Azar and J. Burton (eds), *International Conflict Resolution: Theory and Practice* (Brighton, Wheatsheaf; Boulder CO, Lynne Rienner, 1986), pp. 92–4.

13 Habermas, *The Theory of Communicative Action* I, p. 10.

14 *Ibid.*, pp. 10–12.

15 M. Oakeshott, *Rationalism in Politics and other Essays* (London and New York, Methuen, 1984), pp. 1–36 and 83–7.

16 M. Weber, *Max Weber: Selections in Translation*, ed. W. G. Runciman and trans. E. Matthews (Cambridge, Cambridge University Press, 1978), pp. 28–9.

17 R. Brubaker, *The Limits of Rationality: An Essay on the Social and Moral Thought of Max Weber* (London, Allen & Unwin, 1984), pp. 4, 36 and 51–3.

18 Weber classifies formal and substantive rationality, subjective and objective rationality and *Zweckrationalität* and *Wertrationalität*. See Brubaker, *The Limits of Rationality*.

19 J. Dryzek, *Discursive Democracy: Politics, Policy, and Political Science* (Cambridge, Cambridge University Press, 1990), pp. 3–6.

20 For a summary see Nicholson, *Rationality and the Analysis*, pp. 49–50.

21 The notion of motivation is problematic in this context. As Hogarth and Reder note, economists and psychologists who refer to the paradigm of rational choice alike agree on the importance of motivation but disagree about what constitutes appropriate motivation. For economists motivation is appropriate only if rewards are an increasing function of the correctness of responses. Psychologists, on the other hand, have greater difficulty in specifying the conditions under which subjects are appropriately motivated. Hogarth and Reder, 'Introduction', p. 11.

22 M. Hollis and S. Smith, *Explaining and Understanding International Relations* (Oxford, Clarendon Press, 1991), p. 77. Nicholson, *Rationality and the Analysis*, p. 50. Herbert Simon holds the view too. He claims that in its treatment of rationality, neoclassical economics (and the traditional rational choice paradigm) is silent about the content of goals and values. In contrast, according to him, other social sciences in their treatment of rationality seek to determine empirically the nature and origins of values and their changes with time and experience. H. Simon, 'Rationality in Psychology and Economics', in R. Hogarth and M. Reder (eds), *Rational Choice: The Contrast between Economics and Psychology* (Chicago and London, University of Chicago Press, 1987), p. 26. The gap between the aims of economics and other social sciences has not, as Burton's case exemplifies, prevented social scientists from adapting some elements of the rational choice paradigm.

23 Hollis, *The Cunning of Reason*, pp. 23–4.

24 Denzin, 'Reading Rational Choice Theory', p. 175.

25 Hollis, *The Cunning of Reason*, pp. 22–4.

26 Avruch and Black, 'Ideas of Human Nature', pp. 222 and 226–7.

27 Burton, *Global Conflict*, pp. 145–7. Burton, 'About Winning', p. 75. Burton, *Conflict: Resolution and Provention*, p. 43.

28 Burton, *Conflict: Resolution and Provention*, p. 22. See also Burton, *Deviance, Terrorism and War*, p. 52, pp. 110–11 and 118. J. Burton, 'The Facilitation of International Conflict Resolution', in L. Kriesberg (ed.), *Research in Social Movements: Conflict and Change* VIII (London and Greenwich CT, Jai Press), p. 42. J. Burton, 'The Means to Agreement: Power of Values?' in D. Bendahmane and J. McDonald, Jr (eds), *Perspectives on Negotiation: Four Case Studies and Interpretations* (Center for the Study of Foreign Affairs, Foreign Service Institute, US Department of State, Washington DC, 1986), p. 240. J. Burton, *Resolving Deep-rooted Conflict: A Handbook* (London and New York, University Press of America, 1987), p. 23. J. Burton, 'Conflict Resolution as a Function of Human Needs', in R. Coate and J. Rosate (eds), *The Power of Human Needs in World Society* (Boulder CO and London, Lynne Rienner, 1988), p. 197. Burton, *Conflict: Resolution and Provention*, pp. 27, 47, 88, 167 and 217.

29 The word 'pragmatic' refers also to the pragmatist movement in philosophy. It should be emphasised that, although pragmatists are referred to in this section, the aim is not to study that heterogeneous philosophical approach. Attention will be drawn only to John Dewey's account of experience and the formulation of problems, William James's idea of human needs as a measure of metaphysical views, and the general notion of problem-oriented action.

30 Burton and Dukes, *Conflict: Practices*, p. 20. See also J. Burton, 'Conflict Resolution as a Political System', in V. Volkan, J. Montville and D. Julius (eds), *The Psychodynamics of International Relationships* II (Lexington MA, Lexington Books, 1991), p. 75.

31 Burton and Dukes, *Conflict: Practices*, p. 20.

32 For challenges of Burton's view see, for example, P. Lawler, 'Pragmatism, Existentialism, and the Crisis in American Political Thought', *International Philosophical Quarterly*, 20: 3 (1980), 327–38. R. Rorty, 'Overcoming the Tradition: Heidegger and Dewey', *Review of Metaphysics*, 30: 1 (1976), 280–305. R. Rorty, *Consequences of Pragmatism* (Brighton, Harvester Press, 1982). J. Smith, *Purpose and Thought: The Meaning of Pragmatism* (New Haven CT, Yale University Press, 1978).

33 Smith, *Purpose and Thought*, p. 86.

34 *Ibid.*, p. 86. Smith refers to Santayana's discussion of Dewey.

35 *Ibid.*, pp. 78–87. See also M. Hollis, 'The Self in Action', in R. S. Peters (ed.), *John Dewey Reconsidered* (London, Routledge, 1977), pp. 56–75.

36 Burton, *Conflict: Resolution and Provention*, p. 72.

37 Smith, *Purpose and Thought*, pp. 94–5.

38 Burton, *Conflict: Resolution and Provention*, Part IV. Burton, *Violence Explained*, p. 44.

39 R. Bernstein, 'Introduction', in John Dewey, *On Experience, Nature, and Freedom*, ed. R. Bernstein (Lanham IN and New York, Bobbs-Merrill, 1960), pp. xxvii–xxxiii.

40 Burton speaks about 'reality testing', which means that the parties are helped in the workshop to test their perceptions of the conflict situation against 'reality'. J. Burton, *World Society* (Lanham MD, University Press of America, 1987), p. 160.

41 Smith, *Purpose and Thought*, p. 39.

42 Burton, *Dear Survivors*, p. 119.

43 Smith, *Purpose and Thought*, pp. 88–9.

44 See Burton, *Dear Survivors*, p. 120. Burton, *Global Conflict*, p. 135. Burton, *Conflict: Resolution and Provention*, p. 204.

45 The notion of discursive rationality is developed by John Dryzek in his *Discursive Democracy*. Dryzek himself uses the term 'communicative rationality'. In this study, however, the term 'discursive rationality' is preferred, because it emphasises the dialectic and contextual nature of that type of rationality. The word 'dialectic' refers in this work solely to dialogue.

46 There are several differences between Habermas's and Dryzek's views. Dryzek claims that, instead of limiting discursive rationality to the sphere of the life-world of social interaction, he expands it to the spheres of the 'social' and 'systemic'. It follows that he does not see the domains of instrumental and communicative rationality as separate and incompatible. Dryzek also tries to overcome the critique levelled at Habermas's objectivistic position which seeks an objectivistic solid ground for both truth and morality. Moreover, he advances the view according to which communicative rationality provides only procedural, not substantive, criteria about how disputes and arguments might be resolved and about how principles might be constructed. *Ibid.*, pp. 14–22.

47 *Ibid.*, p. 14.

48 *Ibid.*, pp. 20 and 53–4. See also Habermas, *The Theory of Communicative Action* I, pp. 10 and 95–101.

49 Dryzek, *Discursive Democracy*, p. 43.

50 *Ibid.*, pp. 42 and 90–108.

51 It is worth noting that, for example, in *World Society* there is no discussion of interaction at all. Nor does the word 'interaction' appear in any of his indexes.

52 J. Burton, *Conflict and Communication: The Use of Controlled Communication in International Relations* (London, Macmillan, 1969), pp. 11, 23 and 49–59. See similar views also, Burton, 'Resolution of Conflict', pp. 17, 21, 23 and 27.

53 Burton, *Conflict and Communication*, p. 55.

54 Burton, 'The Facilitation', p. 40.

55 J. Burton, 'Three Qualities of a Secure Nation', in M. Macy (ed.), *Solutions for a Troubled World* (Boulder CO, Earthview Press, 1987), p. 245. See also Burton, *Deviance, Terrorism and War*, pp. 117–18. Burton, *Conflict: Resolution and Provention*, pp. 42, 45, 78 and 195.

56 Burton, *Global Conflict*, p. 135. See also Burton, *Dear Survivors*, pp. 70–4. Burton, *Global Conflict*, pp. 131–6. Burton, 'Conflict Resolution as a Function', pp. 190–1 and 199. Burton, *Conflict: Resolution and Provention*, pp. 183–7.

57 Burton, *Conflict: Resolution and Provention*, p. 204.

58 *Ibid.*, pp. 206–7.

59 See especially Burton, *Resolving Deep-rooted Conflict*.

60 A. R. Louch, *Explanation and Human Action* (Berkeley CA and Los Angeles, University of California Press, 1966), p. 70. See also critiques of expertise of needs thinking, I. Illich,

'Needs', in W. Sachs (ed.), *The Development Dictionary: A Guide to Knowledge as Power* (London, Zen Books, 1992), pp. 88–101. E. D. Watt, 'Human Needs, Human Wants, and Political Consequences', *Political Studies*, 30: 4 (1982), p. 538.

61 Burton, *Conflict: Resolution and Provention*, p. 199.

62 *Ibid.*, p. 204. See also Burton, *Deviance, Terrorism and War*, pp. 116–22. Burton, *Dear Survivors*, pp. 119–23. Burton, *Global Conflict*, pp. 149–52. Burton, *Violence Explained*, p. 13. Burton and Dukes, *Conflict: Practices*, p. 144.

63 Oakeshott, *Rationalism*, pp. 83–95.

64 P. Springborg, *The Problem of Human Needs and the Critique of Civilization* (London, Allen & Unwin, 1981), pp. 195–6.

65 *Ibid.*, p. 196.

66 Smith, *Purpose and Thought*, p. 94.

67 See Burton, *Resolving Deep-rooted Conflict*.

68 Habermas, *The Theory of Communicative Action* I, pp. 145–51.

69 *Ibid.*, p. 151.

70 Jean-Pierre Cot places Burtonian workshop rationality in a more recent tradition. He writes: 'Burton's views belong to a respectable stream of thought, illustrated by the Quakers and by certain apostles of international conciliation. A patient discussion among reasonable men can solve any problem. A panel of specialists (even before World War I, Ludwig von Bar and Effremoff had proposed a council of wise men) must help the parties by giving them some technical information on their difficulties.' J.-P. Cot, 'Critical Remarks on John Burton's Paper on Resolution of Conflict with Special Reference to the Cyprus Conflict', *International Studies Quarterly*, 16: 1 (1972), p. 33.

71 See especially Burton, *Dear Survivors*, pp. 22–6. Burton, *Global Conflict*, pp. 16–24. Burton, *Conflict: Resolution and Provention*, pp. 30–5. Burton, *Violence Explained*, p. 13.

72 Burton's methodological principle is abduction. He is not an empiricist in a strict sense.

73 Habermas, *The Communicative Theory of Action* I, p. 102.

74 P. Winch, *The Idea of a Social Science and its Relation to Philosophy* (London, Routledge, [1958] 1973). See also P. Winch, 'Understanding a Primitive Society', in B. Wilson (ed.), *Rationality* (Oxford, Blackwell, 1974), pp. 78–111. Hollis and Smith, *Explaining and Understanding*, pp. 82–8.

75 Winch, *The Idea of a Social Science*, p. 15.

76 M. Hollis and S. Lukes, 'Introduction', in M. Hollis and S. Lukes (eds), *Rationality and Relativism* (Oxford, Blackwell, 1982), pp. 10–11.

77 I. Hacking, 'Language, Truth and Reason', in M. Hollis and S. Lukes (eds), *Rationality and Relativism* (Oxford, Blackwell, 1982), p. 49.

78 *Ibid.*, p. 65.

79 R. Horton, 'Tradition and Modernity Revisited', in M. Hollis and S. Lukes (eds), *Rationality and Relativism* (Oxford, Blackwell, 1982), p. 256. See also R. Horton, 'African Traditional Thought and Western Science', in B. Wilson (ed.), *Rationality* (London, Blackwell, 1974), pp. 131–71.

80 S. Lukes, 'Relativism in its Place', in M. Hollis and S. Lukes (eds), *Rationality and Relativism* (Oxford, Blackwell, 1982), pp. 301–5.

81 *Ibid.*

82 Habermas, *The Theory of Communicative Action* I, p. 102.

83 *Ibid.*, pp. 102–3.

84 His explanation does not involve him in theorising, for example, on true beliefs, risks, probabilities or limited information. Nor does it explain *all* behaviour by referring to the paradigm.

5

Cultural dimensions
of the social world

BURTON'S VERSION OF human needs theory is an inseparable part of his conflict and conflict resolution theory, as demonstrated in earlier chapters. Burton establishes an 'onion model', and gives biologically based needs priority over culture in the structuring of human existence. This part of the book discusses the social constructionist view of human being and social world offered by the phenomenologist Alfred Schutz. His view erects non-biological foundations for human existence and, thereby, challenges the Burtonian biological account. It provides us also with conceptual tools which can be employed to give the problem-solving workshop a phenomenological interpretation.

In order to understand the philosophical context of phenomenology a short study of its general features is presented. It is important to see how phenomenology differs from positivist social science and especially from political behaviouralism. It is also vital to understand the points of departure between such phenomenologists as Edmund Husserl and Alfred Schutz whose philosophy is inclined towards phenomenological sociology. Given that Schutz's main focus is on the social world, his theories offer notions which are applicable to the study of conflict and conflict resolution. The second part of the chapter discusses the dimensions of the social world on the basis of Schutz's views. The last part continues the discussion, but shifts the emphasis to the idea of socially constructed reality, needs and identity.

Phenomenological philosophy and sociology stress the 'subjectivist' viewpoint: the point of view of the experiencing 'I' (consciousness) which is the starting-point of experiences, actions and interpretations in and of the social world. Unlike many other philosophical approaches, it derives from structural accounts of everyday experiences and the everyday world. It does not hide behind the notion of a philosopher who is an outside observer, a purified mind. This feature of phenomenological literature explains the way the pronoun 'I' is employed in the text as a parallel to the pronoun 'we'.

Phenomenology and the theory of science

Phenomenology is described as a return to the traditional task of philosophy, that is, to a search for wisdom and an understanding of the nature of the cosmos and the position of human being in it. By the end of the nineteenth century the scope of a part of philosophy had become severely limited, because the success of natural science in describing the physical world had given rise to the conviction that there is nothing about the physical world that cannot be investigated by empirical means. The acceptance of the Cartesian division of mind and body led many philosophers to the study of 'objective realities as they are in themselves', with the result that the subjective factor in consciousness was ignored as irrelevant and of no philosophical importance. A kind of philosophy developed which attempted to treat consciousness as an empirical phenomenon, as an objective reality, that can be investigated by the quantitative methods of natural science.[1]

In the same spirit, in some approaches of the social sciences the study of human beings became understood as a genuine natural science of individuals in society, differing in degree but not in kind from the well established natural sciences. The centrality of empirical theory characterised this, in many other ways heterogeneous, social science movement. Two models of legitimate knowledge became recognised by the 'positivist temper', as Richard Bernstein calls the essence of the movement, namely the empirical or natural sciences and formal disciplines such as logic and mathematics. The focus on empirical theories was based on the idea that, once we arrive at empirical theories in the social disciplines, those disciplines become genuine 'natural' sciences. The task of the social scientist was thought to be, therefore, to describe and explain social phenomena as accurately as he or she can and not to advocate normative positions.[2] Bernstein summarises the 'positivist temper' as it manifests itself in the social sciences of the twentieth century:

> At the core of this naturalistic interpretation is the conviction that the aim of the social sciences is the same as that of the natural sciences. Collecting and refining data, discovering correlations, and formulating testable empirical generalisations, hypotheses, and models, all have important roles to play, but they are not sufficient to establish the social disciplines as mature sciences. There must be the growth of testable and well-confirmed theories which explain phenomena by showing how they can be derived in nontrivial ways from our theoretical assumptions. At the heart of scientific explanation there must be discovery of and appeal to laws or nomological statements.[3]

The naturalistic interpretation of the social sciences was – and to a certain extent still is – based on the assumption that there is a distinction between empirical and normative theory. It was assumed that theory is different from praxis; theory has its own sphere and praxis its own. The task of the social scientist is to theorise from the point of view of a disinterested observer. The objects in the social world are accessible to a study in a similar way to those in the natural world, because there is no qualitative difference between the two worlds. In other words, the quantitative and experimental methods of natural science were expected to be suitable for the social sciences. For this doctrine of science, theories and laws were formulated for the sake of prediction, which was seen to be an essential feature of scientific explanation.

Some remains of the 'positivist temper' can be still found, for example in political behaviourism, whose *a priori* method and presuppositions are largely based on the ideals of the natural sciences. In political behaviourism a clear distinction is made between what is human and what is merely natural. The starting-point for the analysis of human behaviour is the meaning the actor attaches to his or her action. The meaning of action is studied from the point of view of overt behaviour. The study of large areas of the intended meanings of the actor is neglected. As Hwa Yol Jung argues, 'political behaviourism as a scientific method abandons the relevance of the vast universe of experiential data of everyday life simply as "subjective" or "private" and thus unscientific and unempirical'.[4] 'Private' and motivational phenomena are reduced to 'public' and observable events or the external components of action, with the result that the intentional meaning structure of human conduct becomes completely rejected by political behaviouralists. Similarly, the internal structure of consciousness is interpreted narrowly or not noted at all.[5]

Edmund Husserl's *The Crisis of European Sciences and Transcendental Phenomenology*[6] is a seminal critique of the limited and distorted interpretation of the modern natural sciences. Husserl's point of departure is an analysis of Galilean physics, which created, according to him, the Galilean style of science. The Galilean style is characterised by a cleavage between the world as it presents itself in the perceptual experience of everyday life and the world as it is in scientific truth and in 'reality'. According to Husserl, modern science of the Galilean type refuses to accept the perceptual world at face value. Instead, reality is believed to contain, embody and conceal a mathematical structure. The universe is seen by modern science as a construction which results from, correlates with and is a conceptualisation of idealisations, mathematisations, algebraisations and formalisations. As a consequence, the universe is thought to be uncovered by means of mathematical notions.

Husserl's explication of the presuppositions of modern science does not mean their denial or nullification. Rather, it means the delimitation of their legitimate validity. He argues that the reference to an ideal mathematical order must be eliminated from our experience of the world and the latter must no longer be seen from the perspective of the former. For Husserl the mathematisation of nature implies the ever growing alienation of the universe of physics from the world of perceptual experience. The restoration and reinstating of the life-world is, therefore, one of his main themes in *Crisis*.[7]

Schutz's works are an advancement of Husserl's insights, which Husserl himself never systematically developed with regard to the social sciences: Schutz lays the phenomenological foundations of the social sciences.[8] Schutz does not explicitly discuss the Galilean sciences, although he agrees with Husserl's conclusions. His starting-point is a critique of the Weberian understanding of the concept of subjective meaning. Schutz accepts Weber's axiom that the social sciences must be value-free. He likewise accepts Weber's methodological individualism and his contention that social phenomena are properly understood in terms of ideal types.[9] However, Schutz maintains that Weber fails to state clearly the essential characteristics of understanding (*Verstehen*), of subjective meaning and of action. In *The Phenomenology of the Social World*[10] Schutz questions the Weberian idea that subjective meaning is attached to experience or action, and studies how lived experience gets meaning rather through reflection. On the basis of Henri Bergson's philosophy of life, Schutz discovers the importance of the meaning-giving stream of consciousness, *durée*, and states that 'meaning is a certain way of directing one's gaze at an item of one's own experience'.[11] He, then, distinguishes subjective meaning from objective. According to Schutz, an action or experience has only one subjective meaning, that of the actor himself or herself.[12]

Schutz's clarification of the Weberian understanding of the task of the social sciences implies a challenge to the basic Cartesian ontological and epistemological dichotomy that infects the various forms of naturalism and empiricism. The dichotomy between behaviouralists who study what is observable and psychologists who limit themselves to the study of what is mental is overcome by Schutz. Schutz's thesis is, in Bernstein's words, that 'to understand human action we must not take the position of an outside observer who "sees" only the physical manifestations of these acts; rather we must develop categories for understanding what the actor – from his own point of view – "means" in his actions'.[13]

Schutz, likewise Husserl, turns to the study of the everyday world to understand the actor. He considers the everyday world to be the social reality which the social sciences have to investigate and upon which understanding as a method peculiar to the social sciences needs to be founded. The way the social sciences should approach this world is through second-degree constructs (ideal types), which must include a reference to the subjective meaning an action has for the actor.[14]

Although Schutz's contribution to the issue of understanding in the social sciences is based on original thought, there is a hermeneutical tradition in Western philosophy which discusses the topic. For example, Wilhelm Dilthey and Heinrich Rickert argued at the turn of the twentieth century that there is a fundamental difference between natural science, on the one hand, and studies such as history, jurisprudence and economics, on the other. Dilthey maintained that the distinction is one of content, and he insisted on using the term *Geisteswissenschaften* to refer to sciences of sociohistorical phenomena. He focused on mind and especially on *Erlebnis*, lived experience or immediate experience, which achieves an outward expression. According to Dilthey, by interpreting this outward expression in terms of what lies behind it, we come to understand others. Understanding takes place by reconstituting our own lived experience in the other person. Rickert introduced the term *Kulturwissenschaften*. The content of these sciences was, according to him, the study of cultural products and institutions. It is these and their meanings the cultural sciences seek to understand, not inner psychological processes, as some other hermeneutically oriented philosophers would claim. In Rickert's view, *Kulturwissenschaften* dealt with values, because it is in terms of values we approach actuality and organise reality.[15]

Three things should be emphasised from Schutz's and Weber's position in relation to this tradition. First, Weber and Schutz claim that the task of the social sciences is to understand the subjective meaning of the other. However, the interpreter never comprehends the meaning in its totality, because the other's stream of consciousness always eludes that of the interpreter. They do not consider understanding to be simply re-experiencing and reconstructing the experience of an author, as Dilthey saw it to be. Second, Schutz is in agreement with Weber that Dilthey's basic approach is unscientific, because Dilthey's notion of understanding is unsatisfactory, and his theory lacks the conception of ideal types as a resource of scientific objectivity. Third, on the basis of Rickert's discussion of values, Schutz and Weber argue that, although questions are asked in terms of a value or interest, they can be answered from an objective, that is, scientific, point of view.[16]

In addition to Schutz's attempt to lay the phenomenological foundations of the social sciences and to clarify the task and concepts of those sciences, his impact on other philosophers and social scientists has been remarkable. In the contemporary social sciences, the impulse of Schutz's work is most prominently displayed in ethnomethodology and recent developments in the sociology of knowledge. For example, Harold Garfinkel's *Studies in Ethomethodology*[17] studies the everyday world and that which is taken for granted by actors within it. The study is conducted by experimentally disturbing and testing the limits of the everyday world. Peter Berger and Thomas Luckmann's *The Social Construction of Reality*,[18] on the other hand, has a Schutzian origin in terms of its focus on the distribution of knowledge in the life-world. The book studies what people 'know as reality' in their everyday, non- or pre-theoretical, lives. For Berger and Luckmann the task of the sociology of knowledge is to concern itself with the social construction of reality.

Intentionality, life-world and phenomenological reduction

According to Husserl, all conscious acts have a fundamental directional character: they point towards some object, whether it is objectively real or not. All thinking is thinking of or about something and all remembering is remembering of something. All consciousness is consciousness of something. This is an essential feature of intentionality. For phenomenologists, intentionality of consciousness does not mean planned or purposeful thought as the commonsense usage of the word suggests. Rather, intentionality in Husserl's sense refers primarily to the phenomenological structure of acts of perception, in the broad Cartesian sense of the term 'perception'. Nor are acts of intentionality psychological events. The structure of intentionality is purely *a priori*, that is, logically necessary. The object intended (*noema*), as intended to, corresponds to the objective side of intentional experience. The intentive process (*noesis*), the intending as such, is a subject dimension within the structure of the intentional act.[19] *Noesis* and *noema* are the poles of the structure of consciousness which cannot be separated from each other. Schutz describes the connection by saying that 'every experience is, thus, not only characterised by the fact *that* it is a consciousness, but it is simultaneously determined by the intentional object *whereof* it is a consciousness'.[20]

Earlier in this chapter there have been references to the everyday world of the social actor as the basis of philosophy and the social sciences. The everyday world, the life-world (*Lebenswelt*) as it is called by phenomenologists, is encountered in everyday life. It is given in direct and immediate experience – especially perceptual experience and its derivatives, memory, expectation, and the like – independent of and prior to scientific interpretation. The life-world is the world within which we pursue all our goals and carry on all our activities, including scientific ones.[21] Schutz describes the life-world:

> The following considerations concern the structure of what Husserl calls the 'life-world' (*Lebenswelt*) in which, in the natural attitude, we, as human beings among fellow-beings, experience culture and society, take a stand with regard to their objects, are influenced by them and act upon them. In this attitude the existence of the life-world and the typicality of its contents are accepted as unquestionably given until further notice.[22]

Schutz's description brings up some fundamental elements of the life-world. First, it is a cultural world and refers to a social group. According to Gurwitsch, the term 'life-world' has a sociohistorical meaning: there is no life-world *per se*. Every concrete life-world refers to a certain social group at a certain phase of its history. Every life-world gets its interpretation and is conceived of by a social group whose life-world it is. Second, the natural attitude prevails in the life-world. Through the natural attitude the world appears to us taken for granted and self-evidently real 'until further notice'. In other words, in that attitude we do not question the existence of the intersubjective life-world and its objects.[23] Third, since the life-world is the world within which we act, within which we can understand our fellow men and women, and be understood by them, it is our paramount reality. Fourth, we act and operate not only within the life-world but also upon it: we modify it and it modifies our actions by setting limits to them. As a world of action and work the life-world is pervasively determined by a pragmatic motive. Fifth, in the life-world we confront objects and events from the outset in their typical character.[24]

The sociohistorical meaning of the life-world refers also to its intersubjective nature. Schutz states that 'the world of everyday life is from the outset an intersubjective one'.[25] That is, the life-world is shared with fellow men and women, experienced and interpreted by others: it is a world common to all of us. The life-world is also the area where we encounter the other, and it is the area where we perform our acts directed toward others. The life-world does not depend on our birth or death, because it is historically based. It is historical in terms of moral codes, economic situations, religious practices, etc. The life-world is intersubjective also in respect of future generations.[26]

In order to understand the origins of Schutz's phenomenology and a seminal difference between Schutz and Husserl, we need to return to the notions of the natural attitude and intersubjectivity.[27] Although Husserl and Schutz share the claim that we have to go back to the life-world to find the most fundamental ground for philosophy and the social sciences, their approaches are different. Husserl attempts to establish a transcendental philosophy upon a transcendental ego, whereas Schutz rejects the Husserlian transcendental interpretation of the problem of intersubjectivity and maintains that intersubjectivity is a mundane problem.

In order to uncover the sphere of transcendental subjectivity, Husserl introduces a phenomenological method based on reductions. The reductions are the device of phenomenology for going beyond the natural attitude of a human being living within the world he or she accepts. The purpose of such a technique is to reach a level of indubitable certainty which lies beyond the realm of mere belief. The aim is, in other words, to disclose the pure field of consciousness. The means of conducting reductions is called 'bracketing', which implies 'putting in brackets' the existence of the outer world, along with all the things in it, including fellow men and women, cultural objects and society. Our belief in the validity of our statements about this world has to be suspended too. Not only our practical knowledge of the world but also the propositions of all the sciences dealing with the world have to be brought within brackets. Similarly, I,[28] the human being as a psycho-physiological unit, have to be bracketed: I have to suspend belief in my mundane existence as a human being within the world.[29]

In more technical terms, the bracketing is the methodological suspension of what Husserl terms the 'general thesis of natural standpoint'. That means placing in phenomenological doubt my traditional commonsense taking the very reality of the everyday world for granted. As a result, I now review reality with a phenomenological attitude. This changing of the natural attitude to the phenomenological attitude is called by Husserl 'performing the *epoché*' or 'transcendental phenomenological reduction', which brackets the very worldliness of the ego and returns to the pure stream of consciousness as such. What is left after this reduction is the transcendental ego in whose constitutive activity the world arises.[30] Steven Vaitkus describes the result of the reduction:

> Having carried out this reduction in which transcendental ego is isolated from all references to others, it now becomes possible to describe the constitution of the sense of 'the other' from within this primordial sphere of ownness and, in so doing, to demonstrate that the transcendental ego is indeed the founding stratum upon which the constitution of intersubjectivity is based.[31]

Schutz, however, asks, 'How can the isolated philosopher, the nonparticipating transcendental observer who performs *epoché*, mediate with someone else?'[32] He notes the danger of solipsism with regard to the transcendental ego. Schutz's conclusion concerning Husserl's reduction is that the attempt to constitute transcendental intersubjectivity in terms of the operations of the consciousness of the transcendental ego does not succeed. According to Schutz, it is clear that intersubjectivity is not a problem of constitution which can be solved within the transcendental sphere, but it is a problem belonging fundamentally to the lifeworld. He argues that the products of the sense determination of other subjectivities and our consciousness of them are socially determined. Schutz's philosophical project carries out a 'relative natural analysis' of intersubjectivity in the everyday world by providing an analysis of the relative natural conception of the world[33] held by the actors in everyday life. He analyses the fundamental structures by which the actors take for granted and produce a particular social world for themselves, and establishes the foundation for intersubjectivity to the mundane sphere. Schutz's suspicious attitude to the transcendental ego does not mean that he moves into the realm of the empirical social sciences where the focus is on the content of the natural attitudes of different social groups. Rather, he is interested in seeking the *a priori* structures to be found in any relative natural conception of the world.[34]

Schutz's constitutive phenomenology of the natural attitude which rejects the study of intersubjectivity as a transcendental problem permits the inclusion of sociality. As mentioned, Schutz's theory does not involve the assumption of a solipsistic ego. His notion of person points to the intrinsically social and cultural character of consciousness. His philosophical project points to the analysis of the dimensions of the social world, such as cultural patterns, intersubjectivity, interaction, communication, social groups, institutions and language. The following sections examine the dimensions of the social world in order to lay a foundation for the study of conflict and conflict resolution from the social constructionist perspective.

Typifications, interests and systems of relevance

In the natural attitude, things in the factual world are from the outset perceived as types: my experience of the world takes place in terms of typifications. The outer world is not experienced as an arrangement of individual unique objects, dispersed in space and time, but as, for example, 'books', 'lakes', 'animals', 'fellow men and women'. Typifications are taken for granted, that is, I do not question them until further notice. Typifications become problematic when my attention is directed to some feature not included in them. Since a type is originally formed by ignoring certain individual features not pertinent to the situation or purpose in which or for the sake of which it arises, new relevant information may make it necessary to revise, expand or form a new type. When a new typification is formed it will be deposited in my stock of knowledge and it will be valid until further notice.[35]

Typifications represent the world to me in typical form. Four aspects of typifications need to be highlighted. First, typifications include expectations of the world. For example, I expect cats to behave in a typical way, and I would be surprised to find an animal which looks like a cat but enjoys fetching sticks thrown for it. Second, my network of typifications does not simply consider human individuals, it also considers their course of action patterns, their motives and goals and the social products which originated in their actions. Third, every typifying of objects, events and others necessarily involves self-typification, taking on roles. Fourth, as described earlier, typifications are stored in my stock of knowledge.

Why, then, are certain typifications selected from my stock of knowledge to be employed in certain situations? Why am I merely concerned with some aspects of particular typified objects? Schutz argues that all types are in relation to the particular purpose in hand. This purpose is nothing but the theoretical or practical problem: whatever types I employ to interpret experience will depend on my practical interest and the problem at hand. The relationship between interest and a set of typifications is mutual. Typifications determine the interest, because in the light of a certain set of typifications certain objects or aspects of objects stand out for me in any experience and certain objects or aspects will go unnoticed. A set of typifications itself carries with it interests which, in turn, determine types.[36]

In *Reflections of the Problem of Relevance* Schutz discusses in a detailed manner interest structures or, rather, what he calls relevance structures, and answers why certain typifications come into play in certain circumstances. He studies why and how our attention is focused on this or that object or aspects of them, and how the experience of objects becomes thematic. For Schutz, even perception involves choice, because one may choose which perceptual elements will become thematic, and hence subject to interpretation. Something becoming subject to interpretation does not mean that it becomes predicative: all this may happen at the pre-predicative level. The basic concepts with regard to the systems of relevance are 'theme' and 'field'. When something becomes a focal theme of thought it is presented in a field, in relation to a 'background'. A part of the field

– for example, the autobiographical situation which is unique to me alone – is given, that is, the history of my past experiences as it is deposited in my stock of knowledge.[37]

Schutz's thesis concerning relevances and typifications is that that which is relevant to a person in his or her current situation, and for his or her current purposes, serves to select traits for subsumption under a typification. Schutz distinguishes three types of relevance: topical, interpretative and motivational. By virtue of topical relevance something is constituted as problematic in the midst of an unstructuralised field of unproblematic familiarity. Topical relevance is, thus, the relevance by virtue of which an object is made a problem, made the theme or topic of thought, is segregated from the background of unquestionable and unquestioned familiarity. Topical relevance brings material from the unquestioned and marginal background, from the habitual knowledge, into the thematic field. Topical relevance can be either imposed or intrinsic. If an unfamiliar experience imposes itself upon me by its very unfamiliarity, the relevance can be called imposed. On the other hand, the relevance is intrinsic if an object becomes topically relevant to me through voluntary attention. The categories of imposed and intrinsic extend themselves to other relevances as well.

When something has become a theme of my thought, it needs to be interpreted. That is, it needs to be subsumed under the various typical prior experiences which constitute my actual stock of knowledge in hand. In interpretative relevance an aspect of present or previous experience takes on importance for interpreting a new set of perceptions. By virtue of interpretative relevance certain typifications are selected as relevant to the interpretation of an object or aspect of it. The selection is done on the basis of the recognition of similarity and difference. Motivational relevance, on the other hand, is founded on the interpretative decision for the planning of future conduct. Motivational relevance can be in the form of 'in order to' and 'because' relevances. The 'in order to' relevances emanate from the already established project of action and the 'because' relevances deal with the motivation for the establishment of the paramount project itself. The forms of relevances (topical, interpretative and motivational) are interdependent.[38]

The systems of relevance are items of one's stock of knowledge in hand. The stock of knowledge itself is a collection of typifications, deposited from previous experiences and formed according to the relevance systems. It is made up of typifications of the commonsense world. Through these typifications the objects in the life-world are perceived typically and within a horizon of familiarity. Experiences and interpretations of the world included in the stock of knowledge are mainly handed down from the social stock of knowledge. In other words, knowledge included in the individual stock is largely socially derived, distributed and approved. The stocks of knowledge, and the systems of relevance as parts of them, are not static. Rather, they are in a constant process of change.[39]

The study of the relevance systems is important in the context of problem-solving workshop conflict resolution, because they form a precondition for communication. Schutz claims that communication presupposes the holding of common relevance systems by the partners in the communication. He states that 'successful communication is possible only between persons, social groups, nations, etc., who share a substantially similar system of relevances'.[40] The disparity of the systems of relevance makes the establishment of a common discourse impossible.

Intersubjective understanding

In several problem-solving conflict resolution theories the notion of understanding is taken for granted and, therefore, not clarified. It is assumed that an understanding of the position of the other party can be gained in the problem-solving workshop. Burton implicitly establishes his notion of understanding in the idea of universal human needs. Needs are assumed to be the common human denominator from which the understanding of an other person derives. Intersubjective understanding is, however, not that simple. Nor should it be regarded as a psychological concept which denotes empathy or feelings. In order to discuss intersubjective understanding we need to return to the notion of the life-world.

In the life-world I look at the world within the natural attitude. What is characteristic of the natural attitude is that in it I take the existence of fellow men and women for granted, just as I take for granted the existence of natural objects. I assume that intelligent fellow men and women exist as elements of the life-world. I also assume that the objects of the life-world are, in principle, accessible to the experience of other persons. Schutz calls these two assumptions the fundamental axioms of the natural attitude.[41]

The axioms rest upon two idealisations. First, the idealisation of the 'interchangeability of standpoints' consists of the idea that if I were there, where he or she is now, I would experience things in the same perspective, distance and reach as he or she does. And, if he or she were here where I am now, he or she would experience things from the same perspective as I. Second, the idealisation of the 'congruence of relevance systems' implies that he or she and I learn to accept as given that the variances in apprehension and explication which result from differences between my and his or her biographical situations are irrelevant to our present practical goals. These two idealisations together form, according to Schutz, the 'general thesis of the reciprocity of perspectives'. For Schutz the thesis is the presupposition for a world of common objects and therewith for communication.[42]

The Schutzian theory of alter ego and intersubjective understanding gets its full meaning in the context of the discussion on the spatial and temporal structures of the life-world. According to Schutz's view, I experience the world as spatially organised so that the place my body occupies at a certain moment within this world is the starting-point from which I take my bearing in space. Schutz describes the body as a zero coordinate in the space in relation to which other objects are perceived:

> It [my body] is, so to speak, the centre '0' of a system of coordinates which determines certain dimensions of orientation in the surrounding field and the distances and perspectives of the objects therein: they are above or underneath, before or behind, right or left, nearer or farther. And, in a similar way, my actual 'Now' is the origin of all the time-perspectives under which I organise the events within the world, such as the categories of fore and aft, past and future, simultaneity and succession, sooner or later, etc.[43]

It is the temporally, spatially and socially structured life-world which forms the basis of the understanding of the alter ego. Although my body is the natural 0 coordinate around which my world is arranged, I accept the existence of fellow men and women in the everyday world. I accept that their bodies form their 'here' and that their time is organised around their 'now'. I also assume that they have access to the objects of the life-world, and that we can gain sufficiently congruent relevance systems for the purposes of practical goals in the everyday world. Despite these assumptions prevailing in the natural attitude, the intended (subjective) meaning of the other is to a certain degree unreachable to me.

In the everyday world, in the sector of it which is accessible to my immediate experience, I do not merely experience the body of another person as an object, I also experience it as a field of expression. As a field of expression it expresses something about other consciousness. Through his or her expressive movements or acts[44] I can know something about the other person's consciousness and thoughts. However, the body I perceive refers to something I cannot perceive, to 'inwardness', to his or her inner life. This inner life is something which transcends my immediate and direct experience. Schutz calls this phenomenon 'medium transcendencies of the boundaries of the life-world'. Through these transcendencies a distinction is made between one's own and something other.[45]

In the natural attitude, I take for granted that I can master the medium transcendencies: the boundaries of experience that I run into are crossable. I can cross the boundaries, for example, with the help of indications, marks, signs and symbols as means of conveying news from beyond the boundaries of immediate experience.[46] Signs, and especially language as a system of signs, are important from the point of view of this study, because even though essentially newsbearers, they are a precondition for communication with other people. Given that language is a precondition for communication, the study of it could be at the centre of the theories of problem-solving workshop type of conflict resolution. This is not, however, the case: the area is under-theorised in many problem-solving conflict resolution theories as well as in many mediation theories.[47]

In sum, language as a system of signs facilitates the crossing of the boundary between fellow men and women. Although signs facilitate intersubjective understanding, they do not make it automatic. The subjective and occasional meanings of signs add something 'vague' and 'uncertain' to interpretation, and the interpreter never fully discovers the subjective meaning of the speaker. Language is neither an ahistorical nor a neutral sign system. On the contrary, language is socially, culturally and historically given: its structures are built up intersubjectively, stored historically and transmitted socially. Schutz writes:

> In any case, one thing ought to be clear with respect to human society: the multiply grounded forms of communication in social action presuppose language as a quasi-ideal system, as the authority for clarification, appeal, and mediation. Language is the principal means for the social construction of every *human* reality; but it is also the chief medium for transmitting a particular, hence historically and socially already-constructed reality.[48]

Language is a storehouse of typifications, and it pre-typifies the world to us. In other words, by using language we accept certain ways of typifying the world; we accept a pre-constructed reality.[49]

Schutz's and Burton's views of understanding clearly differ. Burton assumes that there are fundamental similarities, arising from human needs, between people, and that these form the foundation of intersubjective understanding, and therefore such issues as communication and language do not appear problematic in his theory. Schutz's theory of intersubjective understanding, on the other hand, points to the preconditions for communication. As argued above, we can never fully discover the subjective meaning of the other, of his or her experience, action and speech. However, the general thesis of the reciprocity of perspectives implies that a sufficient understanding for the purposes of everyday life can be gained, and language facilitates that understanding. Language as a socially constructed system of signs which consists of typifications forms the most fundamental element of communication.

Action, social action and interaction

Burton's theory of conflict resolution sees the resolution process from the point of view of the behaviour of the individual. His emphasis is on behaviour which originates in needs and which aims at individual utility maximisation. Schutz's theory shifts the emphasis from behaviour to action and from action to interaction, which is the domain of communication. He differentiates action from act. The term 'action' means human conduct devised by the actor in advance, that is, conduct based on a preconceived project. The term 'act' designates the outcome of the ongoing process, the accomplished action. Action, or performance, as Schutz also calls it, may be covert or overt. By 'working' he means overt actions which require bodily movements and which aim at changing the surrounding world. What is crucial in action is that it consists of projecting. Projecting is anticipation of future conduct by way of 'fantasising', of placing oneself in fantasy at a future time when the action will already have been accomplished.[50]

Actions are motivated behaviour. Schutz redefines the concept of motive by distinguishing the 'in order to' motive from the genuine 'because' motive. The 'in order to' motive means the state of affairs, the end, which brings about the action that has been undertaken. The 'because' motive, on the other hand, refers to the point of view of the actor and his or her past experiences which have determined him or her to act as he or she did. For example, we may say that the motive of a doctorate student for finishing his or her studies is to get a lectureship. That is the 'in order to' motive. We may say also that the student has been motivated to undertake doctoral studies because he or she grew up in this or that environment, had these or those experiences at school, etc. That is the 'because' motive.

Action has different meanings for the actor and for the outside observer. Since action gets its meaning through a meaning-bestowing process, through a reflective glance in the consciousness of the actor, the meaning cannot be the same for the actor and for the observer. The 'in order to' motive is, according to Schutz, an essentially subjective category and is revealed to the observer only if he or she asks what meaning the actor bestows on his or her action. The genuine 'because' motive, however, is an objective category and accessible to the observer, who can reconstruct from the accomplished act the attitude of the actor to his or her action.[51]

Examples of social behaviour are feelings of sympathy and antipathy, erotic attitudes, and feeling activities of all kinds. If such experiences have the character of being previously projected they are, according to Schutz, social action. When social action has as its 'in order to' motive the bringing about of a certain conscious experience in the other person it is 'socially affecting'. For example, I can originate a sign for someone else to interpret which implies that I am affecting another by an act of communication. Interaction, on the other hand, is based on an act of affecting another with the aim of leading the other to have conscious experience of a desired sort.[52] In Schutz's words:

> An interaction, then, exists, if one person acts upon another with the expectation that the latter will respond, or at least notice. It is not necessary that the partner reciprocally affect the actor or even act himself. All that is required is that the partner be aware of the actor and interpret what he does or says as evidence for what is going on in his mind. All the partner's subjective experience will, naturally, be modified by his attention to the actor. Every interaction is, therefore, based on an action of affecting another within a social situation.[53]

Schutz considers social interaction to be a motivational context. There is a reciprocal change of motives by the partners in social interaction. In interaction, I expect the 'in order to' motive of myself to become the 'because' motive of my partner and, conversely, he or she is prepared to regard my 'in order to' motive as the genuine 'because' motive of his or her behaviour. Thus interaction involves mutual expectations of behaviour and reactions. However, as Schutz notes, the intermeshing of motives does not necessarily mean agreement of interest and goals.[54]

Social relations originate in social action and interaction. Schutz's thesis is that the motivational context of interaction derives its validity from the direct social relationship of which all other interactions are mere modifications. In the direct relationship the partners are face-to-face, their streams of consciousness are synchronised, geared to each other, and each immediately affects the other. Schutz calls this type of direct social relationship a We relationship. If the face-to-face relation and the directness of experience are essential for the We relationship, in a They relationship, on the other hand, the relation is more remote, indirect and anonymous. In the They relationship the other person is not known to me in his or her vivid present. Rather, he or she is indirectly accessible to me in the form of general types: he or she is an ideal construct of my own. The terms 'anonymity' and 'intimacy' relate to social relationships. Every concrete experience of others is experienced with some degree of intimacy or anonymity. For example, making love with my partner involves a higher degree of intimacy than buying a stamp from a postal clerk. As Schutz seems to suggest, the mediate They relationship based on a hypothetical personal type is characterised by a greater degree of anonymity than the direct We relationship.[55]

In the face-to-face relationship 'what you are' is continuously available to me. In the We relationship I can constantly check my interpretations of what is going on in your mind by observing your expressions and by asking you about the interpretative schemes which you are applying to our common environment. In the process I can correct, expand and enrich my own understanding of you. In other words, I do apprehend the other through typificatory schemes even in the face-to-face situations, but, as Berger and Luckmann note, these schemes are more 'vulnerable' to interference than in 'remoter' forms of interaction. I can also modify my typifications in more anonymous They relationships. The modification occurs, however, only to a small extent, and only as long as the sphere of interest which determines the use of type remains unchanged.[56]

Schutz argues that the face-to-face relationship is important also in harmonising relevance structures between partners in interaction:

> In the second place, every communication with other men in the life-world presupposes a similar structure of at least the thematic and interpretational relevancies. This similar structure will occupy a privileged position within the social domain involving fellow-men in face-to-face situations because the sector of the spatial life-world, common to partners, by necessity makes some elements to be equal thematic relevancy for both partners, and furthermore because the body of the partner with

his field of physiognomic expression, his gestures, his actions and reactions discloses an interpretationally relevant field which otherwise would not be accessible to the same extent.[57]

Although the face-to-face relationship may impose some elements of equal thematic relevance to partners in the situation, experiences which do not become problematic do not change typifications and other relevance structures. In other words, unless an experience is presented as a problem, it rather confirms the efficacy of 'old' relevance structures and typifications than modifies them.[58]

Before moving to a more detailed application of Schutz's theory to conflict and conflict resolution, two preliminary conclusions can be drawn from his account of intersubjective understanding and interaction. First, seen from the point of view of conflict resolution, interaction, although based on the intermesh of motives, does not create common interests and goals in the conflict resolution situation. The study of the processes of communication and typification as well as of the formation of relevance systems is needed to obtain more sophisticated conceptual tools with which we can approach problem-solving workshop conflict resolution. Second, if all interaction is affecting the other, as Schutz claims, the solitary and utility-maximising ego postulated by Burton as a foundation for conflict resolution theory is irrelevant, or, at least, it is not fruitful. As demonstrated in the previous chapter, in Burton's theory interaction is largely reduced to the sum of choices made by each actor. His view is not fruitful, because it does not create space for communication. Schutz's theory has brought us to the point where it is necessary to reject the Burtonian theory of behaviour, which emphasises the solitary ego, if we want to study communication, language and interaction as a means through which shared typifications and a common reality are created in the problem-solving workshop.

Rationality

Burton postulates two main types of rationality when explaining behaviour. For him, instrumental rationality founded on utility-maximising calculations is the most prominent. On other hand, Burton hints at the possibility of discursive rationality too. Schutz's account of the rationality of action differs fundamentally from Burton's views. Schutz's main thesis is that the everyday action may be reasonable, but not rational. People act in everyday life on the basis of routines and rules of thumb rather than on the basis of instrumental calculations. Schutz writes:

> We may say that a man acted sensibly if the motive and the course of his action is understandable to us, his partners and observers. This will be the case if his action is in accordance with a socially approved set of rules and recipes for the coming to terms with typical problems by applying typical means for achieving typical ends. If I, if We, if 'Anybody who is one of us' found himself in typically similar circumstances

he would act in a similar way. Sensible behaviour, however, does not presuppose that the actor is guided by insight into his motives and the means–ends context.[59]

Schutz also calls this type of rationality 'practical rationality'. Practical rationality becomes constituted under the limiting conditions of everyday reality. Actions based on it are rational relative to subjective factors and everyday goals. A course of action can be perfectly rational from the point of view of the actor and appear non-rational to the partner or observer.[60]

Schutz justifies the 'non-rationality'[61] of everyday action by claiming that the knowledge of the actor is always incoherent and confused. In the stock of knowledge at hand, clear and distinct experiences are intermingled with vague conjectures and prejudices with well proven evidences. Motives, means, ends, causes and effects are strung together without clear understanding of their real connections. There are also rules, habits and principles whose origin and validity are beyond our control and never verified. In short, our knowledge in daily life is approximate and typical. Schutz argues that in the everyday world 'we are satisfied if we have a fair chance of realising our purposes'.[62] In everyday life we have a 'cookery book' or 'recipe' type of knowledge with the help of which we anticipate the likelihood of events and orient ourselves in the life-world rather than engage in strictly rational means–ends calculations.[63]

Given that the knowledge of the actor is of such a kind, the question 'Is rational choice of action possible?' arises. And if we assume that it is possible, what are the criteria of knowledge that guide rational choice? Points of departure between the traditional rational choice paradigm and Schutz's theory are evident. The rational choice paradigm takes the first question for granted and tries to answer the second. As noted earlier, for example, Burton, who employs elements from the paradigm while explaining the entry and workshop stages, does not question the idea that the parties in conflict are capable of instrumentally rational choices.

Schutz's answer clarifies first the criteria of the rationality of knowledge. He argues that the rationality of knowledge presupposes that all the elements from which the actor has to choose are clearly and distinctly conceived by him or her.[64] The choice itself is rational if the actor selects, from all means within his or her reach, the most appropriate for realising the intended end. Rational action presupposes that the actor has clear and distinct insight into ends, means, secondary results, alternative means to the end, relations of the end to other possible means and different possible ends. The complications increase when the action in question is social, that is, when it is directed towards other people. Then clear and distinct knowledge of the situation as defined by the partner is needed. Schutz concludes by claiming that this ideal of rationality, rational action and interaction is not and cannot be a peculiar feature of everyday thought and action. He, thereby, disagrees with the rational choice model.[65]

103

Schutz's theory of action and rationality differs from Burton's views of human behaviour at least in three major respects. First, Schutz does not assume that simple instrumental, means–ends, rationality prevails in the everyday world. His theory of choice – which Schutz does apply, but to rare situations where the usual rules of thumb no longer yield results that fit the expectations – is complex and takes into account situational factors. Burton, on the other hand, does not recognise that the workshop participation can be routine action which does not constitute a problematic situation for the participants. In other words, the participants do not necessarily calculate utility.

Second, Schutz's emphasis is on the socially formed stock of knowledge of the individual. Given the social construction of knowledge, the origins of the choices and actions of the individual are in the social world, in its interactive and communicative processes. Schutz's main theme is not the action of the individual and the choices made by the individual. It is, rather, how typifications and relevances intersubjectively regulate social action, interaction and communication. In Schutz's theory the 'because' motives of the actors are important, whereas Burton does not attach any importance to this 'social background' of the actor. For Burton the actor is the solitary ego whose 'because' motives are not relevant. The Burtonian solitary ego is not culturally and socially conditioned; rather, it is largely biologically determined. There is no need, in Burton's view, to discuss the culturally constructed interactive and communicative processes in and through which the individual, his or her stock of knowledge, relevance structures, typifications and 'realities', are formed.

The third point of departure derives from the second: Schutz's theory allows the study of social groups and their notions of rationality, whereas Burton limits his theory to the study of the individual actor. Owing to his limited understanding of interaction, Burton dismisses the influence of the socially approved rules on conduct. Unlike Burton's views, Schutz's views make it possible to understand how social groups influence, for example, decisions. According to Schutz, the actor orients his or her action on standards which are culturally and socially approved as rules of conduct by the in-group he or she belongs to.[66] Moreover, to follow these socially constructed standards is not to imply that they are rationally understood. Thus the ultimate origin of the entry into and action within the problem-solving workshop is in socially approved conduct. This conduct is founded on the relatively similar typifications and relevance systems of the members of the group the participant represents.

In sum, several of Schutz's themes and ideas, such as the 'because' motive, the idea that the basis of rationality is in the social world and the notion of socially approved standards of conduct, shift the attention to socially and culturally conditioned human existence. The theory of the alter ego, as Schutz presents it, on the other hand, establishes the foundations for the study intersubjective understanding and communication in the problem-solving workshop.

Cultural patterns and social groups

Problem-solving workshop approaches to international conflict resolution stress that the resolution of a conflict must be based on an analysis of the needs, motivations, hopes and fears of the conflicting parties. A question arises: are needs, motivations, hopes and fears individual and 'subjective' mental – or even 'objective' biological – factors or are they, rather, intersubjective and produced in the processes of the social world? Burton derives needs and motivations from biology and ends up emphasising the solitary actor. Schutz, on the other hand, focuses his phenomenological analysis on the life-world and the relative natural views of the social groups. Following the tradition of seeing human existence as socially constructed, as the most recent sociological terminology expresses it, this part of the study challenges the image of the solitary ego postulated by Burton and continues to study how social actors are constructed in and through the social world and how they, in turn, construct their reality, needs and identity in that world.

Schutz approaches the question of socially constructed reality in terms of cultural patterns. According to him, the cultural pattern peculiar to a social group functions for its members as an unquestioned scheme of reference. The cultural pattern consists of all the peculiar valuations, institutions, and systems of orientation and guidance (e.g. mores, laws, habits, customs and fashions) which characterise or constitute any social group at a given moment in its history. Schutz claims that 'any member born or reared within the group accepts the ready-made standardised scheme of the cultural pattern handed down to him by ancestors, teachers, and authorities as an unquestioned and unquestionable guide in all situations which normally occur within the social world'.[67] The knowledge included in the cultural pattern consists of 'recipes' for interpreting and for handling things in the social world. These 'recipes' work also as guides to actions which tell what to do to gain certain results in certain social situations: the cultural pattern provides in its 'recipes' typical solutions for typical problems available for typical actors.[68]

Any society considers itself as a little cosmos, and the maintenance of the cosmos requires symbols to keep it together. Societies, social groups, need their central myths, or dominant ideologies, to justify and to establish foundations for self-interpretation. Social groups can be distinguished by virtue of their commonly held relevance systems from which typifications arise. Typifications included in cultural patterns vary from one social world or culture to another.[69] As M. Barber claims, 'social conditionness is an essential property of typifications'.[70]

A group has a relative natural world view which is taken for granted and commonly shared. On the basis of the relative natural world view all subjects organise their experiences as members of the group. Furthermore, on the basis of the view they understand the other as a member of their group. The group has, according to Schutz, the subjective and objective meaning. It has a subjective meaning to a person who considers himself or herself a member of it and speaks of it in terms of 'we'. The objective meaning is that which the group has for outsiders who speak of its members in terms of 'they'.[71]

Schutz discusses the processes through which a member of an out-group adapts to a new group. The stranger does not have 'tools' offered by the cultural pattern of the in-group for acting or reacting typically in the new group. He or she does not know what kind of conduct to expect from the members of the in-group. What is missing is a 'scheme of translation' according to which the stranger may translate and interpret the cultural pattern of his or her own group into the new group and vice versa. The knowledge he or she has about the new group is not necessarily adequate, because it does not provide him or her with tested 'recipes' for behaviour. It may provide him or her with 'recipes' for interpretation, but not with 'recipes' for action which have been tried out in actual situations. The process of cultural adjustment takes place through trial and error, and is slow, according to Schutz.[72]

The Schutzian account of the outsider and cultural adaptation offers a viewpoint for the conceptualisation of the problem-solving workshop. In the case of the workshop, the other party does not need to adapt to the world view or culture of the other. Rather, both parties need to find ways to encounter each other in the workshop without one-sided adaptation. The parties as well as the facilitator need to find a 'scheme of translation' in order to understand each other and to create a shared reality. The workshop is a place where 'strangers' meet without well tested 'recipes' for the interpretation of and action in the situation, and where trial and error are a means of slow adaptation to a shared culture.[73]

Individuals, institutions and social structures

Berger and Luckmann's analysis of socially constructed reality focuses on the relation between the individual actor and institution through habitualised actions, that is, actions which are repeated frequently. Habitualisation implies also that the action in question may be performed again in the future in the same manner and with the same economy of effort. Habitualised action becomes instutionalised 'whenever there is a reciprocal typification of habitualised actions by types of actors'.[74] The reality of everyday life contains typificatory schemes in terms of which other people and objects of the life-world are apprehended and dealt with. What is peculiar, according to Berger and Luckmann, to the typifications of habitualised actions that constitute an institution is that typifications are shared by the actors participating in reciprocal action. The relationship between the actor and typifications is also mutual: typifications are available to all members of the institution in question and the institution, on the other hand, itself typifies individual actors as well as individual actions. Institutions control human conduct by setting up predefined patterns of action and interpretation and, thereby, participate in the creation and definition of realities.[75]

Berger and Luckmann's account rejects the study of organisational or institutional structures as such, as social realities of their own. Although organisational structures are created in an interplay between the actor and institution, the actor may experience the institution possessing a reality of its own, a reality that confronts the individual as an external and coercive fact. As long as institutions are, according to Berger and Luckmann, constructed and maintained only in the interaction of A and B, their objectivity remains tenuous and changeable. The case is different when the institution is transferred to the new generation. Then the individual confronts a comprehensive and given reality which may not be altered and which appears as self-evident. An institutional world is experienced as an objective reality.[76]

How does the actor act as a member of an institution or organisation? Acting as a member of an organisation does not differ essentially from acting as an individual. There is something also in the organisational world which is taken for granted by the actor: the organisation presents him or her with a number of anonymous and functional typifying schemes that are 'passively' received and that help him or her to orient his or her behaviour and interpret the world. The actor becomes socialised to the organisational world too. The relationships in that world are organised on the basis of anonymous roles which guarantee the smooth functioning of the organisation. However, face-to-face relationships within the organisational structure influence typifications in a way that the actual experience the organisational member has of the other members rarely maintains the characteristics of pure anonymity.[77]

Larger social structures (e.g. feudalism, industrial society) condition human existence too. According to Schutz, they offer the individual a range of typical biographies:

> The individual experiences the social world which is already given to him, and objectivated in the relative-natural world view, as a scale of subjective probabilities related to him, as an ordering of duties, possibilities, and goals attainable with ease or with difficulty. In other words, the social structure is the rigid boundary in which his age, his life-plans, and thus his priority structures and daily plans gain concrete form.[78]

Social structures are, in this view, differentiated through their degree of freedom in the various courses of life. The individual places himself or herself in the social structure through biographies, and typical biographies work as a means of socialisation, for the knowledge of typical biographies, consisting of the what and how type of knowledge, is socially transmitted to the individual in different phases of his or her life.[79]

In sum, reality or, rather, 'what is known as reality' is socially and intersubjectively constructed and shared. Schutz sees the influence of the group on the individual in terms of the cultural patterns which form a basis for a shared reality, whereas Berger and Luckmann emphasise institutionally defined reality. In Schutz's view the cultural pattern offers an unquestioned scheme of orientation in the social world. According to Berger and Luckmann's theory, on the other hand, the individual is influenced by the institutions which provide him or her with knowledge and rules of conduct. Despite these differences, they share the view that the reality of an actor is defined through knowledge which consists of typifications of the world and which is mainly handed down to him or her by other actors belonging to the same social group or institutional world.

Given this notion of reality, the study of conflict and conflict resolution presupposes the study of social groups and institutions. The way groups and institutions distribute knowledge, define reality through shared typifications and use language becomes a fundamental issue for conflict studies. Similarly, it is seminal to study the points where typifications break down, shared reality collapses and communication becomes impossible.

Culturally constructed needs and identities

If we accept the view that reality is socially constructed, the notions of needs and identity get a new interpretation. The emphasis shifts, from the universalist definition of needs and identity to such questions as how the actor experiences them, what meaning they have for him or her and how they are created.

Peter Manning and Horacio Fabrega's study of self and body offers analytical tools to criticise Burton's universalist needs theory from a phenomenological point of view. Manning and Fabrega study structure and meanings in one area of cultural practices, namely health and illness. They claim that social scientists tend to postulate a 'radical equalisation of the social significance of the human body'. Manning and Fabrega's analysis can be applied to Burton's version of needs theory where there is a 'radical equalisation of the social significance of human needs'.

Manning and Fabrega argue that social scientists suppose that 'since the body is composed of universal features, it necessarily is experienced as such; furthermore, given this "universality", it need not be accounted for within any special system of propositions bearing on the explanation of human behaviour'.[80] The universalist, and often also biological, view of the body consists of seven assumptions: (1) the body can be partitioned internally into named organs, systems and functional relationships; (2) unless external or internal causes intervene the body functions normally; (3) the senses are universal; (4) disease is universal; (5) boundaries between the self and the body are non-problematic; (6) death is a biological process that occurs when the body ceases to function and (7) the body should be seen as a natural, objective, valuationally neutral entity.[81]

108

The Burtonian view of human needs assumes that needs can be partitioned into named parts such as a need for identity, a need for security and a need for cooperation, and that there are functional relationships between these parts. Burton's argument is that when, for example, elites hinder needs satisfaction conflict will result. When individuals are free to satisfy their needs, society functions normally. Needs are universal in Burton's theory: everybody has them. Consequently, according to Burton, deviance and conflict are a universal and cross-culturally invariant phenomenon. Boundaries between the self and needs are non-problematic, in Burton's view, because needs express themselves through and in the self. Finally, needs should be seen as an objective and neutral entity, because seeing them as such is the very precondition for successful conflict resolution and the avoidance of violent conflict.

Burton assumes also that needs are universally experienced as such, that is, needs are experienced such that variations between persons, situations, groups, and even larger social units are of minor empirical significance. He does not deny that needs are expressed through different cultures: they may find cultural expression. These differences, however, are of minor importance from the point of view of theory formation, conceptualisation and, finally, conflict resolution. Seen from the angle offered by Manning and Fabrega, Burton's theory – which clearly equalises the social significance of needs – denies the social and cultural construction and production, if not expression, of human needs.

Needs are produced in social practices – instead of their being independent of the context of their production, as Burton argues. Needs are a socially constructed reality which is closely dependent on the concepts of, for example, professional practitioners. Attention should be focused on the contexts of needs and the ways practitioners use the concept of needs in different situations and to different effect.[82] This view of socially produced needs does not deny the importance of the needs concept in social practices. Rather, it denies the universalist understanding of needs.

For example, in the Burtonian type of problem-solving context the notion of needs is often employed by the facilitator to point out interests the participants seem to have in common. The fact that the facilitator uses the notion should not be confused with the idea that the participants actually have objective and universal needs which are recognisable in the conflict resolution workshop. The participants may participate in the needs discourse created by the facilitator in order, for example, rhetorically (by convincing and persuading) to justify certain actions, but that should not be interpreted as proving that there are universal and biologically based needs independent of the milieu in which they are discussed.[83] In other words, if the concept of needs is employed in conflict resolution practices and in theorising on conflict and conflict resolution, the process of its creation and its situational nature should be reflected.

Closely related to the issue of the social production of needs is the question of identity. Burton maintains that identity is a need in which behaviour originates. According to Schutz, on the other hand, identities are structured in accord with the numerous social groups to which we pertain and that pressure us from different directions. There is no single identity; rather, there are multiple identities. Multiple membership of numerous groups is experienced as a set of self-typifications. A conflict may arise within the personality, because the endeavour to live up to the various expectations inhering in membership of various groups is difficult. Despite the difficulty, the individual, or rather his or her identity, is not determined by the social group, because he or she is free to choose for himself or herself with which part of his or her personality he or she wants to participate in group membership.[84] In Schutz's theory there is no single coherent identity which can be the source or the aim of behaviour, as Burton suggests. Nor can identity be denied. Its expression can be suppressed, and the ways of confirming it can be banned, but that does not necessarily imply deviant behaviour as Burton argues in his conflict theory.

Realities are defined through and in the social groups. Conflict is also a reality which is defined in social processes: what counts as conflict is culturally constituted. Similarly, a problem-solving workshop is a socially constructed reality. The participants bring to the conflict resolution situation their definitions of reality, conflict and conflict resolution which are mediated through socially constructed typifications. As a consequence, in order to understand and study a conflict, the sets of understandings about conflict held by the people involved in a dispute are crucially important. By shifting the focus from the functional questions of what causes conflict and what conflict accomplishes materially and politically to the contextual and interpretative question of how people think about conflict, we start to see the importance of the culturally constructed interpretations of the world for the study of conflict.[85]

Culture is seen in many conflict and conflict resolution theories as an artificial label or custom which simply produces differences between the parties in conflict. Burton's conflict theory does not expand the view, because in his theory culture is interpreted in an individualistic and instrumental manner. Culture is vital, however, because, for example, the 'identity' of a person is created through the social groups and in accordance with the cultural patterns which prevail in the groups the person belongs to. Even the use of language implies being influenced by the cultural pattern. This view, which denies the existence of the person independently of the cultural patterns, challenges also the Burtonian notion of the conflict resolution workshop as a filter through which cultural influences can be filtered away. As the next chapter shows, with the help of the social constructionist view, 'cultural influences' can be set at the very centre of conflict and conflict resolution theory.

NOTES

1 D. Stewart and A. Mickunas, *Exploring Phenomenology: A Guide to the Field and its Literature*, second edition (Athens OH, Ohio University Press, 1990), pp. 4–5.

2 R. Bernstein, *The Restructuring of Social and Political Theory* (London, Methuen, 1979), pp. xi–xxiv and 4–54.

3 *Ibid.*, p. 43.

4 Hwa Yol Jung, 'A Critique of the Behavioral Persuasion in Politics: a Phenomenological View', in M. Natanson (ed.), *Phenomenology and the Social Sciences* II (Evanston IL, Northwestern University Press, 1973), p. 139.

5 *Ibid.*, pp. 138–43. For a similar criticism see also A. Schutz and T. Luckmann, *The Structures of the Life-World* II (Evanston IL, Northwestern University Press), 1989, p. 294. On behaviourism see also H. Wagner, *Phenomenology of Consciousness and Sociology of the Life-World: An Introductory Study* (Edmonton, Alta, University of Alberta Press, 1983), pp. 11–15.

6 E. Husserl, *The Crisis of European Sciences and Transcendental Phenomenology: An Introduction to Phenomenology*, trans. D. Carr (Evanston IL, Northwestern University Press, 1970).

7 A. Gurwitsch, *Phenomenology and the Theory of Science*, ed. Lester Embree (Evanston IL, Northwestern University Press, 1974), pp. 17–19 and 34–8. For a detailed analysis of the processes of matematisation, formalisation and idealisation see *ibid.*, pp. 33–59. See also Husserl, *Crisis*, pp. 52–3 and 65–6. A. Schutz discusses the issue too. He writes: 'The phenomena of productive subjectivity, which alone constitute the life-world, remain closed off to the mathematical/natural-scientific point of view for essential reasons, and the natural scientist forgets that he himself, with his subjectivity which produces science, cannot find an understanding of himself and his action in any objective science. Only recourse to this sphere of productive subjectivity, which is of course made use of by natural science and by psychology which is oriented toward the natural sciences although it is never brought to a self-understanding, can on the one hand free mathematical natural science from the crises concerning its foundations and on the other hand ground for a true science of man (*Geisteswissenschaft*).' The quotation is from Schutz's letter to Aron Gurwitsch in R. Grathoff (ed.), *Philosophers in Exile: The Correspondence of Alfred Schutz and Aron Gurwitsch, 1939–59* (Bloomington and Indianapolis IN, Indiana University Press, 1989), p. 11.

8 Bernstein, *The Restructuring*, pp. 135–6.

9 Ideal types or second degree constructs, as Schutz calls them, are constructs of the social world, action and actor produced by the social scientist in accordance with the scientific problem he or she sets for himself or herself. They are based on the first-degree constructs of the thought objects constructed by the commonsense thinking of men living their daily lives within the social world.

10 A. Schutz, *The Phenomenology of the Social World*, trans. G. Walsh and F. Lehnert (Evanston IL, Northwestern University Press, [1932] 1967).

11 *Ibid.*, p. 42

12 *Ibid.*, pp. 15–44.

13 Bernstein, *The Restructuring*, pp. 138–9. Understanding has multiple meanings which, according to Schutz, must be distinguished from each other. Understanding is: (1) the experiential form of commonsense knowledge of human affairs; (2) an epistemological problem, and (3) a method peculiar to the social sciences. A. Schutz, *Collected Papers* II, *Studies in Social Theory*, ed. A. Brodersen (The Hague, Nijhoff, 1964), p. 56.

14 A. Schutz, *Collected Papers* I, *The Problem of Social Reality*, ed. M. Natanson (The Hague, Nijhoff, 1962), pp. 57–66, 149 and 209–10. See also Gurwitsch, *Phenomenology*, pp. 128–31.

15 G. Walsh, 'Introduction', in A. Schutz, *The Phenomenology of the Social World*, trans.

G. Walsh and F. Lehnert (Evanston IL, Northwestern University Press, [1932] 1967), pp. xix–xx. See also J. Bleicher, *The Hermeneutic Imagination: Outline of a Positive Critique of Scientism and Sociology* (London, Routledge, 1982), pp. 52–68. F. Dallmayr, 'Phenomenology and Social Science: an Overview and Appraisal', in D. Carr and E. Casey (eds), *Explorations in Phenomenology* (The Hague, Nijhoff, 1973), pp. 135–8 and 146–8. I. Srubar, 'On the Origin of Phenomenological Sociology', *Human Studies*, 7: 2 (1984), 164–70.

16 *Ibid.* It should be strongly emphasised that although there are several similarities between Weber's and Schutz's projects, Schutz criticises and clarifies many of Weber's views. See a summary, M. Barber, *Social Typifications and the Elusive Other* (London and Toronto, Associated University Press, 1988), pp. 25–33. Schutz's account of ideal types as a resource of scientific objectivity will be discussed in the next chapter.

17 H. Garfinkel, *Studies in Ethnomethodology* (Englewood Cliffs NJ, Prentice Hall, 1967). See also a summary of Garfinkel's views and their relation to Schutz's phenomenology, G. Psathas, 'Ethnomethodology as a Phenomenological Approach in the Social Sciences', in D. Ihde and R. Zaner (eds), *Interdisciplinary Phenomenology* (The Hague, Nijhoff, 1977), pp. 73–98.

18 P. Berger and T. Luckmann, *The Social Construction of Reality: A Treatise in the Sociology of Knowledge* (London, Penguin Books, 1991).

19 R. Cox, *Schutz's Theory of Relevance: A Phenomenological Critique* (The Hague, Boston MA and London, Nijhoff, 1978), p. 61. M. Natanson, 'Introduction', in M. Natanson (ed.), *Essays in Phenomenology* (The Hague, Nijhoff, 1966), pp. 14–15. Stewart and Mickunas, *Exploring Phenomenology*, pp. 8–9.

20 A. Schutz, Alfred, *Collected Papers* III, *Studies in Phenomenological Philosophy*, ed. I. Schutz (The Hague, Nijhoff, 1966), pp. 4–5.

21 Gurwitsch, *Phenomenology*, p. 3.

22 Schutz, *Papers* III, p. 116.

23 Gurwitsch, *Phenomenology*, p. 57. In the natural attitude of everyday life the following is taken for granted without question: (1) the corporeal existence of other human beings; (2) that these bodies are endowed with consciousness essentially similar to my own; (3) that the things in the outer world included in my environs and that of my fellow men and women are the same for us and have fundamentally the same meaning; (4) that I can enter into interrelations and reciprocal actions with my fellow men and women; (5) that I can make myself understood to them; (6) that a stratified social and cultural world is historically pre-given as a frame of reference for me and my fellow men and women and (7) that therefore the situation in which I find myself at any moment is only to a small extent purely created by me. A. Schutz and T. Luckmann, *The Structures of the Life-World* I (London, Heinemann, 1974), p. 5.

24 *Ibid.*, pp. 3–8.

25 Schutz, *Papers* I, p. 312.

26 Stewart and Mickunas, *Exploring Phenomenology*, p. 127. See also Schutz, *Papers* III, p. 312.

27 These writers have distinct periods in their thinking whose study is rejected in this account of phenomenology.

28 It is the conscious and concrete 'I' which can perform the reduction, not an abstract 'we'.

29 Natanson, 'Introduction', pp. 7–14. This description of the phenomenological reduction is the most primitive. For more detailed studies see, for example, *ibid.* Schutz, *Papers* I, pp. 104–9 and 122–6. S. Vaitkus, *How is Society Possible? Intersubjectivity and the Fiduciary Attitude as Problems of the Social Group in Mead, Gurwitsch, and Schutz* (Dordrecht, Boston MA and London, Kluwer, 1991), p. 138. Wagner, *Phenomenology*, pp. 40–5.

30 Wagner, *Phenomenology*.

31 Vaitkus, *How is Society Possible?*, p. 138.

32 Schutz, *Papers* III, p. 80.

33 The relative natural conception of the world is a conception which is given in society as an *a priori* to individual experience. The conception, although it is relative to a particular soci-ohistorical situation, appears to the individual as the natural way of looking at the world.

34 Schutz, *Papers* III, p. 82. Barber, *Social Typifications*, p. 64. Vaitkus, *How is Society Possible?*, p. 141.

35 Schutz claims, however, that I may take the typical apperceived object as an exemplar of the general type, but I do not need by any means to think of, for example, the concrete cat as an exemplar of the general concept of 'cat'. For example, the cat of my neighbour, Jonas, shows all the characteristics which the type 'cat', according to my previous experience, implies. But what he has in common with other cats does not concern me. I look at him as my friend, as such distinguished from all other cats. Thus, without a special motive, I am not induced to look at Jonas as a mammal, an animal, an object of the outer world, although I know that he is all that too. Schutz, *Papers* I, pp. 7–9 and 306. Schutz, *Papers* II, pp. 233–4. A. Schutz, *Reflections of the Problem of Relevance*, ed. R. Zaner (New Haven CT and London, Yale University Press, 1970), pp. 56–64. A. Schutz, *On Phenomenology and Social Relations: Selected Writings*, ed. H. Wagner (Chicago and London, University of Chicago Press, 1970), pp. 116–20. Schutz and Luckmann, *Structures* I, pp. 142–6. Cox, *Schutz's Theory of Relevance*, pp. 5–10. Gurwitsch, *Phenomenology*, pp. 115–16 and 140–1.

36 Schutz, *Papers* II, pp. 124–7. Barber, *Social Typifications*, p. 37. Cox, *Schutz's Theory of Relevance*, p. 9.

37 Schutz, *Reflections*, pp. 3–5. Cox, *Schutz's Theory of Relevance*, p. 72. See also Schutz, *Papers* I, pp. 9–10.

38 Schutz, *Papers* III, pp. 122–32. Schutz, *Reflections*, pp. 26–30, 35–6, 45–52 and 68–71. On relevances see also Schutz and Luckmann, *Structures* I, pp. 182–229. For an excellent summary of Schutz's theory of relevance see Cox, *Schutz's Theory of Relevance*, pp. 72–91. Schutz's example (here simplified and modified), originally presented by the Greek sophist Carneades, suggests the following. I come home from a pub and perceive that there is something unexpected in the corner of my room. I think that it may be either a pile of rope or a coiled snake. Thus the object has become by virtue of topical relevance a theme of my thought. By virtue of interpretational relevance I subsume this unknown object under the type 'pile of rope' instead of the type of 'snake', because in my stock of knowledge there is the type 'rope' which corresponds with or, rather, is relevant to this experience. The inter-pretational decision to choose the type of 'pile of rope' determines my future action in such a way that I go to bed and start reading James Joyce's *Ulysses* instead of taking a knife and stab the object.

39 All temporal and social arrangements of subjective experience of the life-world are funda-mental elements of the stock of knowledge. The focus is here on the social arrangements. In sum, the types of knowledge included in the stock are the knowledge of the fundamen-tal structures of the life-world, the routine knowledge (including skills and useful knowl-edge), and the specific knowledge at hand. For a summary of these see Vaitkus, *How is Society Possible?*, pp. 94–8. For detailed discussions on the stock of knowledge see Schutz, *Papers* II, pp. 120–34. Schutz and Luckmann, *Structures* I, chapter 4. Cox, *Schutz's Theory of Relevance*, p. 111. For the social nature of the stock of knowledge see Schutz and Luckmann, *Structures* I, pp. 261–2.

40 Schutz and Luckmann, *Structures* II, p. 261. See also Schutz, *Papers* II, p. 238. Schutz, *Papers* III, p. 132. Schutz, *On Phenomenology and Social Relations*, p. 121.

41 Schutz, *Papers* I, pp. 11–13. Schutz, *The Phenomenology of the Social World*, pp. 97–9. Schutz and Luckmann, *Structures* II, pp. 208–9.

42 Schutz, *Papers* I, pp. 11–13 and 315–16. Schutz and Luckmann, *Structures* I, pp. 59–61. Barber, *Social Typifications*, pp. 41–2. See also a case study, M. Pollner, 'Mundane Reasoning', *Philosophy of the Social Sciences*, 4 (1974), 35–54.

43 Schutz, *Papers* I, pp. 306–7.

44 According to Schutz's terminology, expressive movements have meaning only for the observer, whereas expressive acts have meaning for the actor too.

45 Schutz and Luckmann, *Structures* II, pp. 109–17.

46 A sign has three different types of intermingled meanings. A sign (e.g. word) has an objective meaning within a sign system (e.g. language) when it can be intelligibly coordinated with what it designates independently of whoever is using the sign or interpreting it. A sign has also a subjective meaning which arises when the user or the interpreter of the sign associates the sign a certain meaning having its origin in the unique experience in which he or she once learned to use the sign. A sign has always in it something of the context in which it is used, that is, it has an occasional meaning. *Ibid.*, pp. 131–47. Schutz, *The Phenomenology of the Social World*, pp. 124–5.

47 For an exception see, for example, J. Folger and T. Jones (eds), *New Directions in Mediation: Communication Research and Perspectives* (Thousand Oaks CA, London and New Delhi, Sage Publications, 1994).

48 Schutz and Luckmann, *Structures* II, p. 154.

49 Schutz, *Papers* II, pp. 100–1.

50 Schutz, *Papers* I, pp. 19–20 and 67–9. Schutz, *The Phenomenology of the Social World*, pp. 57–66. Schutz and Luckmann, *Structures* II, pp. 6–18.

51 Schutz, *Papers* I, pp. 21–2 and 69–72. Schutz, *The Phenomenology of the Social World*, pp. 25–43 and 86–99. Schutz and Luckmann, *Structures* II, pp. 18–21. Subjective means in Schutz's terminology the meaning for the actor and objective the meaning for the observer. Objective meaning does not, thus, refer to 'detached' or 'scientific' meaning.

52 Schutz, *The Phenomenology of the Social World*, pp. 144–55.

53 *Ibid.*, pp. 158–9.

54 Schutz, *Papers* II, pp. 22–4. Schutz, *The Phenomenology of the Social World*, pp. 159–63. Schutz and Luckmann, *Structures* II, pp. 84–6.

55 Schutz, *Papers* II, pp. 109–12. Schutz, *The Phenomenology of the Social World*, pp. 163–207. Schutz and Luckmann, *Structures* I, pp. 61–92. Vaitkus, *How is Society Possible?*, pp. 126–8. Vaitkus suggests that one can choose either intimacy or anonymity independent of the relationship. He writes: 'He [the person] is able, if he so desires, to act quite intimately within the context of the anonymous typifications of a region or, vice versa, to act quite anonymously within the given context of the specific typifications of a region.' *Ibid.*, p. 186. It can be argued, on the other hand, that a relationship can be so structured that this choice does not arise. See also D. Druckman and B. Broome, who use the terms 'familiarity' and 'lack of familiarity' in the context of conflict resolution. D. Druckman and B. Broome, 'Value Differences and Conflict Resolution: Familiarity or Liking?' *Journal of Conflict Resolution*, 35: 4 (1991), 571–93.

56 Berger and Luckmann, *The Social Construction of Reality*, p. 43–5. Schutz, *The Phenomenology of the Social World*, pp. 169, 171, 185, 192 and 204. Schutz and Luckmann, *Structures* I, pp. 68, 77 and 85. Barber, *Social Typifications and the Elusive Other*, pp. 46–7. In the phenomenological literature based on Schutz's ideas there are two approaches to typification and to the understanding of the subjective motives of the actor. Richard Zaner emphasises that refraining from typifying is required to grasp the other's subjective meaning. Maurice Natanson, on the other hand, claims that a degree of typification and anonymisation is needed for understanding. Vaitkus, *How is Society Possible?*, p. 87. See also R. Zaner, 'Theory of Intersubjectivity: Alfred Schutz', *Social Research*, 28: 1

(1961), 71–93. M. Natanson, *Anonymity: A Study in the Philosophy of Alfred Schutz* (Bloomington IN, Indiana University Press, 1986). See also Druckman's and Broome's discussion. They seem to be closer to Zaner's position than Natanson's, although they do not employ phenomenological terminology. Druckman and Broome, 'Value Differences', pp. 571–93.

57 Schutz, *Papers* III, p. 132. See also Schutz and Luckmann, *Structures* I, p. 254. It should be emphasised that equal relevance does not imply identicality. Rather, it implies the congruency of relevance systems.

58 Schutz and Luckmann, *Structures* I, p. 226.

59 Schutz, *Papers* I, p. 27.

60 *Ibid.*, pp. 29–30. Schutz and Luckmann, *Structures* II, pp. 58 and 229.

61 Schutz does not actually claim that action is irrational or non-rational. He, rather, wants to redefine the notion of rationality. For him, rational action is 'always action within an unquestioned and undetermined frame of constructs of typicalities of the setting, the motives, the means and ends, the courses of action and personalities involved and taken for granted'. Thus it is reasonable to speak about degrees of rationality or partial rationality. Schutz, *Papers* I, p. 33.

62 Schutz, *Papers* II, p. 73

63 *Ibid.*, pp. 72–4. Schutz defines the 'cookery book' type of knowledge: 'This kind of knowledge and its organization I should like to call "cook-book knowledge". The cook-book has recipes, lists of ingredients, formulae for mixing them, and directions for finishing off. This is all we need to make an apple pie, also all we need to deal with the routine matters of daily life. . . . Most of our daily activities from rising to going to bed are of this kind. They are performed by following recipes reduced to automatic habits or unquestioned platitudes. This kind of knowledge is concerned only with the regularity as such events in the external world irrespective of its origin.' *Ibid.*, pp. 73–4.

64 See a more detailed list of the criteria of knowledge, *ibid.*, pp. 79–80. See also Schutz and Luckmann, *Structures* II, pp. 58–65.

65 Schutz, *Papers* I, pp. 27–34. Schutz, *Papers* II, pp. 77–80. Hartmunt Esser challenges the interpretation that Schutz disagrees with the rational choice paradigm. Esser studies the moment of choice in Schutz's theory of action, and notes that Schutz assumes that action that has now become habitual, and may be categorised as sensible or reasonable, once originated in action that was problematic, and therefore was chosen on the basis of subjective expected utility. Esser concludes that, in fact, there is no contradiction between Schutz's theory of action and rational choice theory. H. Esser, 'The Rationality of Everyday Behavior: a Rational Choice Reconstruction of the Theory of Action by Alfred Schutz', *Rationality and Society*, 5: 1 (1993), pp. 7–31. See also Ilja Srubar's critique of Esser, 'On the Limits of Rational Choice', *Rationality and Society*, 5: 1 (1993), pp. 32–46.

66 See, for example, Schutz, *Papers* I, pp. 32–3. Schutz and Luckmann, *Structures* II, pp. 230–1.

67 Schutz, *Papers* II, p. 95.

68 *Ibid.*, pp. 91–105. The scheme of orientation is unquestioned 'until further notice'. Thus it may break down in unexpected and new situations.

69 *Ibid.*, pp. 244–5.

70 Barber, *Social Typifications*, p. 78.

71 Schutz, *Papers* II, pp. 95–104, 113–14, 121, 129, 227, 230, 236 and 255. Vaitkus, *How is Society Possible?*, p. 82.

72 Schutz, *Papers* II, pp. 91–105.

73 Benjamin Broome uses the phrase 'third culture' to describe culture in which the parties in conflict resolution are able to operate. According to him, the creation of such a culture

is a precondition of successful problem-solving workshop conflict resolution. B. Broome, 'Managing Differences in Conflict Resolution: The Role of Relational Empathy', in D. Sandole and H. van der Merwe (eds), *Conflict Resolution Theory and Practice: Integration and Application* (Manchester and New York, Manchester University Press, 1993), p. 104.

74   Berger and Luckmann, *The Social Construction of Reality*, p. 72.

75   *Ibid.*, pp. 65–109. See also Roger Jehenson's application of the idea of institutionalisation to the study of a psychiatric hospital and its shared typifications. R. Jehenson, 'A Phenomenological Approach to the Study of the Formal Organization', in G. Psathas (ed.), *Phenomenological Sociology: Issues and Applications* (New York, Wiley, 1973), pp. 219–47.

76   Berger and Luckmann, *The Social Construction of Reality*, pp. 76–7. Berger and Luckmann employ the concept of role as a mediation between the objectivated reality and the subjective conception of it. By playing roles the individual participates in a social world, and by internalising these roles the same world becomes subjectively real to him or her. It is important to note that the actor can establish a distance between himself or herself and his or her role-playing. *Ibid.*, pp. 91–6 and 108.

77   Jehenson, 'A Phenomenological Approach', pp. 219–47.

78   Schutz and Luckmann, *Structures* I, p. 95.

79   *Ibid.*, pp. 94–6.

80   P. Manning and H. Fabrega, 'The Experience of Self and Body: Health and Illness in the Chiapas Highland', in G. Psathas (ed.), *Phenomenological Sociology: Issues and Applications* (New York, Wiley, 1973), p. 254.

81   *Ibid.*, p. 255. For a similar critical account of needs see G. Smith, *Social Need* (London, Routledge, 1980), pp. 66–7.

82   Smith, *Social Need*, pp. 65–85.

83   The idea of the rhetorical justification is from a study which discusses how medical practitioners employ different frames to justify certain actions in relation to dying patients. A. Peräkylä, *Kuoleman monet kasvot: identiteetin tuottaminen kuolevan potilaan hoidossa* (Multiple Faces of Death: The Production of Identities in the Care of the Dying Patient) (Tampere, Vastapaino, 1990).

84   Schutz, *Papers* II, p. 254. Barber, *Social Typifications*, p. 60. See also Schutz, *Papers* I, p. 14. Berger and Luckmann, *The Social Construction of Reality*, pp. 194–200. Schutz's position does not imply social determinism. Although cultural patterns offer us approved knowledge for conduct, the selection of 'recipes' for conduct to a given situation is done by us. In other words, cultural patterns do not determine which 'recipes' we employ in a given situation, although they offer us a selection of 'recipes'.

85   For similar views see also P. Black and K. Avruch, 'Some Issues in Thinking about Culture and the Resolution of Conflict', *Humanity and Society*, 13: 2 (1989), pp. 187 and 193. K. Avruch and P. Black, 'Conflict Resolution in Intercultural Settings: Problems and Prospects', in D. Sandole and H. van der Merwe (eds), *Conflict Resolution Theory and Practice: Integration and Application* (Manchester and New York, Manchester University Press, 1993), p. 132. C. Greenhouse, 'Cultural Perspectives on War', in R. Väyrynen (ed.), *The Quest for Peace* (London, Sage, 1987), p. 34.

6

Phenomenological interpretation of problem-solving workshop conflict resolution: limitations and possibilities

I N THIS CHAPTER a phenomenological understanding of conflict and problem-solving conflict resolution is presented. Problem-solving workshop conflict resolution is reassessed and its area of applicability evaluated. The chapter continues the discussions introduced in the previous chapter: it clarifies the role of relevance structures, typifications, language and discursive rationality in conflict and conflict resolution processes. Some new themes are included. For example, power and politics are discussed in relation to conflict resolution. Attention is paid also to the double role of the facilitator. The sources of his or her expertise, ethical conduct and theorising are explored. Given that the facilitator is assumed to be both the third party and the social scientist, the notion of participant observation offers a fruitful metaphor to describe those roles.

Conflict as a breakdown of shared reality

Conflicts are characterised by a breakdown of shared reality. The individual makes his or her world through typifications, through interpretations. This does not, however, imply solipsism: typifications are produced and distributed in and through the processes of social interaction. Typifications are also a foundation for 'sociality' and cooperation. In other words, a common reality is defined through shared typifications. Maurice Natanson maintains that to be with others is to share typifications, to respond to them, to participate in them and to assume that others typify in the same way as I (or we) do. He argues that 'when such typification breaks down or is for certain reasons denied or severely circumscribed, then we have, at least in descriptive terms, evidence of fundamental differences or basic prejudices'.[1] If shared typifications break down, a common reality, the undergirding structure of shared reality, collapses. The breakdown of language and communication is merely a symptom of 'fractured sociality'. When breakdown is far-reaching, according to Natanson, we have some form of *anomie* in the society.[2] Natanson's idea can be further developed by claiming that *anomie* may take the form of conflict, and what finally counts as conflict is culturally constructed.

What is at the centre of conflict, what is characteristic of it, is not the denial of needs satisfaction. At the centre there is a far-reaching breakdown of shared definitions of reality or a fundamental clash of typifications, and what finally counts as conflict is culturally constituted through the processes of intersubjective typification. Conflict may appear either within an in-group which used to share typifications or between an in-group and an out-group whose typifications clash in the most rudimentary manner. Examples of the breakdown of shared typifications can be found in several internal conflicts. The collision, on the other hand, took place, for example, in the conquest, colonisation and destruction of the Aztecs by the Spaniards in the sixteenth century.

The location of conflict is over definitions of reality. Conflict involves the struggle to impose one's definition of reality upon the other. The question is whose description of reality is taken seriously, and even acted upon. Since the location of conflict is over definitions of reality, the study of power is of great importance for conflict analysis. Power should not be understood as manifest in conflicts and visible in overt actions of coercion and domination. Nor should it be thought to lie in relationships and be manifest in the suppression of differences. Rather, power should be considered as an attribute of discourse and manifest in the production and contestation of consensus.

Struggles to discipline and control definitions of reality involve the play of power which takes place in 'knowledgeable practices'. These practices of power are not negative. Nor do they *necessarily* give rise to conflict. The practices of power are continuous as well as productive, because they participate in the defining and transforming of the social world, often without conflict. Given the notions of conflict and power introduced, the study, not only of the sets of understandings about conflict held by the people involved in a dispute, but also of the machinery in and through which dominant definitions and positions are reconstituted in both conflict and conflict resolution practices, is important for the understanding of a conflict.[3] In short, conflict and conflict resolution practices are not free from power. They are also 'machinery' in which and through which definitions of a reality are reconstituted. They are practices which produce 'power structures and sociocultural grids of communication and interpretation at the present which limit the identity of the parties to the dialogue', which set 'the agenda for what are considered appropriate or inappropriate matters of institutional debate' and which 'sanctify the speech' of some parties over others.[4]

The idea of conflict entertained above differs from that of traditional conflict theories at least in two major respects. First, it differs from subjectivist and objectivist approaches to conflict which claim that conflict is caused either by subjective perceptions, misunderstandings and attitudes or by objectively recognisable, often structural, factors. The view introduced, on the other hand, pays attention to the interplay between the individual actor and the social group. Definitions of reality, as well as the breaking down of these definitions, are dependent on socially shared typifications. Second, the approach does not postulate a universal causal explanation of conflict. That is, it does not establish the cause or causes of conflict (e.g. structures, human needs, communication, misperception) outside the notion of 'fractured sociality'. There is space for situational factors to enter into the explanation or, rather, into the interpretation. For example, Natanson's unspecified notion of 'denied shared typifications' implies that shared typifications may be denied for several reasons which we, as cultural analysts – to use Avruch and Black's expression – need to study and understand separately, depending on the case.[5]

If we accept the idea that 'sociality' and cooperation are based on shared typifications, and that there are 'fractured' interpretations of reality, 'no longer shared' or 'not yet shared' typifications, at the centre of conflict, we need to return to the relevance systems from which typifications arise. The systems of relevance are important also because they form a precondition for communication. The native language of a given linguistic group is one of the most important forms of relatively congruent systems of relevance. Robert Cox writes about the relevance structures and social groups:

> In fact, to a very large measure, various groups may be defined by the relevance systems held in common by the members of that group. Further, the relevance systems may function to (1) perpetuate the group, (2) polarise the group (the in-group) from another (the out-group), and (3) even constitute the basic *raison d'être* for the group itself.

He continues by giving examples:

> As examples of these, consider national loyalties, team spirit, and religious beliefs, which usually contain within themselves the urgency to perpetuate, to pass along to new members of the group, the attitudes and feelings about the group held by the current members. Further, there are groups, such as political parties, iconoclastic religions, and even nations which manifest antagonist stances toward other such groups, this antagonism being rooted in typifications and certain interpretative relevances of the group.[6]

The relevance systems influencing typification and interpretation are thus of vital importance while studying conflict. Applied to conflict resolution, it is necessary for the resolution process to deal with these by harmonising relevance systems and (re)creating shared typifications. The question in what kind of processes the harmonisation of relevance systems and the creation of shared typifications take place brings us to an understanding of conflict resolution. Underlying the idea of conflict resolution is the assumption that relevance systems and typifications need to be changed, and a new interpretation of a reality found, if a form of cooperation is to emerge. A new reality needs to be 'negotiated' in the conflict resolution process. The negotiating of a new reality does not exclude dissociative solutions, i.e. the possibility that the parties agree to disagree without conflict.[7]

Face-to-face interaction in conflict resolution

Problem-solving workshop conflict resolution forms a framework for mutual cultural adaptation. The participants, including the facilitator, need to find a 'scheme of translation' to produce ways to understand each other and to create a shared reality. The other, the alter ego, is always elusive to us, i.e. his or her inner life transcends our immediate and direct experience. We never fully understand his or her subjective meanings as he or she understands them. Language partly bridges the gap between 'us' and 'the other': language as a system of signs facilitates the crossing of the boundary between fellow men and women. Similarly, in the face-to-face situation the subjectivity of the other is available to us through a maximum of symptoms.

Since the problem-solving workshop can be seen to offer a context for mutual adaptation, it needs to be studied how typifications change in that context. Face-to-face interaction between the conflicting parties is one of the core ideas on which most of the problem-solving conflict resolution approaches rely. It is assumed that when conflicting parties have a chance to meet face-to-face in an analytical and supportive environment it will encourage them to change, for example, misperceptions and to 'humanise their mutual images'.[8] The notion of the We relationship is implicitly referred to in many problem-solving approaches when the foundations of interpersonal understanding are theoretically constructed.

There are limits in understanding the problem-solving workshop as a face-to-face encounter. Even in a face-to-face encounter it is possible to maintain an anonymous They relationship. The participants can approach each other through, for example, the anonymous ideal type of 'enemy' in the workshop. It would be, therefore, premature to conclude that a problem-solving workshop as a face-to-face encounter automatically reduces the scope for founding the interaction on anonymous ideal types and, thereby, produces changes in typifications. Second, although face-to-face situations make some elements of equal thematic relevance to both parties, changes in thematic relevance do not necessarily bring about the harmonisation of other relevance structures. It is possible to imagine a case where the face-to-face encounter confirms typifications the participants hold. Third, and most important, enriched and changed typifications of the individual participants of the other participants (i.e. increased interpersonal understanding in the workshop) do not necessarily produce changes in the way the participants typify the conflict in question.

In brief, the harmonisation of thematic relevances, especially if added to enriched typifications of the other, can facilitate interpersonal communication which is one aim of the problem-solving workshop. Two questions remain unanswered. How to broaden the area of interpersonal understanding, and how to transfer that understanding outside the workshop? Problem-solving workshop approaches which solely encourage, for example, 'free expression of feelings' and produce 'interpersonal understanding' are, according to this view, not likely to facilitate the finding of a shared reality which extends beyond the workshop context.

Finding a shared reality

Although thematic relevances harmonise in the face-to-face situation, the problem-solving workshop needs to deal also with the interpretative and motivational relevance structures of the participants. Unless an experience is presented as a problem, it does not change the relevance structures. Something becoming problematic can be either imposed or intrinsic. There are several reasons why a problematic situation may emerge in the workshop context: hypothetical ideal types do not apply, the workshop situation itself is unexpected, a problem may be posed by the facilitator or by the other party so that something becomes relevant and an 'old' typificatory scheme does not apply, etc. Instead of 'solving problems' the workshop is a place where 'something is allowed to become problematic' for the parties. The encouragement of discursive rationality between the participants may also help them to find a shared reality. (Discursive rationality is discussed in the next section.)

Before redefining problem-solving workshop conflict resolution it should be emphasised that the problem-solving workshop has a situational nature, and it never captures the 'whole' conflict. For example, the participants bring into the workshop a 'sector' of a conflict. Although we may agree with Michael Banks and Christopher Mitchell that the principle in the workshop type of conflict resolution 'must be that the conflict situation defines its own parties and issues',[9] it cannot be avoided that the participants determine the 'sector' of conflict which is represented in the workshop by defining and interpreting the conflict and, finally, by 'negotiating' a reality in their own manner.

A new definition, a definition which is more moderate than many other workshop conflict resolution definitions, and a task can be given to the problem-solving workshop. The problem-solving workshop is an attempt to find a shared reality between the parties in conflict for the purposes at hand without causing a further breakdown of 'sociality' and cooperation. The problem-solving workshop deals *mainly* with the interpretative schemes of the participants by giving them a chance to 'negotiate' a shared reality. The finding of a common language game both presupposes and facilitates that. Negotiating a shared reality may lead to agreement on a common disagreement.

The question how to avoid a further breakdown of 'sociality' in the workshop emerges from the definition. A shared acknowledgement of conflict and a shared need for conflict resolution offer a foundation for 'negotiating' a shared reality based on harmonised relevance structures. If the parties themselves ask for problem-solving workshop conflict resolution, their relevance structures have already some similarities: they both acknowledge the existence of the conflict. The conflict is constituted as a problem for both of them. These shared relevance structures facilitate the further harmonisation of relevances.

A problem imposed by the workshop structure can also facilitate the harmonisation. Burton's discussion of functionalist solutions of conflict can be interpreted to point to this idea. For example, the decline of the tourist industry in Cyprus may appear to be a common problem for both the Turkish and the Greek communities of the island. The parties may be willing to discuss the topic in the workshop context and try to find functional solutions. They may be willing to discuss the issue despite the fact that, for example, the causes of the conflict may be differently constituted to them.[10] In Dryzek's words, 'individuals can then seek consensus on *what* is to be done while differing about *why*'.[11] Before the parties can even discuss a common problem, some harmonised relevance structures are required: something appearing as a shared problem presupposes some equal relevances. Unless the parties possess some equal relevances before the problem-solving workshop conflict resolution attempt takes place, it is not likely to produce desired results.

A certain degree of similarity of languages or, rather, language games needs to be found in the problem-solving conflict resolution process in order, at least, for communication to be effective. Dryzek's account of regulatory negotiations in the late 1970s between representatives of the coal industry and environmental groups in the United States describes the importance of language games:

> With a little prodding, the participants began talking in a language new to both sides, that of welfare economics. The overarching value implicit in this language is allocative efficiency, which again was of little prior concern to either side. Now a switch from the language of strategic interaction to the language of welfare economics is perhaps little more than the replacement of one kind of distorted discourse by another that is equally distorted. Yet it suggests the possibility of a reciprocal scrutiny of normative judgements, penetrating beyond particular concerns such as profits of the coal industry or the preservation of a hillside in Utah.[12]

A typificatory schema is given in language. If the schema of a social group differs from the schema of another group, it is reflected in the languages of these groups. Although the native language of a given linguistic group is one of the most important forms of relatively congruent systems of relevance, Dryzek's example demonstrates how different language games can be played with the language. Since the relationship between language and typifications is mutual, a shared language game enforces shared typifications founded on equal relevances.

The role of the native tongue is important in the workshop context. For example, the use of English as a dominant workshop language cannot be justified in all cases. Since it may not be the mother tongue of the participants, they cannot fully participate in language games available in it. The interpretative schemes offered by the language are less clear to the participants than those offered by their native languages. English may well also represent, for example, colonialism and alienation for the parties. In some cases the use of English can be justified: as a foreign language it 'frees' the participants from the interpretative and typificatory schemes built into their mother tongue. Even in that case, English is not a neutral language, because it gives the world to the parties in a certain way.

The harmonisation of relevances does not need to rely on the finding of similarities between the conflicting parties. At a pragmatic level, the concept of human needs serves exactly that purpose: it helps the parties to recognise commonalities they are assumed to share. However, the parties must go 'beyond similarity' and learn 'how to deal with difference', instead of trusting in abstract similarity.[13] Rather than postulating, for example, the abstract notion of a 'need for identity', the facilitator can direct the discussion in the workshop to the issue of multiple and coexistent identities which are defined and emphasised in accordance with situations. Learning to live with these as well as with the continuous struggles and 'negotiations' in which the identities are defined is one aim of problem-solving workshop conflict resolution, rather than the reduction of differences, for example, to the conception of universal human needs.

Problem-solving conflict resolution, like all forms of conflict resolution, is a political activity: the problem-solving workshop is not a 'neutral', 'non-political', space. The struggles over the definitions of reality do not cease to exist in the workshop and their intrusion into it cannot and should not be artificially prevented. In other words, the struggles over meanings and interpretations should not be neutralised in the workshop. Since politics is these continuous struggles, it cannot be argued, as Banks and Mitchell argue, that the workshop 'is not a commitment to anything political at all'.[14] On the contrary, since the workshop produces definitions of reality and creates versions of a world, it is a political process, commitment to politics.

The workshop facilitator participates in the political processes by asking questions, making summaries and shaping the grounds on which agreement and disagreement can take place. The language of the facilitator plays an important role. The psychological language and vocabulary (e.g. emotions, fears, hopes and concerns) which the facilitator may use refer to individuals and their intrapsychic processes, rather than to communication patterns and interpersonal processes. As Sara Cobb and Janet Rifkin argue, 'rather than reduce adversarial communication patterns, the mediator's psychological vocabulary contributes to maintain problematic patterns, obscuring the process of the production of consensus in sessions'.[15] The psychological language allows the political processes and struggles over meanings and interpretations to go unchecked: the psychologised vocabulary dismisses the struggles and 'negotiations' over intersubjective reality by giving priority to individual psychological processes. The facilitator should be, at least, aware of the language he or she employs, and avoid the 'psychologisation' of issues.

Discursive rationality

Everyday action may be reasonable, but not rational, as argued earlier. Action in everyday life is often based on routines and rules of thumb rather than on instrumental utility estimations. In addition to this 'everyday rationality', there are other rationalities. All rationalities are the product of traditions, and historically and culturally constituted: a rationality does not transcend particular traditions. Human beings are capable of different forms of rationality (e.g. instrumental, practical, discursive), but certain structures or frameworks of action encourage certain forms of rationality. For example, the biography of the modern army officer in the twenty-first-century army may encourage instrumental rationality at the expense of discursive rationality. Similarly, the conduct of modern warfare may have a logic which imposes the pursuit of instrumental rationality.

Discursive rationality is fundamental in the context of problem-solving conflict resolution, because it contributes to the prevention of the further breakdown of 'sociality' and facilitates the finding of a shared language game. Discursive rationality ultimately celebrates plurality. Dryzek argues that 'differences across contexts, traditions, opinions, and paradigms of personhood are profound and perhaps ineliminable. But debates among partisans are not only possible but also more or less communicatively rational. And rational consensus is no empty hope.'[16]

The type of rationality which is needed in the problem-solving workshop deals with the typificatory and interpretative schemes of the participants. That mode can be found in discursive rationality whose main domains – because of its dialectic and procedural nature – are both intersubjective understanding and typificatory and interpretative schemes. Since the workshop is an encounter where mutual cultural adaptation can take place, problem-solving workshop conflict resolution consists of discursive possibilities. Through discursive rationality a consensus across cultural and interpretative differences is gained, a consensus which does not arise from instrumental rationality. As Dryzek states, 'important social problems are pervaded by conflicting values, which instrumental action cannot resolve'.[17] Similarly, conflicts are permeated by unshared typifications of reality and, therefore, instrumental rationality which appeals mainly to individual utility maximising does not necessarily contribute to their resolution.

If no substantially shared background of community norms exists in the workshop, 'participants can still reach consensus based on reasoned *dis*agreement, by striving to understand the cultural tradition and/or conceptual framework of the other participants'.[18] In discursive designs and through discursive rationality an understanding of the cultural and conceptual framework of the other party as well as a shared language game can be achieved. This type of understanding advances 'sociality' and cooperation, because it presupposes an openness to the harmonisation of relevance structures through a dialogue. Dialogue demonstrates the will and the readiness to seek understanding with the other. The emphasis need not to be on rational agreement so much as on sustaining those dialogical practices and moral relationships.[19] The facilitator can encourage discursive rationality by helping the participants to overcome their instrumental rationality and instrumental expectations of the workshop outcome. The overcoming can be facilitated by focusing on the preconditions and nature of this type of rationality and by avoiding strategic 'means–ends' as well as psychologised language games.

Discursive rationality refers neither to universal consensus nor to the uniformity of the typifications of the participants. It refers to a limited area of dialectic situations where intersubjective understanding and attempts to find a shared reality are in question. This type of rationality is ultimately limited to the problems in hand. It arises primarily from the reasoning for the purposes of a particular task in hand. The task may be 'practical', but it may also be a question of, for example, ethical principles. The problems dealt with in the workshop context may be generalisable, but they are not universal. The consensus which possibly emerges in the workshop does not derive from universal reason or transcendental intersubjectivity: it derives from the issues which are discussed.

Leaving the workshop structure (re-entry)

Most problem-solving approaches are based on the assumption that something can be transferred, in one way or another, from the workshop to a context outside it, to the 'world of political decision making'. The issue is often reduced to a discussion of the political status of the participants: the higher the level of representation the more will be transferred to 'politics'. The crucial issue is, rather, how the harmonised relevance structures which are gained in the workshop context are transferred outside the workshop. It cannot be assumed that these structures are either lasting or automatically transferred. The relevance structures may be harmonised only for the purposes of the workshop. They may equally be inapplicable to the world outside, especially if they simply create interpersonal understanding. On this view, the issue of re-entry does not pose a psychological problem of how the participants adapt back to their own environment without 'embarrassment'.[20] It poses a question of the importance of the relevance structures.

The importance of the relevance structures is not dependent solely on the status of the participants. It is dependent on the issues through which a shared reality is achieved. If the issues discussed relate to the 'real' problems of the conflicting parties and a shared language game is created to deal with these, the relevances are more likely to be transferred than, for example, in the case where personal feelings are focused on the workshop. If the changes in the relevances do not extend to the level of motivational relevances, they are unlikely to produce new patterns of action. Re-entry can be approached also from the angle of the individual and his or her knowledge. An individual is a 'carrier of social groups', i.e. his or her stock of knowledge is largely socially derived, and individual experiences can be intersubjectively and socially deposited. The experiences of individuals can be incorporated into a common stock of knowledge and, if objectivated in a sign system (e.g. language), can be transmitted from one generation to the next, and from one collectivity to another.[21] Language is fundamental in the process of transmission:

> Language objectivates the shared experiences and makes them available to all within the linguistic community, thus becoming both the basis and the instrument of the collective stock of knowledge. Furthermore, language provides the means for objectifying new experiences, allowing their incorporation into the already existing stock of knowledge, and it is the most important means by which the objectivated and objectified sedimentations are transmitted in the tradition of the collectivity in question.[22]

This insight seems to encourage the transmission of changed typifications from the workshop structure to the tradition of the collectivity in question. It thus challenges the extreme rule of secrecy supported by many problem-solving approaches.

To summarise, in order to cooperate with our fellow men and women in the social world, we need to find shared definitions of the situation in question. The sources of shared definitions are in cultural patterns, institutions and structures as well as in 'negotiations'. Actors do take interpretations of reality for granted, but a person's being in the world is also characterised by continuing 'negotiations' of these definitions. Human beings or reality as such are neither conflictual nor harmonious. The processes of definition are guided by rules.[23] Cultural patterns guide the 'negotiation' processes by offering interpretative and actional frames. In addition typical biographies provide individuals with guiding principles and rules: individuals live up to the social biographies provided by structures, and those biographies consist of rules on how to 'negotiate' and communicate in typical situations. Given that cooperation is based on a joint definition of the situation which is 'negotiated', there is no absolute resolution of a conflict. Problem-solving conflict resolution is, rather, conflict transformation. In it, conflict is transformed into 'negotiations' of reality which are founded upon discursive interest and rationality. Through and in the transformation process the parties can find shared typifications and forms of cooperation for the purposes in hand.

The facilitator and ethical expertise

The facilitator is often assumed to have two roles in the problem-solving workshop: he or she is assumed to be an expert mediator and a social scientist. Some theorists speak about 'action research', which comprises these two elements. Kelman describes the double role of the facilitator:

> While we have not emphasised formal research procedures, however, we are very much engaged in research. Indeed, it is our role as researchers that provides the rationale and legitimacy of our action involvement and that allows representatives of conflicting parties to interact with each other under our auspices in ways that deviate from the norms generally governing their relationship. Our research interest, moreover, cannot be feigned because we would lose credibility very quickly. We must be genuinely interested in learning about conflict in general and about the particular conflict at hand; we must demonstrate this interest and show what we have learned from our action research program through publications . . . and other means. Thus, our action requires involvement in a research program just as our research requires involvement in action program.[24]

Burton, on the other hand, emphasises that the workshop facilitator is an 'outside observer in a scientific role'. Neither of these descriptions of the position of the facilitator is satisfactory. Kelman's view implicitly derives the expertise of the facilitator from his or her academic status. Burton's phrase points to the scientific objectivity as a source of expertise and to the outside nature of the position of the facilitator as a source of legitimacy. The facilitator is neither of these types of expert. He or she is an ethical participant with a theoretical interest whose position arises from three sources: ethicality, participant observation and theorising.

Burton assumes that the facilitator has superior knowledge of the causes and processes of human behaviour, compared with the knowledge of the participants. The expertise of the facilitator is derived from a particular type of knowledge, in Burton's view. What, then, is considered to be good and ethical facilitative conduct? The idea of impartiality or neutrality is employed in many mediation theories to refer to good conduct: impartial behaviour is thought to be ethical behaviour on the part of the mediator.[25] There are also attempts to define a set of rules for desirable behaviour. The most elaborate work is Burton's *Resolving Deep-rooted Conflict*, which sets out a detailed list of principles of ethical conduct for the problem-solving workshop facilitator.[26] Burton justifies the need for rules by claiming that 'ethics used in this context has more of a function connotation than a moral one. There are rules to be observed that are designed to ensure success. It is the possibility of failure because rules were inadequate or were not observed that draws attention to the ethics of intervention.'[27]

Despite this call for rules, the source of good facilitative conduct in Burton's conflict resolution theory can be found ultimately in his theory of human needs. Since the facilitator has distinctive knowledge of human needs and human behaviour related to needs satisfaction, his or her conduct is ethical when it is geared to the recognition and satisfaction of the needs of all the parties in conflict. Facilitative behaviour may take different forms, but the fundamental justification for it as well as the measure of its ethicality can be found in the equal and free satisfaction of human needs. Human needs are employed as an universal tribunal, as ultimate maxims, of ethical behaviour by Burton.

However, the expertise of the facilitator derives from skill acquisition, and his or her ethical conduct follows a similar structure to that of skill acquisition.[28] The conduct of the facilitator can be approached from the point of view of the decisions which are made when he or she faces moral problems; moral problems such as what is good and ethical conduct in a particular situation. The facilitator responds to situations in a manner which involves ethical participation. Ethical expertise is a desired 'quality', a desired way of behaviour, from the angle of the facilitator. This type of expertise is needed in the problem-solving workshop context, because the problem-solving workshop is situational by nature. Edward Azar's evaluation of the limitations of the 'Maryland workshops' of conflict resolution for the conflict in Lebanon illustrates the need for situational conduct and ethics. The example shows how a handbook cannot answer demands which arise from a workshop situation itself. Azar writes about the workshops:

> During both sets of meetings we concentrated on domestic political issues to the exclusion of regional political and economic development issues. This was fine as far as it went, but we exhausted the usefulness of analysing these issues prior to the end of the second forum. Our concern was with avoiding discussion about issues that the participants, and the groups they represented, could themselves do nothing or little about.[29]

The result was:

> There was agreement that the outside actors created problems, but no analysis was made of what the proper role was of these countries in Lebanon. The participants became impatient with the progress, and although they left feeling good about each other as individuals, they did not feel good about the prospects for resolving conflict. This might not have been the case had we incorporated discussion and analysis of substantive and perhaps even technical issues into the two forums.[30]

Skill acquisition consists of five stages: novice, advanced beginner, competence, proficiency and expertise. At the stage of the novice the skill acquisition is based on recognising context-free rules for determining actions. This level is characterised by a 'handbook type of knowledge'. The stage of the advanced beginner includes incorporating situational aspects into instructional maxims. With increasing competence at the third stage, the performer learns to choose a 'plan, goal or perspective which organises the situation and by the examining the small set of features and aspects that he has learned are relevant given that plan, the performer can simplify and improve his performance'.[31] This stage consists of also an 'emotionally involved experience of the outcome', because the choice and successful completion of a goal can be frustrating. Proficiency at the fourth stage is characterised by ceasing to reflect on problematic situations as a detached observer. At this stage a plan, goal or perspective is noticed rather than looked for. A proficient performer sees what needs to be done, but must decide how to do it. An expert performer, on the other hand, knows how to perform the action without calculating and comparing alternatives. The stage of the expertise is based largely on intuition, not on analysis and the comparison of alternatives. The expert does not solve problems. Nor does he or she reason. Rather, he or she spontaneously does what has normally worked.

This five-stage model can be applied to the skill acquisition of facilitative conduct. A beginner tries to follow the rules available, whereas an expert performs the actions needed without deliberation of either rules or a plan, goal or perspective. Learning through experience is a basis of the expertise of the facilitator. The expertise, in this view, does not arise from superior knowledge, it arises, rather, from learning and acquiring skills by performing. Ethical comportment, on the other hand, is a form of expertise and follows a similar structure to skill acquisition. An ethical expert behaves according to the situation, without appealing to rules and maxims. The greater the expertise, the rarer the need for deliberation. Principles and theories serve only for early stages of learning: an expert ethical response to a situation is not grounded on them. In problematic situations the expert deliberates about the appropriateness of his or her intuitions rather than about abstract principles:

> Yet, as we have seen, principles can never capture the know-how an expert acquires by dealing with, and seeing the outcome of, a large number of concrete situations. Thus, when faced with a dilemma, the expert does not seek principles but, rather, reflects on and tries to sharpen his or her spontaneous intuitions by getting more information until one decision emerges as obvious.[32]

Expert performance in ethics is doing what those who are already accepted as ethical experts do and approve. There is an element of convention which derives from the community of the ethical experts. Being a master means also responding to the unique situation 'out of a fund of experience in the culture'. Reaching a stage of maturity does not mean transcending tradition: it implies leaving behind the rules of conventional morality for a new contextualisation, for being more open to the contextual properties of moral dilemmas. In a case of ethical disagreement, two experts should be 'able to understand and appreciate each other's decisions. This is as near as expert ethical judgements can or need come to impartiality and universality.'[33]

Ultimately 'there is no final answer as to what the appropriate response in a particular situation should be'.[34] A single individual and situations he or she responds to are constantly changing, and his or her responses become constantly more refined. A sign of maturity is not reflective detachment from an unique situation to universal principles. On the contrary, maturity means being able to learn from experience, use what one has learned, stay involved and refine one's intuitions. In Seyla Benhabib's words, 'the more we can identify the different viewpoints from which a situation can be interpreted and construed, the more will we have sensitivity to the particularities of the perspectives involved'.[35]

The ethical conduct of the facilitator does not need to rely, therefore, on the maxim of impartiality, a set of rules or the idea of universal human needs. It should rely on openness to different and variable contexts, on openness to 'relativise' each situation. Sensitivity to uniqueness and difference means ethical expertise. That is not to say that rules and maxims may not be needed in the context of problem-solving-workshop conflict resolution. They may be needed, for example, to clarify the idea of the workshop for the participants or to offer instructive advice to an inexperienced facilitator. However, rules should not be understood as universal maxims according to which the facilitator should guide his or her conduct independent of the situation.

Participant observation

The face-to-face relationship is reciprocal between the two or more partners, whereas in direct social observation the relationship is one-sided. In the face-to-face relationship I can verify my assumption that my experiences correspond to those of the other person by directly appealing to an object of the external world which is common to both of us. That is not possible in direct social observation. If it is done, the nature of the relationship changes. The change is described by Schutz:

> But in any direct social observation carried on outside a social relationship, my interpretation of other's behaviour cannot be checked against his own self-interpretation, unless of course I exchange my role as an observer for that of a participant. *When I start asking questions of the person observed, I am no longer a mere observer.*[36]

In direct social observation the observer does not influence the behaviour of the observed. Nor does the interchange of motives take place. On some occasions the observer can be in an advantageous position. When observing two participants in interaction he or she can be aware of the whole interactional situation, whereas the participants themselves tend to be aware only of each other. It may even happen that the observer is acquainted with the interpretative schemes of one participant better than his or her partner.[37]

The problem-solving facilitator is not an outside observer. Rather, he or she is a participant in a communicative situation. The facilitator participates in the workshop situation by facilitating communication, offering theoretical insights and keeping discussion within an analytical framework. The participation constitutes the context of his or her theorising. The facilitator may occasionally adopt the role of the observer, but the type of observing is not accurately grasped in the Burtonian notion of 'scientific observer', which denotes, as demonstrated, a 'purified mind'. A more fruitful metaphor to describe the facilitator and his or her position in the workshop can be found in the conception of 'participant observer'. The metaphor can be employed to describe the active and participant position of the facilitator in the workshop without reference to epistemological commitments. On the other hand, it can be seen to imply certain epistemological stances.

Participant observation is traditionally understood to be a methodological device in conducting anthropological and sociological fieldwork. Although participant observation has this specific and limited meaning which implies a research method, the notion brings up questions and discussions which are also vital in the problem-solving workshop context. Given that the facilitator is a part of an 'action research programme', the epistemological implications of this participation are difficult to dismiss. Participant observation is conventionally defined in the following manner:

> For our purposes we define participant observation as a process in which the observer's presence in a social situation is maintained for the purpose of scientific investigation. The observer is in a face-to-face relationship with the observed, and, by participating with them in their natural life setting, he gathers data. Thus the observer is part of the context being observed, and he both modifies and is influenced by this context. The role of participant observer may be either formal or informal, concealed or revealed; the observer may spend a great deal or very little time in the research situation; the participant-observer role may be an integral part of the social structure or largely peripheral to it.[38]

Participant observation is characterised by two distinct features. First, the status of the investigator of being an outside agent is reduced to a minimum. Second, the emphasis is on dialogue. Participant observation is dialectical in that the 'subject' and 'object' of the research remain in communicative contact. The observer becomes socialised to a certain extent into the life-world of the research 'objects'.[39] The active behaviour of the facilitator displaces his or her role as an outside agent. His or her research activities derive from this active participation where the facilitator is inevitably to a certain extent socialised to the worlds of the participants in the workshop, if not to their entire life-worlds. The facilitator is, as noted earlier, in a communicative contact with the participants, with the 'objects' of the research.

131

The symbolic interactionist tradition claims that the ability of the researcher to perform and to be accepted as a member of the life-world of the 'objects' indicates that he or she knows and can analyse the ways in which 'objects' carry on their activities. It can be argued, on the other hand, that the social scientist is concerned with understanding and explanation and that socialisation into the ways the 'objects' perform their activities is not enough for the search of the formal or invariant properties of human activities.[40] In the case of the problem-solving workshop the participants often expect the facilitator to take a professional role – a role which limits his or her socialisation to the world of the parties.

As a fieldwork method, participant observation is often described by using the notion of 'surrender and catch'. It is assumed that fieldwork begins with the 'surrender' of a social researcher to his or her subject matter so that the difference between subject, act and object disappears. This is thought to imply total suspension of the received notions concerning subject matter, method and theory. In other words, 'surrender' means not to select. 'Catch' is assumed to be a new conceiving or new conceptualising of the result of 'surrender'. At the stage of 'catch' the researcher tries to find out what he or she has 'caught' and returns from the pre-scientific sphere to the scientific sphere. In the scientific domain the researcher, then, proceeds with the help of the conceptual and methodological tools offered by his or her own science.[41]

The idea of 'surrender' refers to the possibility of an 'empty mind', of a *tabula rasa*. However, as argued in the introduction to this book, the precondition for all understanding is in fore-meanings and prejudices, not in an 'emptied mind'. It is not possible to purify one's mind from these, because they are an ontological condition of a person's 'being in the world'. A person trying to understand a text must be sensitive to the text's quality of newness. Sensitivity involves neither neutrality in the matter of the object, nor the extinction of one's self, but the conscious assimilation of one's own fore-meanings and prejudices. The familiar horizons of the interpreter are an integral part of the event of understanding any alien object: his or her prejudices open up an object. The idea of a hermeneutical circle emphasises that all understanding inevitably involves prejudices, which can be critically reflected.[42] The facilitator enters into the workshop with his or her prejudices. These fore-meanings are bound to change when the past and present meet within the situation. If the facilitator aims at theorising on the bases of his or her workshop experience, his or her fore-meanings consist of, for example, his or her understanding of that particular field of science he or she identifies himself or herself with, i.e. its concepts and theories. Giving them up, suspending the notions concerning the subject matter and theories, is not, on this view, possible as the notion of 'surrender' suggests.

Theorising and the sources of objectivity

The problem-solving workshop facilitator is a participant who has a theoretical interest and who, on the other hand, has 'already contributed, as a participant in interaction, to establishing the context of action that he then analyses as an object'.[43] The issues of obtaining data and the validity and 'objectivity' of data arise in a following manner:

> If we conceptually enrich the first-level models of action to the point where interpretation and understanding appear as basic features of social action itself, the question of how the interpretative accomplishments of the social-scientific observer are connected with the natural hermeneutics of the everyday practice of communication, of how communicative experiences can be transformed into data, can no longer be trimmed down to the size of a technical subproblem in research.[44]

The topic can be approached from the angle of viewpoints too. The social world is given us in a complex system of perspectives. There is a fundamental difference between my interpretation of my own subjective experiences and my interpretation of the subjective experiences of someone else. Although the social sciences try to determine what an action means to the actor, they see it from the viewpoint of an observer.[45]

Several positions can be claimed in relation to the question of the sources of scientific objectivity. Burton's discussion of the issue can be described as 'modified positivist' in standpoint. Schutz's answer, on the other hand, illustrates a hermeneutical stance. Although his answer to the quest for objectivity may not be fully satisfactory, it discusses in a highly sophisticated manner several vital ontological and epistemological issues of science. The relativist position advocated by some ethnomethodologists, and the genealogical method employed by poststructuralists, introduce issues which are important also to problem-solving workshop theorising.

For Burton the scientist has a corrective function. The role of the scientist is to find explanations that fit modern conditions and problems better. A paradigm shift in social sciences in general, and in International Relations in particular, is needed, because 'vague thinking' based on false assumptions and imprecise meanings influences reality and causes harmful policies and dysfunctional conflicts. According to Burton the epistemological problems faced by the social scientist are threefold: how to construct imaginative hypotheses through abduction, how to produce corrective hypotheses through deduction and how to test hypotheses. He admits the limits of hypothesis testing and argues that there can seldom be verification; there are, rather, processes of falsification. The ultimate task of the scientist is to offer 'objective' and 'non-ideological' viewpoints on which the construction of universal laws of human behaviour can be based.[46]

According to Schutz, the social scientist obtains his or her data through understanding meanings, meanings which are created by actors in the lifeworld.[47] The social scientist encounters symbolically pre-structured objects on the basis of which he or she constructs the 'objective' reality within which the science operates. Theorising belongs essentially, in Schutz's view, to the 'sub-universe of science' which differs from everyday life. In the 'scientific sub-universe' the theorising self is solitary: it has no social environment and it stands outside social relations. Moreover, in it the social scientist adopts a scientific attitude. Schutz describes the attitude and its implications:

> This attitude of the social scientist is that of a mere disinterested observer of the social world. He is not involved in the observed situation, which is to him not of practical but merely of cognitive interest. It is not the theatre of his activities but merely the object of his contemplation. He does not act within it, vitally interested in the outcome of his actions, hoping or fearing what their consequences might be, but he looks at it with the same detached equanimity with which the natural scientist looks at the occurrences in his laboratory.[48]

In brief, when theorising the scientist detaches himself or herself from his or her biographical situation within the social world. He or she enters into the world of science, which constitutes its own frame with pre-organised knowledge. The scientist shifts himself or herself into the relevance systems of science. All our knowledge of the world, in commonsense as well as in scientific thinking, involves, according to Schutz, constructs, that is, a set of abstractions, formalisations, idealisations, etc. An everyday actor uses the commonsense constructs to orient himself or herself and to act in his or her life-world. The scientific constructs, on the other hand, form a general model of a sector of the social world which is constructed from the point of view of the scientist and his or her particular problem under scrutiny. These 'second-degree constructs' do not refer to unique acts of a unique individual occurring within a unique situation.

The scientific model of the social world creates 'puppets' with artificial consciousness, according to Schutz. When observing social action or interaction the scientist constructs patterns of typical action. Then he or she coordinates to these typical 'course-of-action patterns' a personal type, a model of a typical actor whom he or she imagines to possess a fictitious consciousness. This type of model of the actor does not have biography or history, because it is placed in a situation by the scientist. Furthermore, the 'puppet and his artificial consciousness is not subjected to the ontological conditions of human being'.[49] In such an artificial model of the social world, for example, purely rational acts, choices from rational motives, are possible, because all the difficulties the real actor has in the life-world can be eliminated by the scientist.

Schutz maintains that the social sciences deal in an objective way with the subjective meaning of human action. The question arises how it is possible to gain valid knowledge through scientific models if they are based on the 'subjective creativity' of the scientist? In order to be objective, the models postulated by the social scientist must conform to the canons of verifiability and testability set by the scientific community. Schutz refers to three postulates which restrict the construction of models. The 'postulate of logical consistency' states that the constructs designed by the scientist have to 'be established with the highest degree of clarity and distinctness of the conceptual framework implied and must be fully compatible with the principles of formal logic'.[50] The 'postulate of subjective interpretation' enables the scientist to discern what is distinctive about the models that are appropriate for an adequate social theory. The 'postulate of adequacy' maintains that the model of social action created by the scientist must be constructed in such a way that the act indicated by the model would be understandable for the actor himself or herself in terms of commonsense interpretation of everyday life.

The Burtonian scientist is assumed to have non-arbitrary access to the objective domain of behaviour, and the perspective of the interpreter is supposed to be similar to the perspective of the actor. Schutz's account of science challenges Burton's view. For Schutz the scientist does not have non-arbitrary access to the world and meanings of the actors. The scientific constructs as second-degree constructs offer access, but they are neither equal nor similar to the constructs created by the actors in their life-worlds. Nor do the subjective and objective meanings ever fully coincide: the scientist can never grasp the meanings of the actors as those meanings appear to the actors themselves. Burton's utility-maximising actor can be considered to offer a scientific model. His theory of conflict and conflict resolution as well as his 'need man' can be seen to be one possible model and 'puppet' created by a theorist. However, if evaluated according to the criteria of objectivity suggested by Schutz, it may be the case that Burton's model does not fulfil them. Moreover, both the criteria and the whole notion of scientific objectivity can be disputed.

The argument presented by, for example, some ethnomethodologists who challenge the idea of objectivity can be summarised in the following manner. Social research and theorising can be seen to count only as one particular form of life alongside others. Theoretical work may be distinguished, like, for example, religion and art, by its reflexivity, but that does not imply objectivity. Theorising takes place in the sphere of the life-world as any other activity and, therefore, interpretative (social) sciences can give up the claim to produce any objective knowledge at all. There are no criteria of truth and validity outside the domain in which theorising is carried out. The constructs of the social sciences have the same status as the everyday, first-degree, constructs of lay members, because they too are bound to a social context and values. In other words, the validity standards of science are just as particular as any other types of criteria of validity that function in other departments of life.[51]

The most recent phase of this 'post-empiricist' movement employs the genealogical method to demonstrate that knowledge does not simply reflect or represent the world. Rather, there are discourses of knowledge whose success derives from their connections with networks of power. In all societies, power–knowledge functions to produce some forms of truth and to disqualify others. In modern society the production of truth has taken a disciplinary and normalising form. Geneaology offers a reading of the effect of present social practices which does not claim to correspond either to the everyday under-standing of being in those practices or to a deeper repressed understanding. Genealogy does not, like hermeneutical approaches, seek a frame of analysis that shows how the behaviour of various actors can be recovered if we know their cultures or fields of meanings. It seeks to distance us from the various lin-guistic practices that give us objects, subjects and the more general valuing within which they function. The question of the sources of and the whole quest for scientific objectivity appear in the light of historical discourses for poststruc-turalists.[52]

All these epistemological stances are available to the facilitator who studies problem-solving workshop conflict resolution. He or she can approach the topic from the angle of the meanings held by the persons involved in a conflict and in a conflict resolution attempt. The facilitator can also take part in abstract 'model building' as Burton suggests. The researcher can, on the other hand, study problem-solving workshop conflict resolution practices, such as the practice of neutrality. In that case the focus is on neutrality as a discursive practice that may, for example, function to obscure the workings of power in mediation.[53] Similarly, the emphasis can be, for example, on patriarchal relations, which are reproduced in the power relations of conflict and problem-solving conflict resolution. This type of poststructuralist approach is also hinted at in the book when the political nature of conflict resolution and the elements of power are discussed. Rather than seeing the hermeneutical and poststructural positions as opposite to each other, this chapter has tried to demonstrate points at which they could coincide.

NOTES

1 M. Natanson, *The Journeying Self: A Study in Philosophy and Social Role* (Reading MA, Menlo Park and London, Addison-Wesley, 1970), p. 59.
2 *Ibid.*, pp. 58–60. For a similar view see also A. Schutz and T. Luckmann, *The Structures of the Life-World* I (London, Heinemann, 1974), p. 255.
3 For the traditional views of power see S. Lukes, *Power: A Radical View* (London and Basingstoke, Macmillan, 1979). For more sophisticated accounts see S. Cobb and J. Rifkin, 'Practice and Paradox: Deconstructing Neutrality in Mediation', *Law and Social Inquiry*, 16: 1 (1991), 35–62. R. Ashley, 'Living on Border Lines: Man, Poststructuralism, and War', in J. Der Derian and M. Shapiro (eds), *International/Intertextual Relations: Postmodern Readings of World Politics* (Lexington MA, Lexington Books, 1989), pp. 296–7. For views which discuss conflict and definitions of reality see P. Black and K. Avruch, 'Some Issues in Thinking about Culture and the Resolution of Conflict', *Humanity and Society*, 13: 2 (1989), 192. P. Berger and T. Luckmann, *The Social Construction of Reality: A Treatise in the Sociology of Knowledge* (London, Penguin Books, 1991), pp. 70–109 and 125–7.

4 S. Benhabib, *Situating the Self* (Cambridge, Polity Press, 1992), p. 48.
5 Natanson's account of *anomie* can be given a different interpretation, the interpretation which many traditional conflict theorists would give. According to the traditional view, *anomie* is caused by, for example, unsatisfied human needs, unjust structures, misperceptions, etc. Ultimately we are dealing with the question of the role of theory in the social sciences and with the 'universalistic–particularistic' debate as well as with the 'explanatory–interpretative' stances in the social sciences.
6 R. Cox, *Schutz's Theory of Relevance: A Phenomenological Critique* (The Hague, Boston MA and London, Nijhoff, 1978), p. 113.
7 The idea of 'negotiated reality' is from R. Cohen, 'Negotiating Reality: International Relations and the Metaphor of the Holy Sepulchre', paper presented at the thirty-fifth annual convention of the International Studies Association, Washington DC, 28 March–1 April 1994. Cohen emphasises that reality as a social construct has two interlocking sources: the heritage of the past and negotiation. See also T. Scheff, 'Negotiating Reality: Notes on Power in the Assessment of Responsibility', *Social Problems*, 16: 1 (1968), 3–17.
8 H. Kelman, 'Informal Mediation by the Scholar/Practitioner', in J. Bercovitch and J. Rubin (eds), *Mediation in International Relations: Multiple Approaches to Conflict Management* (Basingstoke and London, Macmillan, 1992), p. 76.
9 M. Banks and C. R. Mitchell, *The Resolution of Conflict: A Handbook on the Analytical Problem Solving Approach* (Fairfax VA, Institute for Conflict Analysis and Resolution, George Mason University, 1993), p. 27.
10 This type of cooperation can originate in grass roots-level interactions. For example, Edith Miguda describes the networks created by interactions among women between the conflicting parties in western Kenya during the 1990s ethnic and land clashes. E. Miguda, 'Harnessing Internal Local Resources for Conflict Resolution and Self-sustaining Peace in the Face of Ethnic Violence', paper presented at the fifteenth general conference of the International Peace Research Association, Malta, 30 October–4 November 1994.
11 J. Dryzek, *Discursive Democracy: Politics, Policy, and Political Science* (Cambridge, Cambridge University Press, 1990), p. 43.
12 *Ibid.*, pp. 47–8.
13 See also B. Broome, 'Managing Differences in Conflict Resolution: the Role of Relational Empathy', in D. Sandole and H. van der Merwe (eds), *Conflict Resolution Theory and Practice: Integration and Application* (Manchester and New York, Manchester University Press, 1993), pp. 104–5. *International Alert*, 'Conflict Resolution and Training in the North Caucasus and Georgia', report of the Piatigorsk seminar, 6–19 June 1993, p. 7.
14 Banks and Mitchell, *The Resolution of Conflict*, p. 63.
15 Cobb and Rifkin, 'Practice and Paradox', p. 60. Cobb and Rifkin demonstrate in their study of more than thirty mediation sessions of community mediation programmes in western Massachusetts how the use of psychological language contributes to the marginalisation of the other disputant and to the reconstruction of the story of the other party as dominant.
16 Dryzek, *Discursive Democracy*, p. 19.
17 *Ibid.*, p. 53.
18 *Ibid.*, p. 42.
19 See also Benhabib, *Situating the Self*, p. 6.
20 See Banks and Mitchell, *The Resolution of Conflict*, pp. 136–7.
21 Berger and Luckmann, *The Social Construction of Reality*, p. 85.
22 *Ibid.*, pp. 85–6. See also Schutz and Luckmann, *Structures* I, pp. 278, 285–6 and 292–9. R. Jehenson, 'A Phenomenological Approach to the Study of the Formal Organisation', in G. Psathas (ed.), *Phenomenological Sociology: Issues and Applications* (New York, Wiley, 1973), p. 234.

23 See, for example, G. Gonos, '"Situation" versus "Frame": the "Interactionist" and the "Structuralist" Analyses of Everyday Life', *American Sociological Review*, 42: 6 (1977), 854–67.

24 H. Kelman, 'Interactive Problem Solving: the Uses and Limits of a Therapeutic Model for the Resolution of International Conflicts', in V. Volkan, J. Montville and D. Julius (eds), *The Psychodynamics of International Relationships* II (Lexington MA, Lexington Books, 1991), p. 149.

25 Not all writers support the idea of neutrality, but it forms one of the core metaphors of mediation theory. See also Cobb and Rifkin, 'Practice and Paradox'.

26 For a handbook see also Banks and Mitchell, *The Resolution of Conflict*. A call, on the other hand, for the 'institutionalisation and professionalisation' of problem-solving workshop conflict resolution is presented in, R. Fisher, 'Developing the Field of Interactive Conflict Resolution: Issues in Training, Funding and Institutionalisation', paper presented at the fourteenth annual scientific meeting of the International Society of Political Psychologist, Helsinki, 1–5 July 1991.

27 J. Burton, *Resolving Deep-rooted Conflict: A Handbook* (London and New York, University Press of America, 1987), p. 27.

28 This section is based on an application of H. Dreyfus and S. Dreyfus, 'Towards a Phenomenology of Ethical Expertise', *Human Studies*, 14: 4 (1991), 229–50. Only direct quotations from the text are noted. The article is levelled at the view that the highest level of moral maturity consists in judging actions according to abstract and universal principles.

29 E. Azar, 'The Analysis and Management of Protracted Conflict', in V. Volkan, J. Montville and D. Julius (eds), *The Psychodynamics of International Relationships* II (Lexington MA, Lexington Books, 1991), p. 107.

30 *Ibid.*, p. 107.

31 Dreyfus and Dreyfus, 'Towards a Phenomenology of Ethical Expertise', p. 233.

32 *Ibid.*, p. 244.

33 *Ibid.*, p. 242. Compare this idea also with the notion of discursive rationality.

34 *Ibid.*, p. 246.

35 Benhabib, *Situating the Self*, p. 54.

36 A. Schutz, *The Phenomenology of the Social World*, trans. G. Walsh and F. Lehnert (Evanston IL, Northwestern University Press, [1932] 1967), pp. 173–4. Schutz's own italics.

37 *Ibid.*, pp. 172–6.

38 M. Schwartz and C. Schwartz, 'Problems in Participant Observation', in G. McCall and J. L. Simmons (eds), *Issues in Participant Observation: A Text and Reader* (Reading MA, Menlo Park and London, Addison-Wesley, 1969), p. 91.

39 J. Bleicher, *The Hermeneutic Imagination: Outline of a Positive Critique of Scientism and Sociology* (London, Boston MA, Melbourne and Henley, Routledge, 1982), p. 143. See also S. Reinhartz, *On Becoming a Social Scientist: From Survey Research and Participant Observation to Experiential Analysis* (San Francisco, Washington DC and London, Jossey-Bass, 1979), pp. 155–7.

40 G. Psathas, 'Approaches to the Study of the World of Everyday Life', *Human Studies*, 3: 1 (1980), 14.

41 H. Wagner, 'Between Ideal Type and Surrender: Field Research as Asymmetrical Relation', *Human Studies*, 1: 2 (1978), 154–6. The idea of 'surrender and catch' as it is introduced here is based on a simplified reading of Kurt Wolff's original idea. See also Wolff's critique of Wagner's article, K. Wolff, 'A Very Brief Commentary on Helmut R. Wagner's "Between Ideal Type and Surrender"', *Human Studies*, 1: 2 (1978), 165–6.

42 H.-G. Gadamer, *Truth and Method*, second edition (London, Sheed & Ward, 1997), pp. 238–9 and 263.

43 J. Habermas, *The Theory of Communicative Action: Reason and the Rationalization of Society* I (London, Heinemann, 1984), p. 125.
44 *Ibid.*, p. 120.
45 Schutz, *The Phenomenology of the Social World*, p. 8. M. Barber, *Social Typifications and the Elusive Other* (London and Toronto, Associated University Press, 1988), p. 31.
46 See, for example, J. Burton, *Deviance, Terrorism and War* (New York, St Martin's Press, 1979), pp. 29–30. J. Burton, 'The Rôle of Authorities in World Society', *Millennium: Journal of International Studies*, 8: 1 (1979), 77–8. J. Burton, 'World Society and Human Needs', in M. Light and A. J. R. Groom (eds), *International Relations: A Handbook* (London, Pinter, 1985), p. 57. J. Burton, *Conflict: Resolution and Provention* (London, Macmillan, 1990), pp. 19–20, 30–3, 44 and 256–7. J. Burton, *Violence Explained* (Manchester and New York, Manchester University Press, 1997), p. 13.
47 The following account of Schutz's ideas is based on A. Schutz, *Collected Papers* I, *The Problem of Social Reality*, ed. M. Natanson (The Hague, Nijhoff, 1962), pp. 5–7, 34–6, 40–4 and 245–55. A. Schutz, *Collected Papers* II, *Studies in Social Theory*, ed. A. Brodersen (The Hague, Nijhoff, 1964), pp. 17–19. On the world of science see also A. Schutz, *Reflections on the Problem of Relevance*, ed. R. Zaner (New Haven CT and London, Yale University Press, 1970), pp. 258–62. Schutz, *The Phenomenology of the Social World*, chapter 5. R. Bernstein, *The Restructuring of Social and Political Theory* (London, Methuen, 1979), pp. 152–6. Cox, *Schutz's Theory of Relevance*, chapter VI. Habermas, *The Theory of Communicative Action* I, pp. 121–4. See also critiques of Schutz, Cox, *Schutz's Theory of Relevance*, pp. 218–28. Bernstein, *The Restructuring*, pp. 167–9. J. Valone, 'A Critical Theory of Knowledge and the Phenomenology of Alfred Schutz', *Cultural Hermeneutics*, 3: 3 (1976), 199–215.
48 Schutz, *Papers* I, p. 36.
49 *Ibid.*, p. 41.
50 *Ibid.*, p. 43.
51 For a summary see Habermas, *The Theory of Communicative Action* I, pp. 126–30. See also, for example, A. Blum, 'Theorizing', in J. Douglas (ed.), *Understanding Everyday Life: Toward the Reconstruction of Sociological Knowledge* (London, Routledge, 1971), pp. 301–19. P. Feyerabend, *Against Method: Outline of an Anarchist Theory of Knowledge* (London, Verso, 1980). P. McHugh, 'On the Failure of Positivism', in J. Douglas (ed.), *Understanding Everyday Life: Toward the Reconstruction of Sociological Knowledge* (London, Routledge, 1971), pp. 320–35.
52 See, for example, H. Dreyfus, 'Beyond Hermeneutics: Interpretation in Late Heidegger and Recent Foucault', in M. Gibbons (ed.), *Interpreting Politics* (Oxford, Blackwell, 1987), pp. 203–20. M. Foucault, 'Nietzsche, Genealogy, History', in M. Gibbons (ed.), *Interpreting Politics* (Oxford, Blackwell, 1987), pp. 221–40. M. Shapiro, *Reading the Postmodern Polity: Political Theory as Textual Practice* (Minneapolis MN and Oxford, University of Minnesota Press, 1992).
53 See Cobb and Rifkin, 'Practice and Paradox'.

7

Conclusion:
ten theses on culture and
international conflict resolution

URTON'S CONFLICT AND conflict resolution theories demonstrate the use of human needs theory and medical metaphors in peace and conflict studies. Implicit denial of the importance of culture in human affairs is at the very core of his theory of international conflict resolution. The strong universalising tendencies constitute his theory as a form of totalist theorising in the social sciences. The Burtonian filter metaphor suggests that problem-solving conflict resolution procedures are not relative to culture, and that the aim of the workshop is actually to filter out cultural factors. Burton's views deny culture its constitutive role in conflict and conflict resolution, and the denial leads to the assumption that there are culture-free techniques of conflict resolution.

Seen from the social constructionist tradition of thinking, culture is vital to becoming and being a moral person. It is argued in this book that, in order for a problem-solving conflict resolution attempt to be successful, a dialogical community is necessary in which the parties can scrutinise each other's views of reality. In such a community the understanding of the uniqueness of the characteristics of the conflict at hand is developed both by the facilitator and by the parties themselves. The facilitator assumes the role of the participant observer who steers the parties towards discursive rationality within which value issues can be discussed and realities 'negotiated'.

The conceptual and theoretical framework suggested in the study can be translated into ten practical non-totalist guidelines – which give culture a foundational role – for international conflict resolution, and especially for problem-solving conflict resolution.

1. It is desirable that the parties in conflict themselves should ask for problem-solving conflict resolution, because it implies that their relevance structures already have some similarities. The conflict is constituted as a problem for them, and their 'horizons of expectation' include the notion of a peaceful resolution. If the relevance structures have enough points of convergence, the parties may be willing to discover solutions for their problems, despite the fact

that the causes of the conflict may be differently constituted for them. The problem-solving workshop provides an outside recognition of the conflict and its parties, and that can have an empowering effect particularly on the party which perceives itself to be in a disadvantaged position. It constitutes a 'subjectivity' for the weaker party in conflict.

2. It is desirable for the facilitator to train the participants in the ideology of this type of conflict resolution before the workshop begins. Training minimises the risk that the participants will have false and empty hopes of the workshop, and builds up more 'realistic' expectations. During the training sessions the limits of problem-solving workshop conflict resolution should be emphasised. The parties should know that the workshop deals mainly with interpretative frameworks, and that it is fundamentally an attempt to find a shared reality between them. It should be also accepted that the parties may not need this particular form of conflict resolution.

3. Although the isolated location of the workshop brings the participants away from the 'reality' of their conflict, and although this itself may harmonise their relevance structures, the political nature of the workshop exercise should not be forgotten or hidden. The struggles over the definitions of reality continue in the workshop, and it should not be artificially isolated from them. The conflict becomes constituted and defined in certain ways in the workshop and, therefore, the workshop 'negotiates' and creates 'versions of reality'. The facilitator participates in these constitutive processes by delivering theoretical talks, asking questions, making summaries and shaping the grounds on which agreement and disagreement take place.

4. The facilitation team should have a shared agenda, and should be well aware of it. The individual facilitators have their images of successful problem-solving workshop outcomes as well as of human nature and 'being'. If the pictures vary, it is reflected in the ways the facilitators conceptualise the conflict and choose facilitative techniques and procedures. For example, a workshop which aims at analysing 'basic human needs' requires different mediation techniques from a conflict resolution attempt which intends to negotiate a set of 'practical action principles'. Similarly, the facilitative techniques which steer the participants towards discursive rationality differ from those which advance instrumental rationality. Discursive rationality presupposes an understanding of the possibility and fruitfulness of dialogue, whereas instrumental rationality presupposes a context of strategic action which can be created, for example, by encouraging the parties to negotiate on their utilities. Although the workshop is always situational by nature, a shared conceptual and theoretical framework among the facilitators brings a structural element into the mediation process.

5. Among the most essential aspects of the facilitative techniques employed in the problem-solving workshop are the theoretical talks delivered by the facilitator. In them the facilitator expresses his or her conceptualisations

and understandings of conflict and creates a basis for a common discourse, for a common point of reference. The facilitator should, for example, emphasise the intersubjective nature of our ways of perceiving conflict. Similarly, he or she should discuss the role of cultural patterns in shaping our interpretations of the world. The characteristic of language as a container of typifications and the importance of the finding of a shared language game should be focused on in the theoretical inputs of the facilitator. Also the ideas that realities are 'negotiated' and that a shared reality can be found through dialogue should be introduced. By doing this, the facilitator steers the parties towards discursive rationality.

The goal of the workshop the facilitator has in mind should be 'going beyond similarity' and learning 'how to live with difference'. The purpose should not be the neutralising of the border between 'we' and 'they' or the reduction of differences to abstract similarities. The facilitative team should be capable of reflecting the ideological and political task it is committed to. It should also be capable of controlling the language games it employs. The team should avoid psychological language games which reject recognition of the struggles and 'negotiations' over reality and the play of power by emphasising an analogy between the psychological processes of the individual and the 'political' processes of the group.

6. One of the strengths of problem-solving workshop conflict resolution compared with many other forms of international conflict resolution is the discursive potential the workshop offers the parties in conflict. The potential should be fully utilised in the workshop context. The workshop gives the parties a chance to express their own typifications and interpretative frameworks of the conflict: in the workshop they can present as well as 'renegotiate' their typifications, definitions of realities. This is vital, because a set of shared typifications is a precondition for the mapping out of cooperative options.

Since the conflict is often constituted in different ways even among one party, the workshop does not grasp the whole conflict. A conflict may be constituted differently for grass-roots people, intellectuals and political decisionmakers. A 'sector' (or 'sectors') of the conflict is represented and interpreted in the workshop. Even the so-called 'contingency models' of conflict resolution are unable to answer the challenge put forward by the notion of the 'sectors of conflict'. Contingency models postulate for conflict a life-cycle, in the form of the stages of conflict, during which different forms of conflict resolution, and especially third-party interventions, are thought to be effective. The idea of a 'sector', on the other hand, suggests that different 'sectors' of the conflict – which ultimately represent the various patterns the conflict is constituted of – may require different forms of conflict resolution. For example, farmers living in a border area may require functional arrangements with farmers living on the other side of the border. The arrangements may presuppose pragmatic rationality which can be advanced in pragmatically oriented conflict resolution attempts. At the same time, a political decision-making 'sector' may require a form of conflict resolution which engages the participants in a dialectic examination of multiple group identities. The tasks of the third party are clearly different in these cases.

7. Instead of conflict resolution, it is better to refer to conflict transformation in the problem-solving workshop. There are conflict transformations in which struggles over, for example, identities are continued by new means. These transformations may become constituted for the parties in conflict as a 'resolution'. By means of the problem-solving workshop conflict can be transformed into 'negotiations over reality' which are founded on discursive interest and discursive rationality.

8. Re-entry does not pose a psychological problem: it poses a question of the importance of relevance structures and of the transfer of those structures outside the workshop context. The overemphasis on interpersonal and psychological understanding in the workshop does not necessarily facilitate the return of the participants to their own communities. Rather, if the issues discussed in the problem-solving workshop are perceived to be 'real' from the point of view of the parties themselves, the changed relevances are likely to be transferred outside the workshop.

9. Follow-up should be a part of the workshop. The following-up process could include, for example, the linking of the various 'sectors' of the conflict with each other and with the parallel forms of conflict resolution attempts.

10. The research agenda and possibilities opened up by the position as participant observer of the facilitator should be fully explored. The position of the participant observer is advantaged, because it offers a means of studying the understandings of the conflict held by the people engaged in it. In other words, it is possible to study what conflict means to the parties and how it is constituted for them. The position affords the means of studying how, for example, ethnic identities are formed in the processes of conflict and conflict resolution and how the dominant definitions of ethnicity are reconstituted through and in conflict resolution processes. These research questions require new, qualitative, methodological devices, whose development has been largely neglected by scholars working on the area of problem-solving workshop conflict resolution.

BIBLIOGRAPHY

Abell, P., 'Denzin on Rational Choice Theory', *Rationality and Society*, 2: 4 (1990), 495–9.

Alevy, D., Bunker, B., Doob, L., Foltz, W., French, N., Klein, E., and Miller, J., 'Rationale, Research, and Role Relations in the Stirling Workshop', *Journal of Conflict Resolution*, 18: 2 (1974), 276–84.

Appley, D., and Winder, A., *T-groups and Therapy Groups in a Changing Society*, London and San Francisco, Jossey-Bass, 1973.

Ashley, R., 'Living on Border Lines: Man, Poststructuralism, and War', in J. Der Derian and M. Shapiro (eds), *International/Intertextual Relations: Postmodern Readings of World Politics*, Lexington MA, Lexington Books, 1989, pp. 259–321.

Avruch, K., *Culture and Conflict Resolution*, Washington DC, United States Institute of Peace Press, 1998.

Avruch, K., 'Introduction: Culture and Conflict Resolution', in K. Avruch, P. Black and J. Scimecca (eds), *Conflict Resolution: Cross-cultural Perspectives*, New York, Westport CT and London, Greenwood Press, 1991.

Avruch, K., and Black, P., 'A Generic Theory of Conflict Resolution: a Critique', *Negotiation Journal*, 3: 1 (1987), 87–100.

Avruch, K., and Black, P., 'Ideas of Human Nature in Contemporary Conflict Resolution Theory', *Negotiation Journal*, 6: 3 (1990), 221–8.

Avruch, K., and Black, P., 'The Culture Question and Conflict Resolution', *Peace and Change*, 16: 1 (1991), 22–45.

Avruch, K., and Black, P., 'Conflict Resolution in Intercultural Settings: Problems and Prospects', in D. Sandole and H. van der Merwe (eds), *Conflict Resolution Theory and Practice: Integration and Application*, Manchester and New York, Manchester University Press, 1993, pp. 131–45.

Avruch, K., Black, P., and Scimecca, J. (eds), *Conflict Resolution: Cross-cultural Perspectives*, New York, Westport CT and London, Greenwood Press, 1991.

Azar, E., 'The Analysis and Management of Protracted Conflict', in V. Volkan, J. Montville and D. Julius (eds), *The Psychodynamics of International Relationships* II, Lexington MA, Lexington Books, 1991, pp. 93–116.

Banks, M., and Mitchell, C. R., *The Resolution of Conflict: A Handbook on the Analytical Problem Solving Approach*, Fairfax VA, George Mason University, Institute for Conflict Analysis and Resolution, 1993.

Barakat, H., 'Alienation: A Process of Encounter between Utopia and Reality', *British Journal of Sociology*, 20 (1969), 1–10.

Barber, M., *Social Typifications and the Elusive Other*, London and Toronto, Associated University Press, 1988.

Bay, C., 'Politics and Pseudopolitics: a Critical Evaluation of some Behavioral Literature', *American Political Science Review*, 59: 1 (1965), 39–51.

Bay, C., 'Taking the Universality of Human Needs Seriously', in J. Burton (ed.), *Conflict: Human Needs Theory*, London, Macmillan, 1990, pp. 235–56.

Bendahmane, D., and McDonald, J., Jr (eds), *Perspectives on Negotiations: Four Case Studies and Interpretations*, Center for the Study of Foreign Affairs, Foreign Service Institute, US Department of State, Washington DC, 1986.

Benhabib, S., *Situating the Self*, Cambridge, Polity Press, 1992.

Benne, K., Bradford, L., and Lippitt, R., 'The Laboratory Method', in L. Bradford, J. Gibb and K. Benne (eds), *T-group Theory and Laboratory Method*, New York, Wiley, 1964, pp. 15–44.

Benvenisti, M., *Conflicts and Contradictions*, New York, Villard Books/Random House, 1986.

Bercovitch, J., 'International Mediation: a Study of the Incidence, Strategies and Conditions of Successful Outcomes', *Cooperation and Conflict*, 21: 3 (1986), 155–68.

Bercovitch, J., 'The Structure and Diversity of Mediation in International Relations', in J. Bercovitch and J. Rubin (eds), *Mediation in International Relations: Multiple Approaches to Conflict Management*, Basingstoke and London, Macmillan, 1992, pp. 1–29.

Berger, P., and Luckmann, T., *The Social Construction of Reality: A Treatise in the Sociology of Knowledge*, London, Penguin Books, 1991.

Bernstein, R., 'Introduction', in John Dewey, *On Experience, Nature, and Freedom*, ed. Richard Bernstein, Indianapolis IN and New York, Bobbs-Merrill, 1960, pp. ix–xlvii.

Bernstein, R., *The Restructuring of Social and Political Theory*, London, Methuen, 1979.

Berry, C., *Human Nature*, London, Macmillan, 1986.

Black, P., and Avruch, K., 'Some Issues in Thinking about Culture and the Resolution of Conflict', *Humanity and Society*, 13:2 (1989), 187–94.

Blake, R., Shepard, H., and Mouton, J., *Managing Intergroup Conflict in Industry*, Houston TX, Gulf Publishing, 1964.

Bleicher, J., *Contemporary Hermeneutics: Hermeneutics as Method, Philosophy and Critique*, London and New York, Routledge, 1980.

Bleicher, J., *The Hermeneutic Imagination: Outline of a Positive Critique of Scientism and Sociology*, London, Boston MA, Melbourne and Henley, Routledge, 1982.

Blum, A., 'Theorizing', in J. Douglas (ed.), *Understanding Everyday Life: Toward the Reconstruction of Sociological Knowledge*, London, Routledge, 1971, pp. 301–19.

Boehringer, G. H., Bayley, J., Zeruolis, V., and Boehringer, K., 'Stirling: the Destructive Application of Group Techniques to a Conflict', *Journal of Conflict Resolution*, 18: 2 (1974), 257–75.

Bolles, R., *Theory of Motivation*, New York, Evanston IL and London, Harper & Row, 1967.

Bradford, L., Gibb, J., and Benne, K., 'Preface', in L. Bradford, J. Gibb and K. Benne (eds), *T-group Theory and Laboratory Method*, New York, Wiley, 1964, pp. vii–x.

Bradford, L., Gibb, J., and K. Benne, 'Two Educational Innovations', in L. Bradford, J. Gibb and K. Benne (eds), *T-group Theory and Laboratory Method*, New York, Wiley, 1964, pp. 1–14.

Broome, B., 'Managing Differences in Conflict Resolution: the Role of Relational Empathy', in D. Sandole and H. van der Merwe (eds), *Conflict Resolution Theory and Practice: Integration and Application*, Manchester and New York, Manchester University Press, 1993, pp. 97–111.

Brubaker, R., *The Limits of Rationality: An Essay on the Social and Moral Thought of Max Weber*, London, Allen & Unwin, 1984.

Bueno de Mesquita, B., 'An Expected Utility Theory of International Conflict', *American Political Science Review*, 74 (1980), 917–31.

Burns, J., 'Wellsprings of Political Leadership', *American Political Science Review*, 71: 1 (1977), 266–75.

Burton, J., 'Regionalism, Functionalism, and the United Nations', *Australian Outlook*, 15: 1 (1961), 73–87.

Burton, J., 'Conflict as a Function of Change', in A. de Reuck and J. Knight (eds), *Conflict in Society*, London, Churchill, 1966, pp. 370–401.

Burton, J., *Conflict and Communication: The Use of Controlled Communication in International Relations*, London, Macmillan, 1969.

Burton, J., 'Resolution of Conflict', *International Studies Quarterly*, 16: 1 (1972), 5–29.

Burton, J., 'Theory and Reality', *Millennium: Journal of International Studies*, 4: 3 (1975), 251–62.

Burton, J., 'Functionalism and the Resolution of Conflict', in P. Taylor and A. J. R. Groom (eds), *Functionalism: Theory and Practice in International Relations*, London, University of London Press, 1975, pp. 238–49.

Burton, J., 'The Dynamics of Change in World Society', *Millennium: Journal of International Studies*, 5: 1 (1976), 64–79.

Burton, J., *Deviance, Terrorism and War*, New York, St Martin's Press, 1979.

Burton, J., 'The Rôle of Authorities in World Society', *Millennium: Journal of International Studies*, 8: 1 (1979), 73–9.

Burton, J., *Dear Survivors*, Boulder CO, Westview Press, 1982.

Burton, J., *Global Conflict: The Domestic Sources of International Crisis*, Brighton, Wheatsheaf, 1984.

Burton, J., 'World Society and Human Needs', in M. Light and A. J. R. Groom (eds), *International Relations: A Handbook of Current Theory*, London, Pinter, 1985, pp. 46–59.

Burton, J., 'About Winning', *International Interactions*, 12: 1 (1985), 71–91.

Burton, J., 'The Facilitation of International Conflict Resolution', in L. Kriesberg (ed.), *Research in Social Movements: Conflict and Change* VIII, London and Greenwich CT, Jai Press, 1985, pp. 33–45.

Burton, J., 'The History of International Conflict Resolution', in E. Azar and J. Burton (eds), *International Conflict Resolution: Theory and Practice*, Brighton, Wheatsheaf, 1986, pp. 40–55.

Burton, J., 'The Means to Agreement: Power or Values?' in D. Bendahmane and J. McDonald, Jr (eds), *Perspectives on Negotiation: Four Case Studies and Interpretations*, Center for the Study of Foreign Affairs, Foreign Service Institute, US Department of State, Washington DC, 1986, pp. 229–41.

Burton, J., 'The Procedures of Conflict Resolution', in E. Azar and J. Burton (eds), *International Conflict Resolution: Theory and Practice*, Falmer, Wheatsheaf; Boulder CA, Lynne Rienner, 1986, pp. 92–116.

Burton, J., 'The Theory of Conflict Resolution', *Current Research on Peace and Violence*, 9: 3 (1986), 125–30.

Burton, J., *Resolving Deep-rooted Conflict: A Handbook*, London and New York, University Press of America, 1987.

Burton, J., 'Three Qualities of a Secure Nation', in M. Macy (ed.), *Solutions for a Troubled World*, Boulder CO, Earthview Press, 1987, pp. 239–48.

Burton, J., *World Society*, Lanham MD, University Press of America, 1987.

Bibliography

Burton, J., 'International Conflict Resolution and Problem Solving', in D. Sandole and I. Sandole-Staroste (eds), *Conflict Management and Problem Solving: From Interpersonal to International Applications*, London, Pinter, 1987, pp. 251–8.

Burton, J., 'Conflict Resolution as a Function of Human Needs', in R. Coate and J. Rosati (eds), *The Power of Human Needs in World Society*, Boulder CO and London, Lynne Rienner, 1988, pp. 187–204.

Burton, J., *Conflict: Resolution and Provention*, London, Macmillan, 1990.

Burton, J., 'International Relations or World Society?' in J. Vasquez (ed.), *Classics in International Relations*, Englewood Cliffs NJ, Prentice Hall, 1990.

Burton, J., 'Unfinished Business in Conflict Resolution', in J. Burton and F. Dukes (eds), *Conflict: Readings in Management and Resolution*, London, Macmillan, 1990, pp. 328–35.

Burton, J. (ed.), *Conflict: Human Needs Theory*, London, Macmillan, 1990.

Burton, J., 'Conflict Resolution as a Political System', in V. Volkan, J. Montville and D. Julius (eds), *The Psychodynamics of International Relationships* II, Lexington MA, Lexington Books, 1991, pp. 71–92.

Burton, J., *Violence Explained*, Manchester and New York, Manchester University Press, 1997.

Burton, J., and Dukes, F., *Conflict: Practices in Management, Settlement and Resolution*, London, Macmillan, 1990.

Burton, J., and Ramsden, H., 'Order and Change', in A. J. R. Groom and C. R. Mitchell (eds), *International Relations: A Bibliography*, London, Pinter, 1978, pp. 128–39.

Burton, J., and D. Sandole, 'Generic Theory: the Basis of Conflict Resolution', *Negotiation Journal*, 2: 4 (1986), 333–44.

Carnevale, P., and Pruitt, D., 'Negotiation and Mediation', *Annual Review of Psychology*, 43 (1992), 531–82.

Coate, R., and Rosati, J., 'Human Needs in World Society', in R. Coate and J. Rosati (eds), *Power of Human Needs in World Society*, Boulder CO and London, Lynne Rienner, 1988, pp. 1–20.

Cobb, S., and Rifkin, J., 'Practice and Paradox: Deconstructing Neutrality in Mediation', *Law and Social Inquiry*, 16: 1 (1991), 35–62.

Cohen, R., 'Negotiating Reality: International Relations and the Metaphor of the Holy Sepulchre', paper presented at the thirty-fifth annual convention of the International Studies Association, Washington DC, 28 March–1 April 1994.

Cohen, S., Kelman, H., Miller, F., and Smith, B., 'Evolving Intergroup Techniques for Conflict Resolution: an Israeli–Palestinian Pilot Workshop', *Journal of Social Issues*, 33: 1 (1977), 165–89.

Colosi, T., 'A Model for Negotiation and Mediation', in D. Bendahmane and J. McDonald, Jr (eds), *International Negotiation: Art and Science*, Center for the Study of Foreign Affairs, Foreign Service Institute, US Department of State, 1984, pp. 15–33.

Connolly, W., *Identity/Difference: Democratic Negotiations of Political Paradox*, Ithaca NY and London, Cornell University Press, 1991.

Coser, L., *The Functions of Social Conflict*, Glencoe IL, Free Press, 1956.

Coser, L., *Continuities in the Study of Social Conflict*, New York, Free Press, 1967.

Cot, J.-P., 'Critical Remarks on John Burton's Paper on Resolution of Conflict, with Special Reference to the Cyprus Conflict', *International Studies Quarterly*, 16: 1 (1972), 31–9

Cox, R., *Schutz's Theory of Relevance: A Phenomenological Critique*, The Hague, Boston MA and London, Nijhoff, 1978.

Curle, A., *Making Peace*, London, Tavistock Publications, 1971.

Dallmayr, F., 'Phenomenology and Social Science: an Overview and Appraisal', in D. Carr and E. Casey (eds), *Explorations in Phenomenology*, The Hague, Nijhoff, 1973, pp. 133–66.

de Maré, P. B., *Perspectives in Group Psychotherapy: A Theoretical Background*, London, Allen & Unwin, 1972.

de Reuck, A., 'Controlled Communication: Rationale and Dynamics', *The Human Context*, 11: 1 (1974), 64–80.

de Reuck, A., 'A Theory of Conflict Resolution by Problem-solving', in J. Burton and F. Dukes (eds), *Conflict: Readings in Management and Resolution*, London, Macmillan, 1990, pp. 183–98.

Denise, T., 'The Concept of Alienation: Some Critical Notices', in F. Johnson (ed.), *Alienation: Concept, Term, and Meanings*, New York and London, Seminar Press, 1973, pp. 141–60.

Denzin, N., 'Reading Rational Choice Theory', *Rationality and Society*, 2: 2 (1990), 172–89.

Denzin, N., 'The Long Good-bye: Farewell to Rational Choice Theory', *Rationality and Society*, 2: 4 (1990), 504–7.

Der Derian, J., *On Diplomacy: A Genealogy of Western Estrangement*, Oxford, Blackwell, 1987.

Deutch, M., 'Conflict and its Resolution', in C. Smith (ed.), *Conflict Resolution: Contributions of the Behavioral Sciences*, London and Notre Dame IN, University of Notre Dame Press, 1971, pp. 36–57.

Dirven, R., and Paparotté, W., 'Introduction', in R. Dirven and W. Paparotté (eds), *The Ubiquity of Metaphor*, Amsterdam and Philadelphia PA, Benjamins, 1985, pp. vii–xix.

Doob, L. (ed.), *Resolving Conflict in Africa: The Fermeda Workshop*, New Haven CT and London, Yale University Press, 1970.

Doob, L., 'A Cyprus Workshop: an Exercise in Intervention Methodology', *Journal of Social Psychology*, 94 (1975), 161–78.

Doob, L., and Foltz, W., 'The Belfast Workshop: an Application of Group Techniques to a Destructive Conflict', *Journal of Conflict Resolution*, 17: 3 (1973), 489–512.

Dreyfus, H., 'Beyond Hermeneutics: Interpretation in late Heidegger and recent Foucault', in M. Gibbons (ed.), *Interpreting Politics*, Oxford, Blackwell, 1987, pp. 203–20.

Dreyfus, H., and Dreyfus, S., 'Towards a Phenomenology of Ethical Expertise', *Human Studies*, 14: 4 (1991), 229–50.

Druckman, D., 'Four Cases of Conflict Management: Lessons Learned', in D. Bendahmane and J. McDonald, Jr (eds), *Perspectives on Negotiation: Four Case Studies and Interpretations*, Center for the Study of Foreign Affairs, Foreign Service Institute, US Department of State, 1986, pp. 263–88.

Druckman, D., 'An Analytical Research Agenda for Conflict and Conflict Resolution', in D. Sandole and H. van der Merwe (eds), *Conflict Resolution Theory and Practice: Integration and Application*, Manchester and New York, Manchester University Press, 1993, pp. 25–42.

Druckman, D., and Broome, B., 'Value Differences and Conflict Resolution: Familiarity or Liking?', *Journal of Conflict Resolution*, 35: 4 (1991), 571–93.

Dryzek, J., *Discursive Democracy: Politics, Policy and Political Science*, Cambridge, Cambridge University Press, 1990.

Eco, Umberto, 'Horns, Hooves, Insteps: Some Hypotheses on three Types of Abduction', in U. Eco and T. Sebeok (eds), *The Sign of Three: Dupin, Holmes, Peirce*, Bloomington IN, Indiana University Press, 1983, pp. 198–220.

Edwards, W., 'Utility, Subjective Probability: Their Interaction and Variance Preferences', *Journal of Conflict Resolution*, 4: 1 (1962), 42–51.

Elshtain, J. B., *Women and War*, Brighton, Harvester Press, 1987.

Elster, J., 'Introduction', in J. Elster (ed.), *Rational Choice*, Oxford, Blackwell, 1986, pp. 1–33.

Eshete, A., 'Appraisal by an Ethiopian', in L. Doob (ed.), *Resolving Conflict in Africa*, New Haven CT and London, Yale University Press, 1970, pp. 85–103.

Esser, H., 'The Rationality of Everyday Behavior: a Rational Choice Reconstruction of the Theory of Action by Alfred Schutz', *Rationality and Society*, 5: 1 (1993), 7–31.

Feyerabend, Paul, *Against Method: Outline of an Anarchist Theory of Knowledge*, London, Verso, 1980.

Fisher, R., 'Third Party Consultation: a Method for the Study and Resolution of Conflict', *Journal of Conflict Resolution*, 16: 1 (1972), 67–94.

Fisher, R., 'Third Party Consultation as a Method of Intergroup Conflict Resolution', *Journal of Conflict Resolution*, 27: 2 (1983), 301–34.

Fisher, R., 'Developing the Field of Interactive Conflict Resolution: Issues in Training, Funding and Institutionalization', paper presented at the fourteenth annual scientific meeting of the International Society of Political Psychology, Helsinki, 1–5 July 1991.

Fisher, R., and Keashly, L., 'The Potential Complementarity of Mediation and Consultation within a Contingency Model of Third Party Intervention', *Journal of Peace Research*, 28: 1 (1991), 29–42.

Folger, J., and Jones, T. (eds), *New Directions in Mediation: Communication Research and Perspectives*, Thousand Oaks CA, London and New Delhi, Sage, 1994.

Foltz, W., 'Two Forms of Unofficial Conflict Intervention: the Problem-solving and the Process-promoting Workshops', in M. Berman and J. Johnson (eds), *Unofficial Diplomats*, New York, Columbia University Press, 1977, pp. 201–21.

Foucault, M., 'Nietzsche, Genealogy, History', in M. Gibbons (ed.), *Interpreting Politics*, Oxford, Blackwell, 1987, pp. 221–40.

Gadamer, H.-G., *Truth and Method*, second edition, London, Sheed & Ward, 1979.

Galtung, J., 'The Basic Needs Approach', in K. Lederer (ed.), *Basic Needs: A Contribution to the Current Debate*, Cambridge MA, Oelgeschlager, Gunn & Hain, 1980, pp. 55–125.

Garfinkel, H., *Studies in Ethnomethodology*, Englewood Cliffs NJ, Prentice Hall, 1967.

Geertz, C., *The Interpretation of Cultures: Selected Essays*, London, Fontana Press, 1993.

Ghosh, P. (ed.), *Third World Development: A Basic Needs Approach*, Westport CT, Greenwood Press, 1984.

Gonos, G., '"Situation" versus "Frame": the "Interactionist" and the "Structuralist" Analyses of Everyday Life', *American Sociological Review*, 42: 6 (1977), 854–67.

Goodman, N., *Ways of Worldmaking*, Indianapolis IN, Hackett, 1978.

Grathoff, R. (ed.), *Philosophers in Exile: The Correspondence of Alfred Schutz and Aron Gurwitsch, 1939–59*, Bloomington IN, Indiana University Press, 1989.

Greenhouse, C., 'Cultural Perspectives on War', in R. Väyrynen (ed.), *The Quest for Peace*, London, Sage, 1987, pp. 32–47.

Groom, A. J. R., 'No Compromise: Problem-solving in a Theoretical Perspective', *International Social Science Journal*, 153: 1 (1991), 77–86.

Groom, A. J. R., and Webb, K., 'Injustice, Empowerment, and Facilitation in Conflict', *International Interactions*, 13: 3 (1987), 263–80.

Gurwitsch, A., *Phenomenology and the Theory of Science*, ed. L. Embree, Evanston IL, Northwestern University Press, 1974.

Habermas, J., *The Theory of Communicative Action: Reason and the Rationalization of Society* I, London, Heinemann, 1984.

Hacking, I., 'Language, Truth and Reason', in M. Hollis and S. Lukes (eds), *Rationality and Relativism*, Oxford, Blackwell, 1982, pp. 48–66.

Hill, B., 'An Analysis of Conflict Resolution Techniques: From Problem-solving Workshops to Theory', *Journal of Conflict Resolution*, 26: 1 (1982), 109–38.

Hobbes, T., *Leviathan*, ed. M. Oakeshott, Oxford, Blackwell, [1651] 1955.

Hogarth, R., and Reder, M., 'Introduction: Perspectives from Economics and Psychology', in R. Hogarth and M. Reder (eds), *Rational Choice: The Contrast between Economics and Psychology*, Chicago and London, University of Chicago Press, 1987, pp. 1–23.

Hollis, M., *Models of Man: Philosophical Thoughts on Social Action*, Cambridge, Cambridge University Press, 1977.

Hollis, M., 'The Self in Action', in *John Dewey Reconsidered*, ed. R. S. Peters, London, Routledge, 1977, pp. 56–75.

Hollis, M., *The Cunning of Reason*, Cambridge, Cambridge University Press, 1987.

Hollis, M., and Lukes, S., 'Introduction', in M. Hollis and S. Lukes (eds), *Rationality and Relativism*, Oxford, Blackwell, 1982, pp. 1–20.

Hollis, M., and Smith, S., *Explaining and Understanding in International Relations*, Oxford, Clarendon Press, 1991.

Holsti, K. J., 'Paths to Peace? Theories of Conflict Resolution and Realities in International Politics', in R. Thakur (ed.), *International Conflict Resolution*, Boulder CO and London, Westview Press, 1988, pp. 105–32.

Horton, R., 'African Traditional Thought and Western Science', in B. Wilson (ed.), *Rationality*, London, Blackwell, 1974, pp. 131–71.

Horton, R., 'Tradition and Modernity Revisited', in M. Hollis and S. Lukes (eds), *Rationality and Relativism*, Oxford, Blackwell, 1982, pp. 201–60.

Husserl, E., *The Crisis of European Sciences and Transcendental Phenomenology: An Introduction to Phenomenology*, trans. D. Carr, Evanston IL, Northwestern University Press, 1970.

Hwa Yol Jung, 'A Critique of the Behavioral Persuasion in Politics: a Phenomenological View', in M. Natanson (ed.), *Phenomenology and the Social Sciences* II, Evanston IL, Northwestern University Press, 1973, pp. 133–73.

Iklé, F., *How Nations Negotiate*, New York, Harper & Row, 1964.

Illich, I., 'Needs', in W. Sachs (ed.), *The Development Dictionary: A Guide to Knowledge as Power*, London, Zen Books, 1992, pp. 88–101.

International Alert, 'Conflict Resolution and Training in the North Caucasus and Georgia', a report of the Piatigorsk seminar, 6–19 June 1993, London, International Alert, 1993.

Israel, J., *Alienation: From Marx to Modern Sociology*, Boston MA, Allyn & Bacon, 1971.

Jabri, V., *Mediating Conflict: Decision-making and Western Intervention in Namibia*, Manchester, Manchester University Press, 1990.

Jabri, V., *Discourses on Violence: Conflict Analysis Reconsidered*, Manchester and New York, Manchester University Press, 1996.

Jehenson, R., 'A Phenomenological Approach to the Study of the Formal Organization', in G. Psathas (ed.), *Phenomenological Sociology: Issues and Applications*, New York, Wiley, 1973, pp. 219–47.

Johnson, F., 'Alienation: Overview and Introduction', in F. Johnson (ed.), *Alienation: Concept, Term, and Meanings*, New York and London, Seminar Press, 1973, pp. 3–25.

Kelman, H., 'The Problem-solving Workshop in Conflict Resolution', in R. Merritt (ed.), *Communication in International Politics*, Chicago, University of Illinois Press, 1972, pp. 168–204.

Kelman, H., 'Foreword', in M. Banks (ed.), *Conflict in World Society: A new Perspective on International Relations*, Brighton, Wheatsheaf, 1984, pp. xvii–xx.

Kelman, H., 'Interactive Problem-solving: a Social-psychological Approach to Conflict Resolution', in J. Burton and F. Dukes (eds), *Conflict: Readings in Management and Resolution*, London, Macmillan, 1990, pp. 199–215.

Kelman, H., 'Interactive Problem Solving: the Uses and Limits of a Therapeutic Model for the Resolution of International Conflicts', in V. Volkan, J. Montville and D. Julius (eds), *The Psychodynamics of International Relationships* II, Lexington MA, Lexington Books, 1991, pp. 145–60.

Kelman, H., 'Informal Mediation by the Scholar/Practitioner', in J. Bercovitch and J. Rubin (eds), *Mediation in International Relations: Multiple Approaches to Conflict Management*, Basingstoke and London, Macmillan, 1992, pp. 64–96.

Kelman, H., and Cohen, S., 'The Problem-solving Workshop: a Social-psychological Contribution to the Resolution of International Conflicts', *Journal of Peace Research*, 13: 2 (1976), 79–90.

Kelman, H., and Cohen, S., 'Reduction of International Conflict: an Interactional Approach', in W. Austin and S. Worchel (eds), *The Social Psychology of Intergroup Relations*, Monterey CA, Brooks/Cole, 1979, pp. 288–303.

Kolb, D., 'To be a Mediator: Expressive Tactics in Mediation', *Journal of Social Issues*, 41: 2 (1985), 11–26.

Lakin, M., *Experiential Groups: The Uses of Interpersonal Encounter, Psychotherapy Groups, and Sensitivity Training*, Morristown NJ, General Learning Press, 1972.

Lakoff, G., and Johnson, M., *Metaphors We Live By*, Chicago and London, University of Chicago Press, 1980.

Laue, J., 'The Emergence and Institutionalisation of Third Party Roles in Conflict', in D. Sandole and I. Sandole-Staroste (eds), *Conflict Management and Problem Solving: Interpersonal to International Applications*, London, Pinter, 1987, pp. 17–29.

Lawler, P., 'Pragmatism, Existentialism, and the Crisis in American Political Thought', *International Philosophical Quarterly*, 20: 3 (1980), 327–38.

Lawler, P., 'Peace Research and International Relations: From Divergence to Convergence', *Millennium: Journal of International Studies*, 15: 3 (1986), 367–90.

Lawler, P., *A Question of Values, Johan Galtung's Peace Research*, Boulder CO and London, Lynne Rienner, 1995.

Lessnoff, M., *Social Contract*, London, Macmillan, 1986.

Lisk, F., 'Conventional Development Strategies and Basic Needs Fulfilment', *International Labour Review*, 115: 2 (1977), 175–91.

Locke, J., *Two Treatises of Government*, ed. P. Laslett, Cambridge, Cambridge University Press, [1689] 1988.

Lockyer, A., '"Traditions" as Context in the History of Political Theory', *Political Studies*, 27: 2 (1979), 201–17.

Louch, A. R., *Explanation and Human Action*, Berkeley CA and Los Angeles, University of California Press, 1966.

Lukes, S., *Power: A Radical View*, London and Basingstoke, Macmillan, 1979.

Lukes, S., 'Relativism in its Place', in M. Hollis and S. Lukes (eds), *Rationality and Relativism*, Oxford, Blackwell, 1982, pp. 261–305.

Manning, P., and H. Fabrega, 'The Experience of Self and Body: Health and Illness in the Chiapas Highlands', in G. Psathas (ed.), *Phenomenological Sociology: Issues and Applications*, New York, Wiley, 1973, pp. 251–301.

Maslow, A., *Motivation and Personality*, third edition, New York, Harper & Row, 1970.

McDonald, J., Jr, and D. Bendahmane (eds), *Conflict Resolution: Track Two Diplomacy*, Center for the Study of Foreign Affairs, Foreign Service Institute, US Department of State, 1987.

McHugh, P., 'On the Failure of Positivism', in J. Douglas (ed.), *Understanding Everyday Life: Toward the Reconstruction of Sociological Knowledge*, London, Routledge, 1971, pp. 320–35.

Merry, S., 'Disputing without Culture', *Harvard Law Review*, 100: 8 (1987), 2057–73.

Merry, S., and Silby, S., 'What do Plaintiffs want? Reexamining the Concept of Dispute', *Justice System Journal*, 9: 2 (1984): 151–78.

Miguda, E., 'Harnessing Internal Local Resources for Conflict Resolution and Self-sustaining Peace in the Face of Ethnic Violence', paper presented at the fifteenth general conference of the International Peace Research Association, Malta, 30 October–4 November 1994.

Mitchell, C. R., 'Evaluating Conflict', *Journal of Peace Research*, 17: 1 (1980), 61–75.

Mitchell, C. R., *Peacemaking and the Consultant's Role*, Farnborough, Gower, 1981.

Mitchell, C. R., 'Necessitous Man and Conflict Resolution: More Basic Questions about Basic Human Needs Theory', in J. Burton (ed.), *Conflict: Human Needs Theory*, London, Macmillan, 1990, pp. 149–76.

Mitchell, C. R., 'Ending Conflicts and Wars: Judgement, Rationality and Entrapment', *International Social Science Journal*, 127: 1 (1991), 35–55.

Mitchell, C. R., 'The Process and Stages of Mediation, Two Sudanese Cases', in D. Smock (ed.), *Making War and Waging Peace*, Washington DC, United States Institute of Peace, 1993, pp. 139–59.

Mitchell, C. R., 'Conflict Research', in A. J. R. Groom and M. Light (eds), *Contemporary International Relations: A Guide to Theory*, London and New York, Pinter, 1994, pp. 128–41.

152

Bibliography

Mitchell, C. R., and Nicholson, M., 'Rational Models and the Ending of Wars', *Journal of Conflict Resolution*, 27: 3 (1983), 495–520.

Mitchell, C. R., and Banks, M., *Handbook of Conflict Resolution: The Analytical Problem Solving Approach*, London, Pinter, 1996.

Mitchell, C. R., and Webb K. (eds), *New Approaches to International Mediation*, Westport CT, Greenwood Press, 1988.

Mitrany, D., *A Working Peace System*, Chicago, Quadrangle Books, 1966.

Mitrany, D., *The Functional Theory of Politics*, London, Martin Robertson, 1975.

Mizruchi, E., 'An Introduction to the Notion of Alienation', in F. Johnson (ed.), *Alienation: Concept, Term, and Meanings*, New York and London, Seminar Press, 1973, pp. 111–24.

Moore, B., Jr, *Injustice: The Social Bases of Obedience and Revolt*, New York, Sharpe, 1978.

Nader, L., 'Some Notes on John Burton's Papers on "Resolution of Conflict"', *International Studies Quarterly*, 16: 1 in the Philosophy of Alfred Schutz, Bloomington IN, Indiana University Press, 1986.

Nader, L., 'Harmony Models and the Construction of Law', in K. Avruch, P. Black and J. Scimecca (eds), *Conflict Resolution: Cross-Cultural Perspectives*, New York, Westport and London, Greenwood Press, 1991, pp. 41–59.

Natanson, M., 'Introduction', in M. Natanson (ed.), *Essays in Phenomenology*, The Hague, Martinus Nijhoff, 1966, pp. 1–22.

Natanson, M., *The Journeying Self, A Study in Philosophy and Social Role*, Reading, Menlo Park and London, Addison-Wesley Publishing Company, 1977.

Natanson, M., *Anonymity, A Study in the Philosophy of Alfred Schutz*, Bloomington, Indiana University Press, 1986.

Neufeld, M., 'Interpretation and the "Science" of International Relations', *Review of International Studies*, 19: 1 (1993), 39–61.

Nicholson, M., *Rationality and the Analysis of International Conflict*, Cambridge, Cambridge University Press, 1992.

Nordstrom, C., *A Different Kind of War Story*, Pennsylvania PA, University of Pennsylvania Press, 1997.

North, R., and Willard, M., 'The Post-behavioural Debate: Indeterminism, Probabilism and the Interaction of Data and Theory', in M. Banks (ed.), *Conflict in World Society: A New Perspective on International Relations*, Brighton, Wheatsheaf, 1984, pp. 22–38.

Nudler, O., 'Human Needs: a Sophisticated Holistic Approach', in K. Lederer (ed.), *Basic Needs: A Contribution to the Current Debate*, Cambridge MA, Oelgeschlager, Gunn & Hain, 1980, pp. 131–50.

Oakeshott, M., *Rationalism in Politics and other Essays*, London and New York, Methuen, 1984.

Olson, W., and Groom, A. J. R., *International Relations Then and Now: Origins and Trends in Interpretation*, London, HarperCollins, 1991.

Oppenheim, A. N., 'Psychological Processes in World Society', in M. Banks (ed.), *Conflict in World Society: A New Perspective on International Relations*, Brighton, Wheatsheaf, 1984, pp. 112–27.

Parsons, T., *The Structure of Social Action*, New York, Free Press, 1967.

Peräkylä, A., *Kuoleman monet kasvot: identiteetin tuottaminen kuolevan potilaan hoidossa* (Multiple Faces of Death: The Production of Identities in the Care of the Dying Patient), Tampere, Vastapaino, 1990.

Peters, R. S., *The Concept of Motivation*, London, Routledge, 1958.

Pettman, J. J., 'Nationalism and After', *Review of International Studies*, 24: 4 (1998), 149–64.

Plato, *Statesman*, trans. J. B. Skemp, London, Routledge, 1952.

Pollner, M., 'Mundane Reasoning', *Philosophy of the Social Sciences*, 4 (1974), 35–54.

Price, R., 'Interpretation and Disciplinary Orthodoxy in International Relations', *Review of International Studies*, 20: 2 (1994), 201–4.

Psathas, G., 'Ethnomethodology as a Phenomenological Approach in the Social Sciences', in D. Ihde and R. Zaner (eds), *Interdisciplinary Phenomenology*, The Hague, Nijhoff, 1977, pp. 73–98.

Psathas, G., 'Approaches to the Study of the World of Everyday Life', *Human Studies*, 3: 1 (1980), 3–17.

Rawls, J., *A Theory of Justice*, Oxford, Clarendon Press, 1972.

Reinhartz, S., *On Becoming a Social Scientist: From Survey Research and Participant Observation to Experiential Analysis*, San Francisco, Washington DC and London, Jossey-Bass, 1979.

Renshon, S., 'Human Needs and Political Analysis: an Examination of a Framework', in R. Fitzgerald (ed.), *Human Needs and Politics*, Oxford and New York, Pergamon Press, 1977, pp. 52–73.

Ricoeur, P., *Hermeneutics and the Human Sciences*, ed. J. Thompson, Cambridge, London, New York, New Rochelle NJ, Melbourne and Sydney, Cambridge University Press; Paris, Editions de la Maison des sciences de l'homme, 1981.

Rorty, R., 'Overcoming the Tradition: Heidegger and Dewey', *Review of Metaphysics*, 30: 1 (1976), 280–305.

Rorty, R., *Consequences of Pragmatism*, Brighton, Harvester Press, 1982.

Rose, S., Lewontin, R. C., and Kamin, L., *Not in our Genes: Biology, Ideology and Human Nature*, Harmondsworth, Penguin Books, 1985.

Ross, M., *The Culture of Conflict: Interpretations and Interests in Comparative Perspective*, New Haven CT and London, Yale University Press, 1993.

Ross, M., *The Management of Conflict: Interpretations and Interests in Comparative Perspective*, New Haven CT and London, Yale University Press, 1993.

Rousseau, J.-J., 'A Discourse on the Origin of Inequality', in J.-J. Rousseau, *The Social Contract and Discourses*, trans. G. D. H. Cole, London, Dent, [1755] 1973, pp. 27–113.

Rousseau, J.-J., *The Social Contract*, ed. M. Cranston, London, Penguin Books, [1762] 1968.

Roy, R., 'Three Visions of Needs and the Future: Liberalism, Marxism, and Gandhism', in R. Coate and J. Rosati (eds), *Power of Human Needs in World Society*, Boulder CO and London, Lynne Rienner, 1988, pp. 59–76.

Roy, R., 'Social Conflicts and Needs Theories', in J. Burton (ed.), *Conflict: Human Needs Theory*, London, Macmillan, 1990, pp. 125–48.

Rubenstein, R., 'Basic Human Needs Theory: Beyond Natural Law', in J. Burton (ed.), *Conflict: Human Needs Theory*, London, Macmillan, 1990, pp. 336–55.

Sandole, D., 'Introduction', in D. Sandole and I. Sandole-Staroste (eds), *Conflict Management and Problem Solving: From Interpersonal to International Applications*, London, Pinter, 1987, pp. 3–12.

Schacht, R., *Alienation*, London, Allen & Unwin, 1971.

Scheff, T., 'Negotiating Reality: Notes of Power in the Assessment of Responsibility', *Social Problems*, 16: 1 (1968), 3–17.

Schmidt, H., 'Peace Research and Politics', *Journal of Peace Research*, 5: 3 (1968), 217–32.

Schutz, A., *Collected Papers* I, *The Problem of Social Reality*, ed. M. Natanson, The Hague, Nijhoff, 1962.

Schutz, A., *Collected Papers* II, *Studies in Social Theory*, ed. A. Brodersen, The Hague, Nijhoff, 1964.

Schutz, A., *Collected Papers* III, *Studies in Phenomenological Philosophy*, ed. I. Schutz, The Hague, Nijhoff, 1966.

Schutz, A., *The Phenomenology of the Social World*, trans. G. Walsh and F. Lehnert, Evanston IL, Northwestern University Press, [1932] 1967.

Schutz, A., *On Phenomenology and Social Relations: Selected Writings*, ed. Helmut Wagner, Chicago and London, University of Chicago Press, 1970.

Schutz, A., *Reflections of the Problem of Relevance*, ed. R. Zaner, New Haven CT and London, Yale University Press, 1970.

Schutz, A., and Luckmann, T., *The Structures of the Life-World* I, London, Heinemann, 1974.

Schutz, A., and Luckmann, T., *The Structures of the Life-World* II, Evanston IL, Northwestern University Press, 1989.

Schwartz, M., and Schwartz, C., 'Problems in Participant Observation', in G. McCall and J. L. Simmons (eds), *Issues in Participant Observation: A Text and Reader*, Reading MA and London, Addison-Wesley, 1969, pp. 89–104.

Scimecca, J., 'Self-reflectivity and Freedom: Toward a Prescriptive Theory of Conflict Resolution', in J. Burton (ed.), *Conflict: Human Needs Theory*, London, Macmillan, 1990, pp. 205–18.

Sebeok, T. (ed.), *The Tell-tale Sign: A Survey of Semiotics*, Lisse, Peter de Ridder Press, 1975.

Seeman, M., 'On the Meaning of Alienation', *American Sociological Review*, 24: 6 (1959), 783–91.

Shapiro, M., *Reading the Postmodern Polity: Political Theory as Textual Practice*, Minneapolis MN and Oxford, University of Minnesota Press, 1992.

Simon, H., 'Rationality in Psychology and Economics', in R. Hogarth and M. Reder (eds), *Rational Choice: The Contrast between Economics and Psychology*, Chicago and London, University of Chicago Press, 1987, pp. 25–40.

Sites, P., *Control: The Basis of Social Order*, New York, Dunellen, 1973.

Sites, P., 'Legitimacy and Human Needs', in J. Burton and F. Dukes (eds), *Conflict: Readings in Management and Resolution*, London, Macmillan, 1990, pp. 117–44.

Sites, P., 'Needs as Analogues of Emotions', in J. Burton (ed.), *Conflict: Human Needs Theory*, London, Macmillan, 1990, pp. 7–33.

Skemp, J. B., 'Introduction', in Plato, *The Statesman*, trans. J. B. Skemp, London, Routledge, 1952, pp. 13–111.

Smith, G., *Social Need*, London, Routledge, 1980.

Smith, J., *Purpose and Thought: The Meaning of Pragmatism*, New Haven CT, Yale University Press, 1978.

Smith, M. B., 'Metapsychology, Politics, and Human Needs', in R. Fitzgerald (ed.), *Human Needs and Politics*, Oxford and New York, Pergamon Press, 1977, pp. 124–41.

155

Smith, S., 'Paradigm Dominance in International Relations: the Development of International Relations as a Social Science', *Millennium: Journal of International Studies*, 16: 2 (1987), 189–206.

Springborg, P., *The Problem of Human Needs and the Critique of Civilisation*, London, Allen & Unwin, 1981.

Srubar, I., 'On the Origin of Phenomenological Sociology', *Human Studies*, 7: 2 (1984), 163–89.

Srubar, I., 'On the Limits of Rational Choice', *Rationality and Society*, 5: 1 (1993), 32–46.

Stewart, D., and Mickunas, A., *Exploring Phenomenology: A Guide to the Field and its Literature*, second edition, Athens OH, Ohio University Press, 1990.

Streeten, P., 'From Growth to Basic Needs', *Finance and Development*, 16: 3 (1979), 28–31.

Streeten, P., and Burki, S., 'Basic Needs: Some Issues', *World Development*, 6: 3 (1978), 411–21.

Taylor, P., 'Introduction', in D. Mitrany, *The Functional Theory of Politics*, London, Martin Robertson, 1975, pp. ix–xxv.

Taylor, P., 'Functionalism: the Approach of David Mitrany', in A. J. R. Groom and P. Taylor (eds), *Frameworks for International Co-operation*, London, Pinter, 1990, pp. 125–38.

Thompson, J., 'Editor's Introduction', in P. Ricoeur (ed.), *Hermeneutics and the Human Sciences*, Cambridge, London, New York, New Rochelle NJ, Melbourne and Sydney, Cambridge University Press; Paris, Editions de la Maison des sciences de l'homme, 1981, pp. 1–26.

Touval, S., 'Biased Intermediaries: Theoretical and Historical Considerations', *Jerusalem Journal of International Relations*, 1: 1 (1975), 51–69.

Touval, S., and Zartman, I. W., 'Introduction: Mediation in Theory', in S. Touval and I. William Zartman (eds), *International Mediation in Theory and Practice*, Boulder CO and London, Westview Press, 1985, pp. 7–17.

Trigg, R., *Understanding Social Science*, Oxford, Blackwell, 1985, pp. 171–2.

UNITAR Research Reports, ed. L. Doob, 'Social Psychological Techniques and the Peaceful Settlement of International Disputes' I, 1970, New York.

Vaitkus, S., *How is Society Possible? Intersubjectivity and the Fiduciary Attitude as Problems of the Social Group in Mead, Gurwitsch, and Schutz*, Dordrecht, Boston MA and London, Kluwer, 1991.

Valone, J., 'A Critical Theory of Knowledge and the Phenomenology of Alfred Schutz', *Cultural Hermeneutics*, 3: 3 (1976), 199–215.

van Weigel, B., 'The Basic Needs Approach: Overcoming the Poverty of *Homo Oeconomicus*', *World Development*, 14: 12 (1986), 1423–34.

Vasquez, J., *The Power of Power Politics: A Critique*, New Brunswick NJ, Rutgers University Press, 1983.

Wagner, H., 'Between Ideal Type and Surrender: Field Research as Asymmetrical Relation', *Human Studies*, 1: 2 (1978), 153–64.

Wagner, H., *Phenomenology of Consciousness and Sociology of the Life-World: An Introductory Study*, Edmonton, Alta, University of Alberta Press, 1983.

Walker, R. B. J., *Inside/Outside: International Relations as Political Theory*, Cambridge and New York, Cambridge University Press, 1993.

Wall, J., Jr, 'Mediation: an Analysis, Review, and Proposed Research', *Journal of Conflict Resolution*, 25: 1 (1981), 157–80.

Wallensteen, P., and Axell, K., 'Conflict Resolution and the End of the Cold War, 1989–93', *Journal of Peace Research*, 31: 3 (1994), 333–49.

Walsh, G., 'Introduction', in A. Schutz, *The Phenomenology of the Social World*, trans. G. Walsh and F. Lehnert, Evanston IL, Northwestern University Press, [1932] 1967, pp. xv–xxix.

Watt, E. D., 'Human Needs, Human Wants, and Political Consequences', *Political Studies*, 30: 4 (1982), 533–43.

Webb, K., 'Structural Violence and Definition of Conflict', in *World Encyclopaedia of Peace* II, Oxford, Pergamon Press, 1986, pp. 431–4.

Webb, K., 'Science, Biology, and Conflict', *Paradigms*, 6: 1 (1992), 65–96.

Weber, M., *Max Weber: Selections in Translation*, ed. E. Matthews, trans. W. G. Runciman, Cambridge, Cambridge University Press, 1978.

Wehr, P., *Conflict Regulation*, Boulder CO, Westview Press, 1979.

Winch, P., *The Idea of a Social Science and its Relation to Philosophy*, London, Routledge, [1958] 1973.

Winch, P., 'Understanding a Primitive Society', in B. Wilson (ed.), *Rationality*, Oxford, Blackwell, 1974, pp. 78–111.

Wittman, D. 'How a War Ends: a Rational Model Approach', *Journal of Conflict Resolution*, 24: 4 (1979), 743–63.

Wolff, K., 'A Very Brief Commentary on Helmut R. Wagner's "Between Ideal Type and Surrender"', *Human Studies*, 1: 2 (1978), 165–6.

Yarrow, C., *Quaker Experiences in International Conciliation*, New Haven CT and London, Yale University Press, 1978.

Young, O., *The Intermediaries: Third Parties in International Crisis*, Princeton NJ, Princeton University Press, 1967.

Young, O., 'Intermediaries: Additional Thoughts', *Journal of Conflict Resolution*, 16: 1 (1972), 51–65.

Young, P., 'Physiological Drives', in *International Encyclopedia of the Social Sciences* IV, 1968, pp. 275–80.

Younghusband, E. (ed.), *New Developments in Casework: Readings in Social Work* II, London, Allen & Unwin, 1966.

Zaner, R., 'Theory of Intersubjectivity: Alfred Schutz', *Social Research*, 28: 1 (1961), 71–93.

Zartman, I. W., and Touval, S., 'Conclusion: Mediation in Theory and Practice', in S. Touval and I. W. Zartman (eds), *International Mediation in Theory and Practice*, Boulder CO and London, Westview Press, 1985, pp. 251–68.

Zartman, I. W., and Touval, S., 'International Mediation: Conflict Resolution and Power Politics', *Journal of Social Issues*, 41: 2 (1985), 27–45.

INDEX

References to footnotes contain the page number followed by 'n' and number of relevant note.

EU authorised representative for GPSR:
Easy Access System Europe, Mustamäe tee 50,
10621 Tallinn, Estonia
gpsr.requests@easproject.com

www.ingramcontent.com/pod-product-compliance
Lightning Source LLC
Chambersburg PA
CBHW060510290526
45791CB00001B/342